THE POWER OF LOVE

LOVE, CONTENTMENT, HAPPINESS AND BLISS

A.V.
A. VENKATASUBRAMANIAN

INDIA • SINGAPORE • MALAYSIA

ISBN

Hardcase 979-8-89446-392-6
Paperback 979-8-89066-768-7

Dedicated

To

Lord Shri Krishna

The God

of

Protection, Compassion, Tenderness and Love

CONTENTS

INTRODUCTION

Focus on the message, NOT on the messenger

This book has been **written with the intent** to SPREAD **love and harmony** around the world. I would like to start by saying that the **FOCUS of any learning**, whether from a teacher, a guru, or for that matter, from tradition, culture, or religion, should be **on the MESSAGE and its ESSENCE.**

The messenger and his vehicle are relatively unimportant.

Often, one ends up sidelining the message and learning; even as one gets fixated on the messenger. Focusing on the messenger distracts from learning the true message and its essence.

To quote a *Sanskrit Slokha* (Sanskrit Verse) as below:

A

'Sanskrit Slokha'

On why a person speaking the real truth is to be valued

सुलभाःपुरुषाराजन्सततंप्रियवादिनः।
अप्रियस्यतुपथ्यस्यवक्ताश्रोताचदुर्लभः॥ -वाल्मीकिरामायण

sulabhāḥ puruṣā rājan satataṃ priyavādinaḥ ।
apriyasya tu pathyasya vaktā śrōtā ca durlabhaḥ ॥

Meaning:

O king, it is always easy to find men who speak pleasing words, but it is difficult to get a speaker and a listener
who use words unpleasant (to the ears) but beneficial (in life).

There is a reason why the 'Truth' is very important. Without the truth, there cannot be any true reflection, and without reflection, there cannot be spiritual and personal growth.

A

'Sanskrit Slokha'

On the Importance of 'Truth'

सत्यमेवपरंमित्रंस्वीकृतेसतिमानवे।
सत्यमेवपरंशत्रुःधिक्कृतेसतिमानवे।।

satyamēva paraṃ mitraṃ svīkṛtē sati mānavē ।
satyamēva paraṃ śatruḥ dhikkṛtē sati mānavē ॥

Meaning:

If we accept truth then truth becomes our best friend.

But if we do not accept the truth and admonish it,

then later in life,

the same truth becomes our enemy.

The Book has SIX Parts. Each Part has a number of Chapters describing the learning and philosophies within the framework of the theme of that part.

The FIRST part (16 Chapters) is titled 'Man in the Mirror' and is meant to be an introspection that is weaved into anecdotes of the author's personal experience and learning.

The SECOND part (14 Chapters) is titled 'Happiness Seen Through the Prism of Money' and deals with the biggest problem people in the material world have, which is their relationship with money. The central idea is to make money work for you, rather than the other way around. The chapter would help a reader use his/her money optimally and hence attain maximum happiness.

The THIRD part (5 Chapters) is titled 'The Three Pillars of Society (Knowledge, Wealth & Power)' and discusses how a society could maximize its wealth and happiness, and do so equitably and fairly.

The FOURTH part (6 Chapters) is titled 'Finding Success and Happiness in Life: Philosophies in a Nutshell' and deals with learning from Sanatana Dharma that have practical applications at a personal and societal level. The objective is to help one 'manage and navigate' the complex material world by growing one's inner spirituality, inner strength, and inner balance.

The FIFTH part (3 Chapters) is titled 'Your Inner 'GPS' [Guru Positioning System]' and deals with principles to guide society from the teachings of Mahatma Gandhi and from ancient Sanskrit texts. It also deals with how one can engage in the material world without being consumed by it. It lays the pathway to enjoyment of the world's offerings, while maintaining a balance. This would give happiness at a personal level while maintaining harmony and balance at a societal level. This section is meant to serve as a guiding light and a compass at an individual and societal level. Ultimately, personal and societal happiness cannot be seen in isolation, as they are interdependent.

The SIXTH part (2 Chapters) is titled 'The World is One Family' and reminds us that we are all interconnected and sends out the message that the 'World is One Family'. We are all together on this beautiful earth, and what affects one will affect the other. By living in harmony and happiness and managing our lives with moderation and balance, we can continue to enjoy the bounties of the world and maximize our happiness and well-being.

The SEVENTH Part (1 Chapter) is the concluding chapter of this book. This part talks about, how we all have that small inner vibration in each one of us.

Each one of us by our actions and choices determine, as to which direction that small vibration is going to take and consequently manifest as. It talks about how EACH one of us has the power of THAT choice. Broadly the choice can stem from a place of 'HATE' or 'LOVE'.

The collective choices we make will determine our collective destiny (and the destiny of our children). We can choose to 'LOVE' and 'UNITE' or we can choose 'HATE' and ultimately 'PERISH'.

Net on net, this book intends to send the message that LOVE is the MOST powerful force in the universe, as it has the power to 'UNITE and MOTIVATE' us to take on and win challenges that we may face at an individual, societal, and universal level.

That is **'THE POWER OF LOVE'** folks!!

So, spread it around!

ACKNOWLEDGEMENT

I would like to express my deepest gratitude to **my parents** who have been my constant support. I thank them for encouraging me during the compilation of this book.

I would like to give special mention to **my little daughter** who has been a source of constant inspiration and purpose that furthered my effort in delivering this compilation.

I would like to thank my **teachers, professors, friends** and **well wishers** who have encouraged me in the endeavour of writing this book.

FOREWORD

PART I

Man in the Mirror

Part I

Chapter 1

RELIGION

Soak in it, but don't get wet!

"Those who can make you believe absurdities, can make you commit atrocities."

– Voltaire

"I believe in God, but not as one thing, not as an old man in the sky. I believe that what people call God is something in all of us. I believe that what Jesus, Mohammed, Buddha, and all the rest said was right. It's just that the translations have gone wrong."

– John Lennon

On the face of it, the world seems to be a very unjust place. While innocent people suffer, some get away with murder. We sometimes question GOD's existence in this context. Many are disillusioned and agnostic; some are even atheists. Many are disillusioned by religion and become atheists. Some are rationalists. They are those who are "too rational" and above the hocus-pocus called religion. Some are ultra-religious. Some are conservative. Some are fanatical. So let us see.

Does GOD Exist?

(An internal Conversation before...)

So let me **first answer this question** upfront from **MY experience.**

Does GOD exist?

The answer is YES.

And who am I to say this?

Q1: Am I "GOD"?

Ans : NO

Q2: Am I a "Messenger of GOD"?

Ans: NO

Q3: Am I a "Prophet"?

Ans: NO

Q4: Am I a "Messiah"?

Ans : NO

Q5: Am I a "Rationalist"?

Ans: I Hope. Closest to who I am actually!. That is what I think, at least!

Q6: Am I a "Fanatic"?

Ans: Hell NO! I have a questioning brain and try to use it!

Q7: Am I "Conservative"?

Ans: NO. I am open to listening to anyone and everyone, but form my own opinion and am not a blind follower or acceptor. I am not a Goat or trying to be a "G.O.A.T" either!

Q8. Am I "Religious"?

Ans: NO

Q9: Am I "Agnostic"?

Ans: NO. I saw reason NOT to be.

Though when you say you are rational you need to be sceptical also. However, we will come to that later.

Q10: Am I an "Atheist"?

Ans: NO.

I believe there is a GOD.... "BUT"

I believe there is a GOD.... "BUT"

BUT??

I believe in GOD... "BUT".

But what?

So let me answer the question upfront from my experience. Does GOD exist?

The answer is YES.

Then, what is this "BUT?"

Ok time for an anecdote.

Children in a room

So there were 'Eleven children' in a room. They were arguing.

The First said, "My Dad is the best because he preaches universal love and brotherhood".

The Second said, "My Dad is the best and has utmost respect for nature".

The Third said, "My Dad is the best because he is peaceful and moderate".

The Fourth said, "My Dad is the best; he never hurt a fly!"

The Fifth said, "My Dad is the best; he has sacrificed his son's life for others".

The Sixth said, "My Dad is the best; he is the purest. All other dads are false or fake".

The Seventh said, "My Dad is the best because he forgives when I mess up".

The Eighth said, "My Dad is the best because he is the wisest".

The Ninth said, "My Dad is the best; he is generous and promotes brotherhood".

The Tenth said, "I don't even think he is my Dad".

The Eleventh said, "Look at this fight; Dad does not exist".

Within moments, the argument in the room heats up.

The first child and third child in the room get into a fight, while arguing about whose dad was better. The first child threatens and banishes the third child into the next room.

The fourth child gets tired of arguing and goes to sleep on the sofa.

The fifth child hates the seventh, and they glare at each other.

Now the fifth child and sixth child get into a violent scuffle and are at each other's throats.

The sixth child is distracted and decides to sit on the first child even as he staves off the fifth.

The ninth child, who is reading a book, abhors what has just happened and tries to broker peace between the sixth and first.

The sixth child pushes the ninth child to the floor and makes him angry by tearing his book. He then sits on both the first child and the ninth child and starts beating them.

The fifth child then joins the fight even as he continues to fight the sixth child.

The fifth and sixth children then stomp on the first and ninth children who are on the floor.

The tenth child does not want to deal with this commotion. He runs away and hides.

The eleventh child just stomps out of the room in a huff, screaming, "I am never coming back".

There is a loud commotion, and a gentleman comes out of the kitchen. He was busy cooking lunch for HIS children and is shocked by what he sees in the room.

Now, if you haven't noticed, I have said HIS children. These eleven children are ALL his children, and he loves them EQUALLY.

He then asks, "WHAT are you children fighting about?"

"WE are fighting over 'Who has the best dad?'" comes the chorus reply.

The dad is taken aback by the absurdity of it all.

All along, as the story unfolded, one thought the children were fighting over whose dad was the best. However, if they had the SAME dad, then, "WHY are they fighting and for WHAT?"

Good question... as absurd as it may seem, read on.

This is exactly what is happening in the world and has been happening since the dawn of CIVILIZATION.

Someone once said, "The jungle may have been cleared, but the laws of the Jungle REMAIN".

"What are you talking about?" you may ask.

Well, let us look at the story AGAIN with a little tweak and from the perspective of the Dad.

Let me tell you the tweak upfront.

The 'Eleven Children' are Hinduism, Paganism, Buddhism, Jainism, Christianity, Islam, Judaism, Zoroastrianism, Sikhism, Agnostic, and Atheist.

Now, let us look at the story AGAIN.

Children in a room (Dad's Perspective)

There were 'Eleven children' in the room. They were arguing.

The First (Hinduism) said, "My Dad is the best because he preaches universal love and brotherhood".

The Second (Paganism) said, "My Dad is the best and has the utmost respect for nature".

The Third (Buddhism) said, "My Dad is the best because he is peaceful and moderate".

The Fourth (Jainism) said, "My Dad is the best; he never hurt a fly!"

The Fifth (Christianity) said, "My Dad is the best; he has sacrificed his son's life for others".

The Sixth (Islam) said, "My Dad is the best; he is the purest. All other dads are false or fake".

The Seventh (Judaism) said, "My Dad is the best because he forgives when I mess up".

The Eighth (Zoroastrianism) said, "My Dad is the best because he is the wisest".

The Ninth (Sikhism) said, "My Dad is the best; he is generous and promotes brotherhood".

The Tenth (Agnostic) said, "I don't even think he is my Dad".

The Eleventh (Atheist) said, "Look at this fight; Dad does not exist".

Within moments, the argument in the room heats up.

The first (Hinduism) child and third (Buddhism) child in the room get into a fight, while arguing about whose dad was better. The first (Hinduism) child threatens and banishes the third (Buddhism) child into the next room.

The fourth (Jainism) child gets tired of arguing and goes to sleep on the sofa.

The fifth (Christianity) child hates the seventh (Judaism), and they glare at each other.

Now the fifth (Christianity) child and sixth (Islam) child get into a violent scuffle and are at each other's throats.

The sixth (Islam) child is distracted and decides to sit on the first (Hinduism) child even as he staves off the fifth (Christianity).

The ninth (Sikhism) child, who is reading a book, abhors what has just happened and tries to broker peace between the sixth (Islam) and first (Hinduism).

The sixth (Islam) child pushes the ninth (Sikhism) child to the floor and makes him angry by tearing his book. He then sits on both the first (Hinduism) child and the ninth (Sikhism) child and starts beating both of them.

The fifth (Christianity) child then joins the fight even as he continues to fight the sixth (Islam) child.

The fifth (Christianity) child and sixth (Islam) child then stomp on the first (Hinduism) and ninth (Sikhism) children who are on the floor.

The tenth (Agnostic) child does not want to deal with this commotion. He runs away and hides.

The eleventh (Atheist) child just stomps out of the room in a huff, screaming, "I am never coming back".

There is a loud commotion, and a gentleman (GOD) comes out of the kitchen. He was busy cooking lunch for his children and is shocked by what he sees in the room.

Now, if you haven't noticed, I have said HIS Children. These eleven children (All Beliefs) are ALL his children, and he loves them EQUALLY.

He then asks, "WHAT are you children fighting about?"

"WE are fighting over 'Who's dad (GOD) is the best?'" comes the chorus reply.

The Dad (GOD) is taken aback by the absurdity of it all.

This is exactly what is happening in the world and has been happening since the dawn of CIVILIZATION.

All HIS (GOD's) children (religions) were fighting over THEIR perception of Dad (GOD) and on whose perception is superior or correct.

In this anecdote, the Dad is GOD and all the eleven children (religions) are HIS (GOD's) Children, born at DIFFERENT TIMES and shaped by THEIR own perceptions of him.

Extension of the Story

"For those who believe in God, most of the big questions are answered. But for those of us who can't readily accept the God formula, the big answers don't remain stone-written. We adjust to new conditions and discoveries. We are pliable. Love need not be a command, nor faith a dictum. I am my own god. We are here to unlearn the teachings of the church, state, and our educational system. We are here to drink beer. We are here to kill war. We are here to laugh at the odds and live our lives so well that Death will tremble to take us."

– Charles Bukowski

(On a Fun note, let us continue the story...)

The Dad is fed up. He exclaims in a huff, "I should never have had so many children. I thought we would be a loving family and more children would increase the love in the family".

Once he said this, the children, who had stopped fighting, now started fighting even more violently and were at each other's throats. They all wanted to be the only child. They were out to kill each other.

The Dad is now exasperated beyond measure. "What is going on?" he exclaims, and smartly turns off the air conditioning in the room.

The room heats up quickly, with the children still fighting. This raises the heat in the room. Finally, the exhausted children are sweating and tired.

It then gets so hot they quit fighting and calm down.

Sometimes, there is nothing like 'collective discomfort!'

'Climate change'... Anybody??

Time for some FUN

As you chew on that, here is **American** singer-songwriter **Sheryl Crow** to lift up your mood with **'Soak Up the Sun'** from her fourth studio album **'C'mon, C'mon',** released in the **year 2002.** Enjoy!!

'Soak Up the Sun'

Sheryl Crow, [Album **'C'mon, C'mon' (2002)**]

SCAN above to see **YOUTUBE** *Video of the Song*

Lyrics

[Soak up the Sun]

My friend, the communist
Holds meetings in his RV
I can't afford his gas
So I'm stuck here watching TV

I don't have digital
I don't have diddly squat
It's not having what you want
It's wanting what you've got

I'm gonna soak up the sun
I'm gonna tell everyone to lighten up
I'm gonna tell 'em that I've got no one to blame
For every time I feel lame I'm looking up
I'm gonna soak up the sun
I'm gonna soak up the sun

I've got a crummy job
It don't pay near enough
To buy the things it takes
To win me some of your love

Every time I turn around
I'm looking up, you're looking down
Maybe something's wrong with you
That makes you act the way you do

I'm, I'm gonna soak up the sun
I'm gonna tell everyone to lighten up
I'm gonna tell 'em that I've got no one to blame
For every time I feel lame I'm looking up
I'm gonna soak up the sun

While it's still free
I'm gonna soak up the sun
Before it goes out on me

Don't have no master suite
But I'm still the king of me
You have a fancy ride
But baby, I'm the one who has the key

Every time I turn around
I'm looking up, you're looking down
Maybe something's wrong with you
That makes you act the way you do
Maybe I am crazy too

I'm gonna soak up the sun
I'm gonna tell everyone to lighten up
I'm gonna tell 'em that I've got no one to blame
For every time I feel lame I'm looking up

I'm gonna soak up the sun
I'm gonna tell everyone to lighten up (to lighten up)
I'm gonna tell 'em that I've got no one to blame
For every time I feel lame I'm looking up (I'm looking up)

I'm gonna soak up the sun
I got my 45 on
So I can rock on

Part I

Chapter 2

IS VEGETARIANISM MORALLY SUPERIOR?

Answer is NOT so straight-forward. It is more complicated than that!

"Only fools argue whether to eat meat or not. They don't understand truth, nor do they meditate on it. Who can define what is meat and what is plant? Who knows where the sin lies, being a vegetarian or a non-vegetarian?"

– *Guru Nanak*

"If slaughterhouses had glass walls the whole world would be vegetarian."

– *Linda McCartney*

The state of Punjab is considered the wheat basket of India. It is fed by the five rivers: Jhelum, Chenab, Ravi, Beas, and Sutlej. Punjab derives its name from 'Punj', meaning 'five', and 'Aab', meaning 'water'. It was so fertile that my father would joke that one just needs to throw the seeds of wheat into the land, and the wheat fields would rise.

Similarly, in the south, Thanjavur is considered the rice bowl of India. It is irrigated and water-fed by the river Cauvery, which is considered one of the seven sacred rivers in India. It so happens that my ancestors, from both my maternal and paternal sides, originated from this fertile region.

Apart from originating from Thanjavur, both my Grandparents had some interesting similarities. They both had tragically lost their fathers before they were even 6 years old. (Losing one of the parents early was, unfortunately, not actually very uncommon in those days when life expectancy could be cruel).

Both struggled but managed to get some education. My Paternal Granddad managed metric but had to drop out at that point because of (as you guessed it) unimaginable financial pressures. Meanwhile, my Maternal Granddad was lucky to have an uncle and then an elder brother help him through college, and he managed a Master's in English Literature and History (a very interesting profile). Both had suffered extreme hardships and had their respective life paths. Interestingly, both joined government service and became accountants (one in Railways and the other in the Defense sector).

They happened to be extremely conservative *Shaivite Brahmins*. Their immediate environment probably contributed to their inclination to study. Interestingly, both were extremely timid and had a high-risk aversion approach, which again probably stemmed from their poverty and maybe extreme conservative Brahmin outlook of contentment.

My Granddad on the Maternal side was a super interesting character. He used to regale me with endless stories of his childhood, college days, and his youth. He had the most fun and quirky personality. More about that later, but the reason I brought them into the picture was to set the context.

'North Indian' Vs 'South Indian'

"I've been a vegetarian for years and years. I'm not judgemental about others who aren't, I just feel I cannot eat or wear living creatures."

– *Drew Barrymore*

"I've been more or less vegetarian for about 40 years. A health diet really helps. I do meditation every day, and either yoga or sport several times a week."

– *John McLaughlin*

When I was in school, we had a lot of 'North Indian' vs 'South Indian' jokes. The North Indian kids would make fun of the rice-eating South Indian kids, and the South Indians would make fun of chapati (wheat flatbread)-eating North Indian kids. All part of the fun and jest, I will add (considering how touchy people of the current generations get over the slightest provocations).

One particular stereotype (if one will) was of the South Indians. They were a heterogeneous group but were bundled into a homogeneous bundle, labeled *'Madrasis'*. The face of the Madrasi was a curd-rice eating Brahmin who was particularly intelligent and especially good at math.

The other stereotype was that of North Indians. They were a heterogeneous group but were bundled into a homogeneous bundle, labeled *'Sardarjis'*. The face of the Sardarji was, as you guessed it, a *chapati* (wheat flatbread) eating (often) Sikh, who was very strong but hot-headed and consequently, supposedly stupid.

Both groups were very proud of their respective staples, often looking down on the other group. In those times, it was often impossible to dislodge them from the perception of the superiority of their dietary preferences.

So, the North Indian kids would have jokes to enforce the stereotypes of South Indian kids, and South Indian kids would have jokes to enforce the stereotypes of North Indian kids. (In jest, I may add).

So, one 'South Indian' counter joke was as follows. A 'Madrasi' is trying to board a train and is unable to lift his heavy suitcase to carry it into his train compartment. A 'Sardarji', who is standing behind in the line, comes around and helps. He casually lifts the heavy suitcase and carries it into the compartment. He then turns to the 'Madrasi' and says, "Roti Kao, Baal Aao". This roughly translates into 'eat chapatis and become strong'. Both men then enter the 3-sleeper compartment and find themselves in adjoining seats.

Nighttime arrives, and it is time to sleep. The Sardar has the middle berth and needs to unhinge and lock the bed in position to be able to use his middle berth as a bed to sleep. The Madrasi, on the other hand, has the lower berth. When the time comes to sleep, the Sardar signals to the Madrasi to get up so that he can unhinge his bed from the partition and lock it. The Sardar tries to unhinge the bed. The Sardar struggles to unhinge the middle bunk bed from its original position. Even after using all his might, the Sardar is unsuccessful.

All along, the Madrasi is quietly watching and waiting. Unless the Sardar gets his bed in position, the Madrasi won't be able to sleep in the lower berth. The Sardar now tries even harder, using all his might, but is unable to dislodge the bed. The Madrasi then quietly signals to say, "Let me help". He works the safety hatch and unhinges the bed. He then raises it and locks it in position, all in a couple of seconds. The Sardar is in awe. The Madrasi then says, "Chawal Kao, Buddhi Aao", which roughly translates into 'Eat rice and get some brains'.

Grand-dad and *Chapatti* dilemma

"But you know, as a kid I would have thought of a vegetarian as a wimp."

– Paul McCartney

"Everyone's a pacifist between wars. It's like being a vegetarian between meals."

– Colman McCarthy

Now back to my Maternal Granddad. As stated earlier, he worked in the accounts department in the Defense Department. The nature of a government job in those days was such that you would be transferred every 3 years. It so happened that, in one of his postings, my Maternal Granddad got transferred to Dehradun. Now, Dehradun was a hill station in Northern India, with particularly cool winters. For my Maternal Granddad, it was cold.

Cold, in the relative context of Thanjavur (his place of origin), whose four seasons were warm, hot, hotter, and hottest. Being originally from Thanjavur, my Maternal Granddad's traditional diet was rice-based. Also, being a conservative Brahmin, he was strictly vegetarian.

Having arrived in Dehradun, it didn't take much time for my Grandad, who was used to South Indian hot weather, to feel the cold right to his bone. Seeing his suffering, a much-amused Punjabi Indian friend in the office recommended that he eat chapattis instead of rice. Chapattis are flatbreads made of wheat and often keep one's body warmer than rice.

My Granddad, in desperation, reluctantly took his colleague's advice and began eating chapattis. He then found himself being able to tolerate the cold better. Chapattis became part of his diet and a staple every day from thereon. My Grandmother and consequently my mother soon became experts at making chapattis, much to the awe of our South Indian friends and relatives over the following decades.

The fact is that South Indian Brahmins were very proud of their traditional diets based on rice. Now, there is nothing wrong with that. It has its advantages. That rice-based diet was adapted to what grew well in the tropics and geographies of South India. Eating local also had advantages. What grows in local regions is often exactly what the body needs. It is actually a science that plants that grow in certain regions provide the exact nourishment required by humans in that climate and location. Rice was more cooling compared to wheat. So, it was no surprise that it was consumed over centuries in the rice bowls and tropics.

The fact is, diets around the world are adapted to geography, climate, location, and what is available in that region and grows well. For instance, Japan, which is surrounded by sea and has rice fields, has 'fish and rice' as a staple. In this way, it is not difficult to see why some cultures have their staples and preferences.

South Indian Brahmins, in general, were vegetarians. They historically originated in regions that had all-round warm weather. Fruits and vegetables often were available all year round. As with any culture or subculture, they were proud of their diet. Added to this was the morally superior posturing that they were "Pure" vegetarians. Pride, buttressed by moral superiority, made them feel superior. Again, nothing wrong with that, except that pride is okay, but nobody is "morally" superior to the other, in reality. Let me explain this differently.

Now, Brahmins, who already basked in the stereotype of being "naturally" intelligent and therefore superior, now somehow had an added dimension. Some of them would love flaunting their vegetarianism as an added badge of being MORE civilized than the meat-eaters. Somewhere, apart from their natural intelligence, they were supposed to be more evolved and spiritually heightened by just their culture, whose one pillar was vegetarianism. This supposedly was evidence of their moral superiority and therefore spiritual growth. Again, nothing wrong with that, except that it is more complicated than that.

Now, back to the story. Dehradun, where my Granddad was transferred, was cold by South Indian standards, alright, but most Scandinavians would probably consider it T-shirt weather. The winter chill of Dehradun converted my Granddad, who was a staunch rice eater and conservative South Indian Brahmin, into a North Indian (by location now) Chapati eater.

However, given my Maternal Granddad's beliefs and religious restrictions, I can guarantee that even if transferred to Scandinavia in the middle of winter, my granddad would not touch meat. He was likely to look for vegetarian options. Given demand, modern logistics could make vegetarian options potentially available even in the coldest of places.

However, I will challenge that if I were to 'time-travel' my Granddad to a Scandinavian winter some 1,000 years ago (in a time when modern logistics were not existent), at some point the cold and hunger would make my Maternal Granddad reconsider his options. Given a spear in hand and left alone, the cold and hunger would even drive my timid Granddad to rise, fight, and hunt. He would either 'hunt and kill' or 'perish trying'.

Under pressure from basic human needs and left to the elements, one's beliefs and convictions would evaporate pretty quickly. Now, I am NOT saying this from any derogatory standpoint. I am just illustrating that we humans are NOT perfect, superior, more intelligent, or in any way different from each other, despite the perceptions of ourselves.

People around the world may dress differently, eat differently, even behave differently, and lecture or judge others from their cozy moral high-grounds. Those high grounds may stem from wealth, health, status, power, perceptions of racial superiority, religion, color, gender, education, and many such superficial distinctions, but given circumstances where survival is at stake, hunger would cause us to steal bread. Caught in the rubble of an earthquake, we would drink our own urine; faced with mortal danger, we would fight or run; and faced with extinction, we would either REACT and fight each other until all die (Apocalypse) or RESPOND and stay together and fight, irrespective of our color, nationality, race, religion, gender, status, money, or situation (like a fight against an alien invasion in a Hollywood movie 😊).

We hope the latter is true, where mankind uses their societal intelligence and comes together to fight the many existential issues it faces, like war and climate change. That would happen when we UNDERSTAND that we are all actually the same, despite our superficial differences.

Understanding, empathy, compassion, courage, and love are common strengths, irrespective of all our differences, and once we understand and multiply that, we will spread beauty and happiness and survive and thrive as a species.

Time for some FUN

Time for the song **'Man in the Mirror'** sung by **American** singer-songwriter **Michael Jackson** from his seventh solo album **'Bad' (1987). 'Man in the Mirror'** was written by **Glen Ballard** and **Siedah Garrett** and produced by **Jackson** and **Quincy Jones.** Enjoy!!

'Man in the Mirror'

Michael Jackson, [Album **'Bad' (1987)**]

SCAN above to see **YOUTUBE** ***Video of the Song***

Lyrics

[Man in the Mirror]

I'm gonna make a change
For once in my life
It's gonna feel real good
Gonna make a difference
Gonna make it right

As I, turn up the collar on
My favorite winter coat
This wind is blowin' my mind
I see the kids in the street
With not enough to eat
Who am I, to be blind pretending not to see their needs?

A summer's disregard
A broken bottle top
And a one man's soul
They follow each other on the wind ya know
'Cause they got nowhere to go
That's why I want you to know

I'm starting with the man in the mirror
I'm asking him to change his ways
And no message could've been any clearer
If they wanna make the world a better place
Take a look at yourself and then make a change

I've been a victim of a selfish kind of love
It's time that I realize
That there are some with no home
Not a nickel to loan
Could it be really me pretending that they're not alone?

A willow deeply scarred
Somebody's broken heart
And a washed out dream (washed out dream)
They follow the pattern of the wind, ya see
'Cause they got no place to be
That's why I'm starting with me

I'm starting with the man in the mirror (oh)
I'm asking him to change his ways (oh)
And no message could've been any clearer
If you wanna make the world a better place
Take a look at yourself and then make a change

I'm starting with the man in the mirror (oh)
I'm asking him to change his ways (oh)
And no message could've been any clearer
If you wanna make the world a better place
Take a look at yourself and then make that
Change

I'm starting with the man in the mirror (oh yeah)
I'm asking him to change his ways (better change)
No message could've been any clearer
(If you wanna make the world a better place)
(Take a look at yourself and then make the change)

(You gotta get it right, while you got the time)
('Cause when you close your heart) you can't
(Then you close your) close your, your mind
With the man in the mirror, oh yeah
I'm asking him to change his ways (better change)
No message could've been any clearer
If you wanna make the world a better place
Take a look at yourself and then make a change

(Oh yeah) gonna feel real good now

I'm gonna make a change
It's gonna feel real good
Come on (change)
Just lift yourself
You know
You've got to stop it
Yourself (yeah)

(Make that change)
I've got to make that change today
(Man in the mirror) you got to
You got to not let yourself brother
(Yeah) you know
(Make that change) I've got to get that man, that man

You've got to
You've got to move
Come on
Come on
You got to
Stand up, stand up (yeah, make that change)
Stand up

Stand up and lift
Yourself, now
(Man in the mirror)

(Yeah, make that change)
Gonna make that change come on
(Man in the mirror)

You know it
You know it
You know it
You know
Change
Make that change

Part I

Chapter 3

WHEN ARE YOU READY FOR LOVE?

Being ready to give and receive love

"Being deeply loved by someone gives you strength, while loving someone deeply gives you courage."

– *Lao Tzu*

"And yet I wish but for the thing I have;
My bounty is as boundless as the sea,
My love as deep; the more I give to thee,
The more I have, for both are infinite."

– ***Shakespeare***, *(Romeo and Juliet)*

I was talking to my Mother the other day, and she was talking about her Grandparents. She talked about how her Grandparents loved their children, as well as their extended family's children and grandchildren, unconditionally. She talked about how they were all happy in one big joint family.

Talking about HER Grandmother, she described how her Grandmother took it upon herself to bring up her entire extended family, including her children and the children of her siblings.

It was amazing that the woman would cook for an entire battalion. My Mother described how in those times, they used firewood and coal for cooking. They used dried cow dung and wood to start a fire in the morning that was sustained by coal pieces. They would have three stoves burning at all times. As a boy, my Maternal Grandfather would be delegated to fetch milk with a rupee in hand. He bought four measures of milk, which was a huge quantity. The milk in those days was very thick, and my Great-Grandmother would pour it into a large container. She would add some water to dilute it and make it sufficient for the children in the entire family. After boiling the milk, she would then take four or more very large scoops of *'Ovaltine'* in a large dish serving utensil and drop it into the large container. After proper mixing, she would transfer the contents into a large kettle and give the kettle to the eldest child along with tumblers (a kind of steel cup). All the children in the family would stand in line with their tumblers first thing in the morning to receive a glass full of milk.

My mother also described how her Grandmother would cook rice in a very large pot for the entire joint family. Those were the days when the pressure cooker was not invented or heard of. Finally, when lunch was ready, the entire family would sit in a very long line to be served, starting from one end to the other, much like an assembly line!

All this fascinated me. My Mother also told me about her loving childhood memories of her Grandmother. My Great-Grandmother, with great affection and love, would take my mother onto her lap. Her tremendous love and affection were truly felt by my Mother, even as she was embraced in the most loving fashion and told sweet endearments.

Now, I know most modern feminists are going to scoff at the joint family concept and talk about how the women were actually exploited. Before you complain, please read on. My Great-Grandmother NEVER felt that she was doing all this "hard work". Her love for her children and extended family propelled her to take up the housework, even if it may be deemed excessive by today's standards. Remember, she never had the luxury of a modern kitchen and all of its accompanying gadgets. Her day was a hell of a lot tougher, and the work was actually grinding and uncompromising. Yet, she was cheerful and happy to be doing it because of her love for her children and love for the children of the extended family. Much like my Mother later, she never even deemed this as "work".

The reason I brought up this anecdote here was to highlight a couple of things. Today, we consider bringing up children to be a chore and a burden. Why is that? Also, why is it that despite having all the modern facilities, entertainment options, and money, we can't find love, happiness, contentment, or satisfaction? Ultimately, having people around you who love you and being cocooned in love is something that money cannot buy. I can go on about how our lives are emptier and loveless despite "having it all".

Well, what are the reasons?

You are ready for Love, when you are ready to Give

"Love is the whole thing. We are only pieces."

– Rumi

"Love is patient, love is kind. It does not envy, it does not boast, it is not proud."

– 1 Corinthians 13

In modern times, we are always chasing things. In the material world, the first thing we are honed to chase is money. We spend a lot of time and energy in pursuit of a better career, in chasing that bigger car, bigger house, more jewelry, and more acquisitions. Our needs are endless, from wanting more gadgets to expensive holidays. Don't get me wrong; there is nothing wrong with all of this. However, in all of this, we exhibit selfish behavior. It is always 'me', 'my wants' and 'my needs'.

The fact is, you will never be ready for love until you have satisfied your needs. Until then, it is human tendency to be selfish. This is actually just natural. So, the point I am trying to make is, until you have achieved your goals (which may be financial or otherwise) or have satisfied most of your needs and wants, you are not really ready for TRUE love.

The paradox is, if you keep expanding your needs and wants and have not settled into a state of contentment, you will never be in a position to truly love. This is because TRUE LOVE is about 'GIVING'. It is about being outwardly focused on the needs of others rather than being focused on only one's needs. Note, I have used the term 'true' love or 'unadulterated' love.

So there are **TWO ways** to achieve **true love.**

1. You hyper-achieve all your goals such that you don't have any more expanding desires. You reach a state of contentment and begin to look outward. I will warn you that if you choose this path of hyper-achieving, you risk burning a lot of 'people and relationships' in the process. Also, I would like to speculate that you may end up being

on a perpetual treadmill of 'running for more', without having the necessary pause to contemplate, before it's too late.

If, however, you do achieve all you wanted to, you now have the ability to give. Potentially, you may become more unselfish and lay the foundation to love humanity and people around you.

2. The second, easier and more achievable way is to limit your desires. For instance, you may choose to be happy with less money as a substitute for more free time. In this way, you may have more time to give your family and hence more love to give. The ability to make sacrifices for your family and others around you in terms of money and time would actually come back as more love. Sometimes, one needs to stop and pause from running on the treadmill of life. In those moments when you pause and contemplate, you are in a better position to reassess your options.

   So the idea is to have a balance of ambition or wants against contentment and stability. This can be done by paring down your ambition, wants, and needs. This road is the 'road to true love', while 'unlimited desire' is the 'road to loneliness and self-destruction'.

Success and money ALONE cannot find you true love. True love, whether it is between you and your parents, you and your spouse, you and your children, or you and your friends, can only be achieved by giving. By giving and sharing what you have—whether your wealth, time, or effort—you can truly begin to experience true love.

My Mother's Grandmother unconditionally put in the effort to care for her joint family. In the process, she found true love, contentment, and happiness in her life. She was NOT the richest, most powerful, well-read, or successful person, but she found love and happiness and unconditionally spread it around.

Look around you, and if you look through the fake veneer, you can quickly ascertain that it is not the richest, most powerful, or successful people alone who find happiness or true love in life. Everybody and anybody with the right attitude can achieve happiness in HIS/HER life. It will take one to reach a state of contentment and giving before one can experience 'True love' in life. You can reach a state of contentment by either achieving all that you wanted (which is unlikely) or taking a pause and thinking about your life and what constitutes happiness to you.

The simple reason for unhappiness in the world (of plenty) is greed and the need for status and power. The reason why this makes you unhappy is that you are always going to be selfish and inward-looking in trying to obtain that money, status, and power. You only get misery if your ambition and wants keep expanding.

Neither is 'ambition or wanting more' wrong. I am just saying you need to pause and ask yourself if you are being too greedy for more to the point you have stopped looking at people and the condition of the world around you. If you really want to be truly happy (and I am not talking about the superficial happiness and dopamine highs of the modern world) and find true love, you need to look outwardly and be giving in terms of money, time, your effort, and sincerity.

Time for some FUN

Time for **'The Power of Love'** from the **Soundtrack** of the **1985 Blockbuster Movie 'Back to the Future'**, performed by **'Huey Lewis & The News'**. Enjoy!!

'Power of Love'

Huey Lewis & The News, [Movie Soundtrack **'Back to the Future' (1985)]**

SCAN above to see **YOUTUBE** ***Video of the Song***

Lyrics **[Power of Love]**
The power of love is a curious thing Make a one man weep, make another man sing Change a hawk to a little white dove More than a feeling, that's the power of love Tougher than diamonds, rich like cream Stronger and harder than a bad girl's dream Make a bad one good, make a wrong one right Power of love will keep you home at night You don't need money, don't take fame Don't need no credit card to ride this train It's strong and it's sudden and it's cruel sometimes But it might just save your life That's the power of love That's the power of love First time you feel it, it might make you sad Next time you feel it, it might make you mad But do be glad baby when you've found That's the power that makes the world go 'round And it don't take money, don't take fame Don't need no credit card to ride this train It's strong and it's sudden, it can be cruel sometimes But it might just save your life

They say that all in love is fair
Yeah, but you don't care
But you know what to do (to do)
When it gets hold of you
And with a little help from above
You feel the power of love
You feel the power of love
Can you feel it?
Mmm

It don't take money and it don't take fame
Don't need no credit card to ride this train
Tougher than diamonds and stronger than steel
You won't feel nothin' 'til you feel
You feel the power
Just feel the power of love
That's the power
That's the power of love

You feel the power of love
You feel the power of love
Feel the power of love

Part I

Chapter 4

WHEN CULTURE CAN BE THAT CANNON BALL TIED TO ONE'S LEG

Why it is NO good to blindly follow the Herd

"We may have different religions, different languages, different coloured skin, but we all belong to one Human Race."

– Kofi Annan

"Difference is an accident of birth and it should therefore never be the source of hatred and conflict."

– John Hume

"Cultural differences should NOT separate us from each other, but rather cultural diversity brings a collective strength that can benefit all of Humanity."

– Robert Alan

I was barely 25 years of age when I started my first business at the turn of the century. To set things in context, I was an engineer with an M.S., with no prior business exposure or experience. My partners were my Father (another engineer!) and an accountant/guide.

Hmm...

My final objective was to develop a discount grocery and supermarket chain. Scaling the business, I reckoned, would give me power with my suppliers and distributors, benefits of which I thought I could pass on to my customers. The rub-off effects of branding would help me draw customers and would help in building a trusted brand.

But, before all those expansion dreams, I needed to prove to myself that the first pilot unit of the store was profitable and sustainable. If profitable, scaling would bring in the benefits of scale; otherwise, if it were a cash-burn type of venture, scaling would only mean scaling of losses entrenched in the business model.

In any case, one fine morning, I arrived at the venture and took stock with the help of my accountant/guide. This gentleman had previously been an accountant in the Middle East for a very large grocery chain and supermarket. I had picked a smaller town to try out my first venture. I had reckoned that there would be less competition, and it would also be an ideal place to set up a discount store.

Once we took stock of the morning situation, we often had time to talk about business and life. The gentleman told me how he had initially spent decades in Iraq as an accountant for similar businesses. But as it panned out, the Gulf War broke out, and he had to leave. He not only had to leave, but he had to leave with just a couple of suitcases and the shirt on his back. The moment the war broke out, Iraq's Saddam Hussein had frozen the exchange of all local currency. So the accountant gentleman had to leave his entire savings back in Iraq as he fled for his life.

He then, at some point, restarted his career in another Gulf country in the Middle East. He would tell me a lot of fun stories about the Gulf and its people. He would tell me about his adventures and challenges. He used to talk about how being a vegetarian in Iraq was a next-to-impossible proposition. Though a few parts of Iraq were fertile and did have a possibility of agriculture, most items were imported. So if a ship landed at port, it could be carrying, say, only one item in a massive shipment. For instance, it could be cabbage. You would then be forced to eat cabbage as a staple for the rest of the month!

More fun stories followed. He talked about how there was a South Korean construction company that had landed a project. They set up an encampment near the prospective site, close to where my accountant/guide worked. A number of Chinese and South Korean semi-skilled laborers were at the site. Also, at the site were a number of stray dogs.

He noticed with time that the number of dogs kept dwindling, and at some point, they had disappeared altogether. He got curious and once asked his office mate, "Where are all those stray dogs?"

"They are a delicacy!" came the cool response as the office mate pointed in the direction of the labor staff camp. True or not, the stories were a fascinating glimpse of life from someone who had spent decades in those countries.

The accountant and I would share stories and finally part late at night when we would take stock of the sales (if any!) and count the cash and close the books for the day. On one particular day, the books did not balance out with the cash on hand. We were short by Rs.20. Being THE accountant that he was, the gentleman kept trying to figure out what the problem was by counting and recounting.

It was getting late, and my stomach started grumbling. My mind began wandering and thinking about what could potentially be waiting for me at the dinner table. I was by now tired, hungry, and impatient. So, at one point, I just took out my wallet and pulled out two ten rupee notes. I then put them into the cash box and declared, "All done!", and walked off, much to the consternation of the cashier and my accountant/guide.

Jokes aside, though my business sank without a trace within a year's time, I had great memories and fun moments from those days. I did learn multiple lessons about business by starting my first venture. Considering that such a business was what one would describe as a 'low entry barrier' business, many businessmen jumped into the fray, starting similar and sometimes identical businesses. I quickly realized I would not survive the squeeze between the 'traditional family-owned' grocery stores and the 'new age' stores coming up like weeds.

The irony was that the traditional street corner grocery stores, which most people would dismiss as being run by illiterate or semi-literate folks, not only gave a tough fight to new age stores started by the MBA types but also outcompeted them. With their level of personalized services and relationships developed, they just would outlast and outlive most of the big entrants.

The fools were basically businessmen like us who studied *Walmart* case studies and then tried transposing those models 'lock, stock, and barrel' into INDIA. Not understanding that these are separate and different scenarios. They have different value propositions and price sensitivities. Also, given the then market size of that small town, so many entrants rushing in would only divide a rather small pie into many small and smaller pieces.

Entering a business with a low-entry barrier was, and is, always risky unless one understands what one can bring to the table that others would not be able to copy or do better. Otherwise, one may end up in a 'race to the bottom', as I learned the hard way.

However, when the time came to make that difficult decision to shutter, I was up to it. Considering that the business did not seem to be viable, sustainable, or profitable, I did take the tough and smarter call to shutter and look to do something else. Throwing bad money after good was not necessarily a winning strategy.

However, during those times of running my first business, my accountant/ guide and I would keep our spirits high as we exchanged stories from our pasts, even as we waited for customers.

One particularly interesting story he narrated was of what transpired in the 1960s in a particular Middle Eastern country, which was desperately poor. It was ruled by a particular *Sheikh* who happened to be a little more on the conservative and traditional side. His sons, however, had studied abroad and were more exposed. Being more exposed, they had new ideas and were more progressive. As one can expect, there were generational differences and clashes between the *Sheikh* and his sons.

This particular Sheikh had passed a law that everyone in the kingdom had to carry a 'lantern' and a 'walking stick'. Now, besides it being a tradition, it did make perfect sense BACK in time. The stick was necessary to probe the sand before one stepped forward, so that one did not step on scorpions, lizards, or snakes. It also served to check for any gaps ahead while walking in the sand. Anyone unlucky enough may sink into those soft spots which behaved like sinkholes. The lantern was for illumination, of course.

This culture was so entrenched that even when people did their folk dance, the walking stick and sometimes lantern were part of the act. All this was just so entrenched in the culture.

Sometime in the early 1970s, gas was struck in the country. The money that came in from the sale of the carbon-based fuel allowed for roads and highways to be laid, electrification to be provided, homes to be built with all accompanying infrastructure. However, the dynamics between the Sheikh and his children also changed. It became more strained and more acutely divergent on many issues.

While lighting was enabled by electricity, money coming into the country allowed for roads and homes to be built. This meant that people actually had no need for the walking stick and the lantern. The Sheikh, however, continued to insist that people carry the walking stick and the lantern. It was, after all, a part of their culture for centuries. 'One should not abandon or discard one's culture' was his refrain.

The sons of the Sheikh were by now at their wits' end. They had to do something about this. Sailing with one leg on a modern cruiser and one leg on a traditional *Dow* was really NOT a practical approach. So the story goes that they got the Sheikh shot in the leg and air-lifted him to a hospital in London for treatment. The Sons of the Sheikh just continued to keep him there, away on one pretext or another and did not allow him to come back. In the meanwhile, they set out to modernize their country. Without the roadblocks of the Sheikh, they could apply their fresh and contemporary approach unhindered.

The anecdote, whether true or embellished, was super fun. While it may be obvious to us from the outside that the culture of carrying a walking stick and a lantern was not practical anymore, it was not so for that Sheikh. You may laugh at the Sheikh and this story, but if you look around, you will find plenty of people who are unable, on one hand, to give up a tradition/culture, while at the same time trying to come to terms with this fast-changing modern world.

As funny as the anecdote is, the Sheikh was NO different from most of us. If one were to look, and look hard in the mirror, one may well find a person who comes close to that Sheikh.

It is human nature and a human thing to cling unto pasts and traditions and do so WITHOUT questioning their relevance or viability. Blindly sticking to traditions gives one a sense of continuity and comfort. This actually is completely 'the normal' and the norm, rather than 'the exception', I may add.

"Change" to most of us can be frightening, threatening, and exhausting. We are all human after all and no different from each other. Often, WITHOUT legacy issues and baggage, the next generation tends to look at things with more lightness and flexibility in their thought processes. This creates generational friction and conflict because of the diverging approaches and perspectives.

There is a saying, "We complain about the headlights of the oncoming car blinding us, even as we drive in full beam, NOT even noticing that OUR car has headlights too, that too in full beam!"

Hence, this change, though, needs to start with the man in the mirror!

Time for some FUN

Time for the song *'Chura Liya Hai Tumne Jo Dil Ko'* starring **Zeenat Aman** and **Vijay Arora** from the Movie *'Yaadon Ki Baaraat'* **(1973).**

Music is by **R.D. Burman** play back singers are **Asha Bhosle** (female) and **Mohammed Rafi** (male). The Movie was directed by **Nasir Hussain** and story was written by pair of **Salim-Javed** (**Salim Khan** and **Javed Akhtar**). Enjoy!!

SONG

'Chura Liya Hai Tumne Jo Dil Ko'

MOVIE

'Yaadon Ki Baaraat' **(1973)**

SCAN above to see **YOUTUBE** *Video of the Song*

Lyrics **['Chura Liya Hai Tumne Jo Dil Ko']**	*Translation* **['Now That You Have Stolen My Heart']**
Chura liya hai tumne jo dil ko Nazar nahin churaana sanam Badalke meri tum zindagaani Kahin badal na jaana sanam	Now that you have stolen my heart Don't avoid/spurn me, my darling After having turned over my life so Don't you ever undergo a change yourself, my darling

Oh, le liya dil, oh haai mera dil Haai dil lekar mujhko na behlaana Chura liya hai tumne jo dil ko Nazar nahin churaana sanam	Darling, you took my heart, yes my heart And now that you have taken my heart don't try to pacify me Now that you have stolen my heart Don't avoid/spurn me, my darling
Badalke meri tum zindagaani Kahin badal na jaana sanam	After having turned over my life so Don't you ever undergo a change yourself, my darling
(Bahaar banke aaoon kabhi tumhaari duniya mein Guzar na jaaye yeh din kahin isi tamanna mein) [x2]	(Like the season of spring, I wish to enter your world I hope that my days do not pass by in this desire) [x2]
Tum mere ho, ho tum mere ho Aaj tum itna vaada karte jaana Chura liya Chura liya hai tumne jo dil ko Nazar nahin churaana sanam Badalke meri tum zindagaani Kahin badal na jaana sanam	You're only mine my sweetheart Just promise me so today, before you leave You have stolen… Now that you have stolen my heart Don't avoid/spurn me, my darling After having turned over my life so Don't you ever undergo a change yourself, my darling
Ho, sajaaoonga lutkar bhi tere badan ki daali ko Lahoo jigar ka doonga haseen labon ki laali ko Sajaaoonga lutkar bhi tere badan ki daali ko Lahoo jigar ka doonga haseen labon ki laali ko	I will adorn/decorate the lovely branches of your body, even if I have to get bankrupt I'll give the blood of my heart to enhance the beauty of your rosy red lips I will adorn/decorate the lovely branches of your body, even if I have to get bankrupt I'll give the blood of my heart to enhance the beauty of your rosy red lips

Hai vafa kya is jahaan ko	This lover of yours
Ek din dikhla doonga main deewana	Will show the world what fidelity is all about one day
Chura liya	You have stolen…
Chura liya hai tumne jo dil ko	Now that you have stolen my heart
Nazar nahin churaana sanam	Don’t avoid/spurn me, my darling
Badalke meri tum zindagaani	After having turned over my life so
Kahin badal na jaana sanam	Don’t you ever undergo a change yourself, my darling
Le liya dil, haai mera dil	Darling, you took my heart, yes my heart
Haai dil lekar mujhko na behlaana	And now that you have taken my heart don’t try to pacify me
Chura liya hai tumne jo dil ko	Now that you have stolen my heart
Nazar nahin churaana sanam	Don’t avoid/spurn me, my darling
Hm hm hm hm, hm hm hm hm [x2]	Hm hm hm hm, hm hm hm hm [x2]

Part I

Chapter 5

WE HANG-ON TO 'WHAT WE GOT'

It is easier on the couch and watching TV, than it is when in the action on the field amidst the heat and dust

"It is not the critic who counts; not the man who points out how the strong man stumbles, or where the doer of deeds could have done them better. The credit belongs to the man who is actually in the arena, whose face is marred by dust and sweat and blood; who strives valiantly; who errs, who comes short again and again, because there is no effort without error and shortcoming; but who does actually strive to do the deeds; who knows great enthusiasms, the great devotions; who spends himself in a worthy cause; who at the best knows in the end the triumph of high achievement, and who at the worst, if he fails, at least fails while daring greatly, so that his place shall never be with those cold and timid souls who neither know victory nor defeat."

– Theodore Roosevelt

"It is not the man who has the most luxurious and coziest bed who sleeps the best. Neither does food taste like heaven for the man who is at a 7-course spread buffet at a 5-Star hotel. It is the man who toils physically through the day and is asleep, even when on a concrete pavement under the moonlight, the ONE, who sleeps the best. Similarly, the man who has strived hard, and who is physically exhausted and hungry, would find that even the humble porridge would taste like nectar."

– Author

I was in my 8th grade and had enrolled in *N.C.C (National Cadet Corps)* at my school. It was an activity that involved us turning up in starched uniforms with belts and boots polished enough that anyone inspecting the boots could see their face.

The uniforms, the belts, the berets, socks, and shoes were given to us free of cost. However, they were hand-me-downs. They had been worn over the decades and were technically decades old. They had been worn by tens of students before us. The uniforms and boots were returned on completion of the 2-year duration of the program. Returned uniforms were then given to the entering batch of students.

Yet, it did not matter; the students turned up in those clothes every Thursday evening after school in fine form. The clothes were suitably mended, stitched for gaps, starched stiff, and ironed prim and proper. This part was done by the Moms of students with fine enthusiasm, I must say!

The belts and shoes, on the other hand, were polished and made to shine by cadets. Using a special bar (like a soap), students applied the polish to their belts. The brass buckles and other parts were polished with *Brasso*. The leather boots, with metal strips in the sole, were shined until we could adjust our berets in our reflection. All this happened on Thursdays, even through our school lunch breaks. The pace was frenetic, and the atmosphere was electric.

Normal School Days

Even on normal school days, students getting ready for the school assembly would be frantically polishing the black leather shoes or applying white liquid polish to their white canvas shoes. If that ran out, students would even use chalk as substitutes. It did not matter that your shoes got dirty in transit on crowded public transport. While the shine on your shoes was often a victim of the rush hour on buses, that was not the school's problem; it was yours as a student.

So, students often carried polish and a brush for leather boots, liquid polish for white canvas shoes. In case the situation got desperate, white chalk was a tempting quick fix, and the humble chalk became worth its weight in gold!

Nails had to be cut to size, and hair cropped suitably short. Clothes needed to be suitably ironed, and belts worn tight. We simply had to come to school on time. Latecomers would be made to wait and undergo another separate process. Habitual latecomers were given suitable physical exercises like frog jumping, push-ups, etc., so that they would prefer getting up early to the snooze button on their alarms.

On Thursday evenings, the N.C.C. group assembled under the command of our commanding officer, who we affectionately called Mr. Suri Sir. The first command would be to stand in ascending order of height. Then began the inspection, where uniforms and turnout were inspected. The boots had to be polished enough that they reflected the commander's face, if he chose to peer. Belts had to be worn tight enough that the commander would not be able to find a gap to hold the buckle. If he thought your belt was not tight enough, he would just hold your buckle and shake you like a leaf as he weeded you out. The beret and the pomp-pom had to be just right. The hair needed to be short enough that he could not grasp it at the back of your head; otherwise, he would get his grip, and you would get your position outside the line. The shirts and shorts needed to be starched, ironed, prim, and proper. The badges on our shoulders and the beret had to be perfect and in position.

After weeding out the slackers, the rest were commanded to perform a maneuver that made us form a three-row assembly in a boat shape by height.

The clothes may have been old, and the heat under the starched clothing was unbearable, but not our resolve. We wore it with pride, and our spirits were high. We had fun too. Even as we began under command to perform the warm-up exercises, there would always be someone who just had a need at some crucial moment to make a comment or crack a joke. Most of us would be trying to keep a straight face and control our laughter. Anyone who laughed would catch the eye of the commander and would be made to stand down, to be given further special treatment.

Once, in a physical training session, I was caught laughing along with two of my colleagues. We were commanded to make rounds of the ground (a public ground behind our school) with dummy wooden rifles above our heads. There were three of us in a line with the guns above our heads making rounds.

The guy who was the source of the joke was suitably in the middle. Incorrigible and the character that he was, he continued telling jokes, even as we were making rounds. I was just behind him. The guy in the middle, however, was on a roll and was rattling out one joke after another, even as we made our rounds.

We tried our best to control our laughter and keep a straight face, even as our commander turned intermittently to keep an eye on us. The ground was large, and the jokes kept coming; at some point, the commander would catch us laughing. Suitably caught, the commander simply made us repeat the dose.

As the jokes kept rolling and the laughter kept bursting through our straight faces, we were simply made to keep running. With the joker in front of me on a roll, the jokes were coming non-stop. We were three clowns in a row, much to the amusement of the rest of the cadets. At some point, as the commander made us do another set of rounds, some of the cadets in the original group could not hold their straight faces. The laughter was totally infectious. The commander was now at his wit's end. "Do any of you guys want to join those monkeys?" he thundered in exasperation.

We 'monkeys' had to keep running around the ground with rifles above our heads, even as this went on for the entire evening. Mercy on us three that it ended when the N.C.C. session finally ended. All throughout, we kept trying to control our laughter and kept trying to dodge our commander, in vain. With our middle-fella in full flight, jokes kept coming, and we kept running. The commander just kept repeating the dose.

At the end of the session when the battalion was asked to disperse, the three of us were flat on our backs with our hands on our stomachs, still unable to control our bursts of laughter. Our stomachs by now were hurting more than our legs or hands.

The *D.A.V. School's (Gopalapuram, Chennai) N.C.C.'s* chapter

The N.C.C. chapter of our school, D.A.V. (Gopalapuram), in its time in the 1980s, was highly rated. From every school around the country, one cadet would be selected to represent the school in the national Republic Day parade. There would be a national competition held for the Best Cadet Award. Those selected cadets sent by their respective schools would be rated based on fitness tests, turnout, march-past, and other skills. Finally, the 'Best National Cadet' would be selected after a grueling competition.

D.A.V.'s (Gopalapuram) N.C.C cadets were no slackers. Often, the **'Nation's Best Cadet Award'** would be the cadet sent from our school.

In our senior batch, N.C.C. Cadet Parameshwaran was awarded the country's Best Cadet Award. In our batch, our classmate N.C.C. Cadet Prahlad.A won the country's Best Cadet Award.

The reason I brought this up is that we were lucky to have such outstanding role models even at that age. Whenever I watched Rahul Dravid (India's famous cricketer) on or off the field, I would recall my classmate Prahlad. A. He was just that kind of guy, 'prim and proper', and a gentleman even when under pressure.

The N.C.C. session always ended with a nice snack. It was often a *Masala Dosa* given in packets, wrapped traditionally in banana leaves (eco-friendly, I may add), and wound with string. After the session, well after sunset, the Masala Dosa packets were handed out and lapped up eagerly by the now hungry cadets.

That was the point when we entered heaven. Hours of grueling schoolwork and after a rigorous N.C.C. drill, tired and ravenously hungry, the Masala Dosa on our laps was just Amrit or Ambrosia ('Nectar of the Gods'). At that moment, we touched heaven.

It is NOT the man who has the most luxurious and coziest bed who sleeps the best. Neither does food taste like heaven for the man who is at a 7-course spread buffet at a 5-Star hotel. It is the man who toils physically through the day and is asleep, even when on a concrete pavement under the moonlight, the one who sleeps the best. Similarly, the man who has strived hard and is physically exhausted and hungry will find that even humble porridge tastes like nectar.

Why We Hang-on Unto 'What We Got'

Having finished the N.C.C. session on that day, I gathered my three bags. On my shoulders are my heavy school bag filled with books. My change of clothes bag was suitably slung around my right shoulder. It had my change of clothes and other accessories which I had brought for my N.C.C. session. The third was my lunch basket, consisting of 3 Tiffin stacked boxes, a large water bottle and towel spread (my lunch basket was lovingly handed to me every morning by my mother. On school days she would get up early to cook and pack my lunch bag with fresh food).

With my shoulders weighed down by my school bag and the change of clothes bag on my right shoulder, I held my lunch basket in my left hand. I then set out for the bus stop to catch my public transport home, with the Beatles song 'A Hard Day's Night', on my lips.

If you would like to sing along as you walk with me to the Bus Stop, here it is below:

'A Hard Day's Night'

Beatles, [Album **'A Hard Day's Night' (1964)**]

SCAN above to see **YOUTUBE** ***Video of the Song***

Lyrics

[A Hard Day's Night]

It's been a hard day's night
And I've been workin' like a dog
It's been a hard day's night
I should be sleepin' like a log

But when I get home to you
I find the things that you do
Will make me feel alright

You know I work all day
To get you money to buy you things
And it's worth it just to hear you say
You're goin' to give me everything

So why on earth should I moan
'Cause when I get you alone
You know I feel okay

When I'm home
Everything seems to be right
When I'm home
Feeling you holding me tight
Tight, yeah

It's been a hard day's night
And I've been workin' like a dog
It's been a hard day's night
I should be sleepin' like a log

But when I get home to you
I find the things that you do
Will make me feel alright, aw!

So why on earth should I moan
'Cause when I get you alone
You know I feel okay

When I'm home
Everything seems to be right
When I'm home
Feeling you holding me tight
Tight, yeah

Ooh, it's been a hard day's night
And I've been workin' like a dog
It's been a hard day's night
I should be sleepin' like a log

> But when I get home to you
> I find the things that you do
> Will make me feel alright
> You know I feel alright
> You know I feel alright

As I sang the lines, "It has been a hard day's night, and I have been working like a dog, It has been a hard day's night, I should be sleeping like a log", the 15-minute walk to the bus stand seemed rather too short. I then stood at the bus stop as I waited for the bus.

The public bus had about a 25-minute frequency, and the time by now was about 7 pm. This was rush hour, and the buses that arrived were jam-packed with people leaving their offices. The crowd was just piling on. I was by now exhausted, just wanting to get home. As I prudently skipped a couple of over-crowded buses, the time was past 8 pm at night. It was an hour's ride home, and it was getting later by the minute.

After another 25 minutes, another bus arrived, and I made the decision to pile on. The only place available was on the footboard of the bus. I will admit that traveling on the footboard is an 'art', and at that point, I was an amateur at it.

Basically, given the rush, there was space for only one foot on the footboard of that bus, which was overflowing with people. If one decided to take the shot, one's body would hang half outside the body of the bus. I transferred my food basket to my right hand and took a step with my left foot into that only space available. As I stepped up with my left foot, I slid my left hand up the slanted handrail (meant to help people board the bus).

While I was foolish enough to board, I was atleast smart enough to slide my hand as deep as possible up the rail, giving myself some cushion and insurance. I took a tight grip with my left hand, even as my left foot found its position on the last step. [Disclaimer: These are things NOT to do, obviously, duh!].

Even as my shoulder bag weighed on my back, I was trying to make sure my change of clothes bag would not slide off my right shoulder. With my lunch basket hanging in the air and held by my right hand, I was juggling three bags, all while my right foot was in the air and my left leg in an awkward and difficult position. To make matters worse, I was further burdened by the partial weight of passengers ahead of me. They, in turn, had the weight of passengers ahead of them. The precarious angle at which we all were positioned only added to the weight transfers.

Being an amateur at 'extreme' footboard traveling, I incorrectly used the smooth and slanted handrail as my hold. Though I was smart enough to grip the topmost part of it, it was smooth-finished and slanting downward. The ride to the next stop was possibly under 10 minutes, but as every second ticked by, my left hand (which had gripped the rail as high and deep as possible) started slipping and sliding.

Letting go was not an option at that point. The angle of my hanging body was such that I would fall on my head if I did let go. Even as every second passed, I was slowly slipping. To make matters worse, it was tense, and my palms were getting sweaty. Bailing out with the bus in motion meant I would hit my head on the asphalt. To make things even worse, the people on the footboard (and ahead of me) had part of their body weight on me. This was simply because of the angle at which they were hanging on. If I did let go, not only would I fall, but most likely, I would have an entire basketball team join me on the asphalt. I don't know how long it took to get to the next stop, maybe 7 minutes, but it felt like forever.

At some point, the bus arrived at the next stop, even as my left hand had reached the edge. By now, my body was at an impossible angle. I got off backward and stepped back. I took a deep breath.

I decided to calmly wait for another hour or so until the crowd thinned out. Finally, I reached home tired and hungry but intact. As I washed my hands and face, I looked into the mirror of the washbasin cabinet and smiled as I thought, 'Getting home LATE was better than reaching the hospital EARLY'.

That was a Bus, How about a Train?

I thought I was alone in this until one day my Father narrated his story. My Father was in far-off Assam in the late 1960s when his uncle passed away. My Father had to travel across the country to attend his uncle's funeral. He tried booking a train, but it was the festive season, and he couldn't secure any reserved seats. He was told he could try the unreserved compartment. Anyone with an unreserved ticket could board an unreserved compartment. The ticket was the cheapest, and it was always crowded.

As luck would have it, the unreserved compartment was full to the brim, except beside the door of the compartment. If one was ready to sit there, one would pretty much be facing the outside with legs hanging outside. However, that was the only option available, a 'take it or leave it' situation. Now, that was risky, but even riskier when you considered that the journey to my Dad's next connection was over 36 hours. The next connection my Dad had was a proper reserved ticket, so that was not a problem, but getting to his next connection was.

My Father had already been short on sleep before even boarding the train. Having taken the seat by the door, and 10 hours into the journey, my Father was beginning to feel it. He put his arm around the vertical handrail (used as a grip when boarding) and held it in a hug, even as he continued to endure the footboard travel.

However, he began to have doubts. He wasn't sure whether he might inadvertently let go in the event he dozed off. With some quick thinking, he took the only thing he had with him, a long thin cloth towel, and tied his left arm to the handrail tightly. It was his insurance. He then took the liberty of intermittently dozing off, confident that he would NOT fall off the train. He ultimately made it to his connecting train on time. Having caught the connecting train, he finally reached his destination just before the cremation, as he had felt obliged to do.

Bus & Train, How about a Plane?

Hanging off a bus is crazy. Hanging off a train is crazier. But, "How about a plane?" Well, hanging off a plane is something only Tom Cruise can do (with safety taken care of), as filmed in the Hollywood movie franchise of the Mission Impossible series.

The fact that Tom Cruise was the only one who could pull it off was something the Afghan gentleman hanging onto the last evacuating U.S. plane leaving Afghanistan found out the hard way. Even as the US military withdrew from Taliban's Afghanistan, the freedom and future of the common Afghan people were at the mercy of the whims of the Taliban.

As for the Afghan gentleman, desperate situations can sometimes call for desperate measures. It is a different story whether you choose to heed that call.

Bus, Train or Plane

"We cannot be sure of having something to live for unless we are willing to die for it."

– Ernesto Guevara

People may laugh at the Afghan gentleman, but you know what? I can feel what he felt. It was a desperate statement he was making. He would rather die, and die trying, than live in a place where his freedom was mortgaged. That plane was his last ticket to freedom. It is a different story that he did not have a real ticket. Not all are as lucky to get one.

Among the three of us—the Afghani gentleman, my Dad, and myself—as converse as it may seem, the biggest fool was myself. Waiting an hour or two and going home late was a small price to pay versus falling off a bus.

My Dad had a more compelling reason; can't blame him. Also, his insurance was way better than mine.

As for the Afghan gentleman, he just had another level of desperation. But you have to give it to him. He was determined, even if maybe he was not completely sensible. But he did make his statement, dramatic as it may have been. I can actually completely understand that, though I would not likely have taken that option in any case.

But, you know what? That is easy to say. Anyone in that position would have considered that option (as crazy as it may seem to us sitting on couches, sipping on our beers, and watching it play on TV around the world). Whether we would have actually taken it, though, depends. Many of us would have been prevented by our fears or a sense of self-preservation. We would have gone on to accept the situation with a sense of resignation.

In the case of that particular Afghan gentleman, 'desperation + audacity + craziness' just got ahead of his sense of 'self-preservation + thought process + common sense'. This made him commit a desperate and fatal act. Some may say he was stupid, but as I said, it is very easy to comment on someone else, that too after the fact.

Conclusion

In our lives, 'We hold on to what we got'. Sometimes, letting go is NOT an option. However, as human and fallible as we all are, thinking through situations would help us reach better outcomes. Sometimes, a tactical retreat is better than suicide. Sometimes, a strategic retreat itself may be the option to consider. You can choose to 'live and fight another day'.

Our 'fight or flight' response is hardwired to make us 'shoot from the hip'. Ultimately, taking fatal risks has to be worth it. The price you pay has to be worth the value you derive. Well, again, all this is easier said than done. We will only know 'WHERE we stand', 'WHEN actually confronted' by such a dilemma.

What we would have and could have done in his place are things that are very easy to say in theory, but God help us if we are put in such a situation and are presented with those impossible choices.

May the Afghan gentleman's soul rest in peace. God Bless!

Time for some FUN

Time to **'Keep the Faith'** with **American** rock star **Bon Jovi** from his album **'Keep the Faith' (1992).** Enjoy!!

'Keep the Faith'

Bon Jovi, [Album **'Keep the Faith' (1992)**]

SCAN above to see **YOUTUBE** ***Video of the Song***

Lyrics

[Keep the Faith]

Mother, mother, tell your children
That their time has just begun
I have suffered for my anger
There are wars that can't be won

Father, father, please believe me
I am laying down my guns
I am broken like an arrow
Forgive me, forgive your wayward son

(Everybody needs somebody to love) mother, mother
(Everybody needs somebody to hate) please believe me
(Everybody's bitching 'cause they don't get enough)
And it's hard to hold on when there's no one to lean on

(Faith!) You know you're gonna live through the rain
Lord, we've gotta keep the faith
(Faith!) Don't you let your love turn to hate
Now we've gotta keep the faith

Keep the faith, keep the faith
Lord, we've gotta keep the faith

Tell me, baby, when I hurt you
Do you keep it all inside?
Do you tell me all's forgiven
And just hide behind your pride? Yeah

(Everybody needs somebody to love) mother, father
(Everybody needs somebody to hate) please don't leave me
(Everybody's bleeding 'cause the times are tough)
Well, it's hard to be strong when there's no one to dream on

(Faith!) You know you're gonna live through the rain
Lord, we've gotta keep the faith
(Faith!) Don't you know it's never too late?
Right now we've gotta keep the faith
(Faith!) Don't you let your love turn to hate
Lord, we've gotta keep the faith

Keep the faith, keep the faith
Oh, we've gotta keep the faith
Keep the faith, keep the faith
Lord, we've gotta keep the faith
Ooh yeah, ooh yeah
Yeah, yeah, yeah!

I've been walking in the footsteps of society's lies
I don't like what I see no more, sometimes I wish I was blind
Sometimes I wait forever to stand out in the rain
So no one sees me cryin', tryna wash away this pain

Mother, father (everybody needs somebody to love)
There's things I've done I can't erase (everybody needs somebody to hate)
Every night we fall from grace (everybody's bitching 'cause they don't get enough)
It's hard with the world in your face (everybody needs)
Tryna hold on, tryna hold on (everybody, keep the faith)

(Faith!) You know you're gonna live through the rain
Lord, you've gotta keep the faith
(Faith!) Don't you let your love turn to hate
Right now we've gotta keep the faith

(Faith!) Keep the faith, keep the faith
Try to hold on, tryna hold on, yeah
(Faith!) Keep the faith, keep the faith
Everybody keep the faith
(Faith!) Keep the faith, keep the faith
Yeah, yeah, yeah, yeah, yeah

(Faith! Everybody needs somebody to love)
Yeah, yeah, yeah, yeah, yeah (everybody needs somebody to hate)
(Faith! Everybody needs somebody to love)
(Everybody needs, everybody, keep the faith, faith!)

<u>Part I</u>

Chapter 6

DISCRIMINATION AND REVERSE DISCRIMINATION

Dead Either way

"Well-developed human resources are the key to open the door to unlimited wealth. Ultimately, all resources—oil, agricultural land, industries, minerals, etc.—are limited. The only thing 'unlimited' is the Human mind."

–Author

"Adults sometimes behave like children, while refusing to allow children to take responsibility like adults."

–Author

Why any Nation or Society that goes down the path of any kind of discrimination and sidetracks merit it is heading down the pipe.

Let us take the example of *caste* as a societal construct in India. For thousands of years, INDIA followed a caste system, in which one's occupation was pre-destined, based on birth. Actually, it is difficult to say whether this was by design or by default. In earlier times, most knowledge and skill were often transmitted from generation to generation WITHIN groups or families. Hence, knowledge and skill were confined to groups.

WIDE dissemination of knowledge and skill did NOT take place. This just fossilized a system that became an 'occupation by birth' kind of social construct, which we referred to later as the caste system in INDIA.

The innovation of the printing press (originally from CHINA but greatly enhanced and harnessed by the WEST) allowed for the creation and the mass printing of books. The caste system, however, had taken root thousands of years BEFORE this groundbreaking innovation.

Even with the invention of the printing press, the problem of dissemination of knowledge was NOT completely solved. This problem existed across societies and nations. The reason is that books cost money to print. Even when mass printed, there was still an affordability barrier that kept most of the inhabitants of this planet unable to afford and/or access them.

When my Father went to undergraduate school to study civil engineering in the 1950s (at V.J.T.I, in then Bombay), he did NOT have money to pay his college fees, let alone buy books. He had a classmate, however, who was relatively well-off. My Father would borrow books from him and return them after having read and taken notes. Having borrowed the books, he would spend nights in the verandah balcony of his two-room **Chawl* and copy them, making notes under streetlight, while his parents and neighbors were asleep. Often, he did NOT have even plain 'A4 sheets' to make notes, so he would accumulate newspapers from neighbors and make notes in the corners wherever he found spaces and gaps.

*A type of Accommodation in MUMBAI (formerly BOMBAY) which often had one room, one kitchen and common communal toilets and bath shared by often 10 families).

Printing books costs money. Many wealthy and smart people in the United States of America recognized this as a significant cost barrier that prevented common folks from benefiting from the learning that came from books. Mass printing did help, but it was still NOT enough. These wealthy and enterprising people recognized that for the greater good of society, it mattered that they create and donate to public libraries.

If you choose to look beyond the superficial glitz and glamour of the United States of America, what will strike you is their high emphasis on 'Public Libraries'. These were places that anyone could go and pick up a book and start reading.

Many of the wealthiest, like the Steel Magnate Andrew Carnegie, had donated huge sums to create humongous libraries. They understood the power of the dissemination of knowledge. They also recognized that to break the cost barrier, it was necessary to build 'Public Libraries'.

Most people think America is rich and wealthy because it has large resources such as endless agricultural land, industries, mines, oil, and unlimited resources, etc. Well, no doubt that is true. However, if you think IT is JUST that, then you are 'Missing the forest for the trees', as they say.

To harness "THOSE unlimited resources", you need to first develop the 'Human Resources'. You need a literate, knowledgeable, creative, and innovative population. Well-developed human resources are the key to opening the door to unlimited wealth. Ultimately, all resources like oil, agricultural land, industries, minerals, etc., are limited. The ONLY thing unlimited is the potential of the 'Human mind'.

For the last 200 years after the dawn of the Industrial Revolution, up until the Information Revolution, the United States laid a foundation of knowledge. Building huge public libraries and land grant universities (like Iowa State University, my alma mater) were part of the plan. It is striking just how big and awe-inspiring libraries at the US universities are.

So, sometimes it is easy to miss the point. Often, we 'miss the signal for the noise'. Rather than looking at the United States of America as a country that got rich because it has natural resources and vast land (which is the noise in the approach), it will suffice to say that the emphasis on (i) Education for the masses + (ii) Free thinking + (iii) Democratic system + (iv) Charter of Equality + (v) Capitalism + (vi) Wealthy Donating to causes, (which as a bundle ARE the signal) allowed the country's most precious resource 'People', to reach for the skies. This is the reason it is called the 'land of opportunity' and the 'land of realizing your dreams', NOT just because it has the Empire State Building, the Brooklyn Bridge, or even the White House. This is what people who get drowned in the noise notice.

The way to look at it is to understand that the Empire State Building, in its time, was a marvel of engineering, as were the Hoover Dam and Brooklyn Bridge. The White House is a symbol of the United States' commitment to '(i) Free thinking + (ii) Democratic system + (iii) Charter of Equality + (iv) Capitalism', and NOT just a seat of power. The POTUS and White House are just the face of that.

The 'Statue of Liberty' (Liberty Enlightening the World; French: La Liberté éclairant le monde), dedicated on October 28, 1886, at Liberty Island in New York Harbor in New York City, was a symbol of what the United States of America stands for. A plaque at the 'Statue of Liberty' reads, "Give me your tired, your poor, your huddled masses yearning to breathe free". (It was a quote by Emma Lazarus, from her poem called 'New Colossus', written for a fundraiser auction to raise money for the pedestal of the statue).

The 'Statue of Liberty' symbolized what the US stood for. There is a saying in America, 'It does NOT matter WHERE you came from, it only matters WHERE you are GOING'.

It would be pertinent to keep in mind the quote, "Never underestimate the determination & capacity of the hungry". I know immigration in recent times has been a complicated and sticky political issue in the USA. However, it still does NOT take away from the fact that the USA was and still is one of the most open-minded and welcoming societies in the world.

When the 'Information Super Highway' (a.k.a. the 'internet') first came to INDIA, an important barrier was crossed. It is important to note that even 'Public Libraries' have limitations. Cost, Accessibility, and Time required to access books in these libraries were still barriers at various levels. With the Internet revolution, and companies like *Google,* this barrier was brought down to a great extent. So, now since the 1990s, these barriers have been broken down further.

However, the internet still required computer and internet access. Even though the cost of computers and internet connection have been coming down, it was still a barrier for most, at least in the 'third world' and in countries like INDIA.

Interestingly, these cost barriers were further broken down with the mobile phone revolution, more particularly the smartphone revolution. The cost of a smart phone has been rapidly decreasing on a per unit basis. Most entry-level smartphones are now more accessible and within reach of billions of people around the world.

The mobile smartphone is one of the most powerful innovations, beyond the discovery of fire, electricity, the printing press, locomotive, or even telecommunication. The mobile smartphone, placed the *Goddess Saraswati* (Goddess of knowledge, learning, and music) into the palms of the most underprivileged. If there could be only ONE boon the poor and underprivileged could ask for, the MOST powerful would be the access to knowledge. The power of this knowledge, has the capacity to open doors to a better life and to raise standards of living globally.

With the mobile smartphone, cost barriers have been brought down to the point where billions of books can be accessed by anyone with 'little money' and 'unlimited desire and determination' to make a better life for themselves and their families. However, while costs have come down, it just needed a little more of a push. We will come to that in a moment.

I often told my DAD, 'You are an Engineer and NOT an Entrepreneur', but I will be the first to admit my Father was a true-born entrepreneur. He just did NOT have the bandwidth and monetary resources to harness that ability in him. His initial poverty and struggle made him risk-averse and emotionally attached to money. So he found it difficult to take risks and maximize his output by combining his savings, entrepreneurial bent of mind, hard work, and talent.

There was a time when as a young teenager, my Dad would hang out around the post offices in Dadar, Bombay (Mumbai). A 'POST CARD' was the most common, economical, and easy method of communication in those days. Most people, who were immigrants to BOMBAY (Mumbai) from far-off villages and towns, would come to the post office to send communications back home.

These migrants were most often NOT literate. This presented a problem. Most people would see it as a problem. Now, where there is a problem, there is an opportunity. Where there is an opportunity, there is an entrepreneur. The entrepreneur in my Dad saw this as an opportunity to make some pocket money. Still in his teens and literate, he saw an opportunity to help those migrants write those POST CARDS. They would dictate while he wrote. They were happy to give him a few coins in return. In this way, my Father would earn a little bit by adding value to society. A little pocket change, if you will, to augment his poor family's income.

Talking of POSTCARDS, the founder of the *Reliance* conglomerate, Late Mr. Dhirubhai Ambani, was once asked whether he would enter a business like telecom. He had a simple answer which NOT just made economic sense, but had deep psychological and societal-economic insight.

He simply said, "I will enter the Telecom business, the day the cost of a 'CALL MINUTE' will be cheaper than the 'COST of a POST-CARD'".

The story of Late Mr. Dhirubhai Ambani, who rose from a gas pump attendant to one who established one of INDIA's greatest conglomerates, is legendary. In the early days, when Mr. Dhirubhai Ambani and his family lived in a chawl, there were stories that his children, Anil and Mukesh, would share clothing. As surprising as it may be to people in the first world, this is completely normal in INDIA, especially in those days.

My Maternal Granddad's brother would attend college, come back, and give his coat & cycle to my Maternal Granddad. My Maternal Granddad would then take both the coat and cycle and attend afternoon/evening classes. (Now, don't ask me why a coat would be required in Chennai weather, that is for later).

My Dad, on the other hand, went to college in shorts. No, it was NOT a style statement. He did not have the money for pants! He was embarrassed to wear shorts, being the only one in his college to do so in those days. No, he did NOT want to stand out for that, but he had no choice.

Ultimately, my Dad did get his pants though. He walked to the University and saved the money he was given for the bus. He at some point accumulated enough to get a pair of pants stitched for himself.

By the time I was born, we as a family had moved up economically and could have been classified as middle class. My Dad's commitment to education, consistent and diligent hard work over 20 years, at that time had taken us to the ranks of the middle class. As I grew up, we moved into the ranks of the upper-middle class. None of this would have been possible without the work ethic, discipline towards health and finance, which my 'Dad and Mom' maintained.

Interesting Family Dynamics

Even then, with the money and prosperity later achieved, there were interesting family dynamics. I had two elder sisters. The eldest would always get new clothes, but my middle sister, much to her dismay, was given the hand-me-downs from her elder sibling. This was a way to conserve costs in those days. This was in the 1980s!! (Ok, BEFORE INDIA liberalized).

Now, thank God! I was a BOY. They did dress me as a girl ONCE though, I must add!

My elder (but middle sister) would often treat me like a doll. In my childhood, she would hang out with me. She would put *Pottu* and Earrings on me to see 'how it looks'. In return, I learned English from her. She was/is a perfectionist. Her English was immaculate, and so it percolated down to me. When I first attended school, my teachers were shocked that I could speak such perfect English as a kindergartener. I will, however, state that with time and more education, it got educated out of my system, and it was only downhill from there!

An interesting tidbit was in the early 2000s when, as a child, my nephew got jealous of the dresses worn by his twin sister and insisted on wearing the clothes she wore. On one occasion, they had to attend a large family marriage function. He threw such a tantrum that my eldest sister had to concede. She dressed him as a girl, in traditional girls' clothing, replete with earrings, Pottu, kajal, and all paraphernalia.

My sister had no choice as my nephew had refused to come to the wedding unless he was dressed equivalent to his twin sister. Once dressed and delivered, he was strutting happily through the wedding function, proud as a peacock, while my eldest sister was following him everywhere, apologetically trying to explain away the curiosity of the people at the function. It was such a hilarious sight!

Coming back to the wisdom and insight with which Mr. Dhirubhai Ambani answered the question of when he would enter the telecom space, one can't help but admire the insight and wisdom in that single statement. Having started out as a gas pump attendant in Eden, he was acutely aware that people who are poor 'DO NOT have the luxury of NOT being price-sensitive'.

He also understood a concept called 'SUBSTITUTION' in Economics. The 'POSTCARD and ONE MINUTE CALL' were perfect substitutes. What can be 'spoken in a minute on a call' is the equivalent of what can be 'written on the space available in a POSTCARD'.

Basically a **'One Minute Call' = 'Content accommodated'** by the **space on** a **Post card.**

When perfect substitutes are presented to a person of limited means, I don't have to elaborate beyond that point on what would happen. I do not know whether Late Dhirubhai Ambani went to college or how much he studied. Honestly, nobody can teach one wisdom and insight in school. It has to be learned through experience, and it will reveal itself only if one is receptive enough. It is a combination of one's native intelligence, experience, receptiveness, empathy, humility, and deep thought. It is only then that wisdom delivers itself. As simple as that statement (made by Late Dhirubhai Ambani) is on the surface, it had great depth and multiple layers of deep insight. I can elaborate further, but I will resist meandering for now.

When one of Mr. Dhirubhai Ambani's sons started *Reliance JIO* (A Mukesh Ambani Company) and launched his mobile data service, he quickly took a position as a cost leader. Mukesh Ambani credits his twin children (Isha and Akash) with seeding him with the idea of JIO.

In Mr. Mukesh Ambani's Own Words

"The idea of Jio was first seeded by my daughter, Isha, in 2011. She was a student at Yale and was home for holidays. She wanted to submit some coursework – and she said, 'Dad, the internet in our house sucks'.

My son Akash said, 'Dad, your generation doesn't get it. In the old world, telecom was voice – and you only make money when one person calls and the other answers. In our new world, everything is digital. We can do a lot more with a digital network than just talk'".

Originally, there were more than 11+ telecommunication companies operating in INDIA, including *Aircel, TATA Docomo, Videocon, MTS India, IDEA Cellular, Bharti Airtel, BSNL, MTNL, Vodafone, Telenor* and *Reliance Communication* (Anil Ambani Company).

The market size of smartphone users who used data at that point was under 80 million Indians. Interestingly, the general NON-DATA users, who were people using feature phones, numbered over 800 million users at that time and were growing. For an entrepreneur/businessman who could dare to think really, really big, and was ready to plan meticulously, run his numbers, and then execute a 'low-cost strategy', the dichotomy of there being 800 million feature phone users and ONLY 80 million Smartphone data users presented a very big and clear opportunity. Most people would see a problem with INDIA being a poor country where only 7-8% of the people could afford mobile data.

Evan Spiegel, the CEO of *Snapchat*, has reportedly said that India is 'too poor a country' for his company to consider investing in. He supposedly said, "His app is ONLY for rich people. I don't want to expand into poor countries like India". I have no doubt that Evan Spiegel is a GOOD entrepreneur; however, there is a difference between a GOOD and a GREAT Entrepreneur.

My Professor of Marketing at ISU (Iowa State University), Mr. Sanjeev Agarwal, once narrated a story. Two executives were dispatched to a distant, dirt-poor country and asked to assess the market. Both of them flew out, spent some time there, made their observations, and returned.

The boss called the first person and asked him what he thought. That executive said that the country was extremely dirt poor, and only 30% of the population wore footwear at all. So he did NOT see it as a viable market, and they should not BOTHER about even trying.

The boss called the second person and asked him what he thought. That executive said that the country was extremely poor, and only 30% of the population wore footwear at all. However, since 70% did NOT wear footwear, it WAS a GREAT opportunity to further understand the needs of the population and build products at price points that can scale. In this way, he proposed that the company could take a position and become a market leader there.

Note, both the executives had made the SAME observation (the country was extremely dirt poor and only 30% of the population wore footwear at all). However, their inferences were DIAMETRICALLY opposite.

The famous professor C.K. Prahalad said, "There is immense fortune at the bottom of the pyramid".

(C.K. Prahalad was a Paul and Ruth McCracken Distinguished University Professor of Corporate Strategy at the University of Michigan, Stephen M. Ross School of Business).

Evan Spiegel, the CEO of Snapchat, is undoubtedly a GOOD entrepreneur, but there is a reason why Mukesh Ambani is a GREAT entrepreneur. There is a difference between GOOD and GREAT.

The late Dhirubhai Ambani had spoken about the telecommunications market about 2-3 decades earlier. His son, Mr. Mukesh Ambani, took the essence of what the Late Dhirubhai Ambani had said. He understood the essence of that one-liner and not just the words alone. Times had changed since Dhirubhai Ambani's time. Now, telecom had moved from fixed-line to feature mobile phones to smartphones.

Beyond that, Mukesh quickly grasped that with apps (such as *Viber, WhatsApp* call), new substitutes had arisen for 'plain talk time' offered by all the existing telecom incumbents. The 'real game', beyond that, was data. People were gradually moving away from talk time and SMSs on the network (for which they were charged) to using calls through either Wi-Fi or using data plans to complete them.

One would think that with 11+ companies, the competitive intensity would bring down costs. Well, it didn't. While 80 million people used data, the rest of the 800 million and growing market were stuck with feature phones and had never accessed the internet, let alone experienced it.

People kept insisting that INDIA is poor, INDIA is poor. People can't afford data, so what to do? Basically, the complainers keep complaining and will keep complaining and take it to their respective graves.

The 'Champs' do something about it. Mr. Mukesh Ambani is a Champ. He took the baton from his father's insight decades ago and ran with it. The rest is history. His genius was, first, his pulse on the market, then his big and far-sighted vision, his grasp on numbers, insight into understanding substitution (and 'which' are the substitutes), the impact of switching costs & switching effort, understanding economies of scale, understanding economies of scope (One data connection could be used for seeing movies, education, shopping, music, reading, news, accessing information, and so on), understanding the strategy of cost leadership, understanding the aspirations of the aspirational class, understanding the socio-economic circumstances of the country's citizens, and the fact that the underprivileged in INDIA had never experienced the power, joy, and learning of the internet. Finally, his audacity and his ability to execute big and rapidly took JIO to being one of the biggest telecom networks in the world.

Before Reliance JIO, there were only 80 million people who used data; the rest of the 800 million were stuck with feature phones. There were more than 11+ companies in the fray. Even with THAT competitive intensity, it was still a gridlock.

Much like the 'Gordian Knot' that people thought was undoable. This gridlock needed action and a thought process much like the way a young 'Alexander the Great' would have thought. Alexander did NOT think like others when challenged to untie the knot. He took one look and straight took out his sword, and cut the knot in two and walked off.

Now, cut to this era, enter Mr. Mukesh Ambani. His sword was simply an astute mind that understood the opportunity at hand, an opportunity that his grip on the numbers had made apparent to him. He saw a huge strategic and tactical opportunity and was daring enough to make the leap, big-time. He knew that to make data plans viable and increase the pie of the market, he needed to employ the most devastating SHAKE-OUT imaginable.

Reliance JIO was launched and offered (Data Plans, SMSs, Talk time, and a whole bundle of services and apps from astrology, sports, news, entertainment, investments, etc.) the entire bundle, all FREE for a six-month period. It was later extended for a further 6 months.

Once, 'the aspirational underprivileged' got a taste of the internet and the mobile apps, etc., it simply got them hooked. Now, Goddess *Saraswathi* (Goddess of knowledge, learning, and music) was tantalizingly close to their palms and within grasp.

INDIA went from being at the bottom in DATA usage worldwide to the top in a couple of years (well ahead of even the US and China, I may add). Mr. Mukesh Ambani simply understood the true power of fixed cost and variable costs. With a grip on numbers, an understanding of the market, and peerless execution at scale, he simply had a strategy that can only be described as 'Shock and Awe'.

The 'chicken and egg' problem of needing capital to build the infrastructure on one hand and the need for revenue on the other hand to accomplish the task needed an 'Alexander-like approach'.

There is a saying in Tamil, "Oru vetu, erundu thundu" (One Strike, Two Pieces). No half measures here. Mr. Mukesh Ambani launched a devastating strike at the right moment. He simply sliced through the market, and the shake-out sent all but 4 of the 11+ other competitors packing. It left only 3 major players (after Idea Cellular and Vodafone merged). There is a saying in English, "Never jump halfway across a well.". You either 'Are' or 'Aren't', and there are no two ways about it.

Now, back to our point, for knowledge to percolate to the underprivileged in INDIA, COST and ACCESS to knowledge needed an overhaul. Mr. Mukesh Ambani just brought the 'Hummer' to the party. Reliance JIO opened the doors not just to knowledge but also to an entire ecosystem of commerce. In this way, not just *Saraswathi Devi* (Goddess of Knowledge, Learning, and Music) but also *Lakshmi Devi* (Goddess of Commerce and Wealth) were, for the first time, in the hands of the underprivileged.

For those underprivileged who are willing to work hard, work smart, be enterprising, and creative, this was a DOUBLE Boon ('Saraswathi Devi' + 'Lakshmi Devi') delivered by the *'Durga'* (Goddess of daring) in the form of Mr. Mukesh Ambani. A DOUBLE chocolate cake, if you will. Now, the smartphone users in INDIA number over 750 million people, up from 80 million before RELIANCE JIO. This number is expected to rise to over one billion by the year 2026.

The entire idea behind the write-up up to this point seeks to illustrate the power of how technology can be used to deliver a better life for all. Neither knowledge, wealth, nor power is the exclusive privilege of a few elite. Most people will look at Mr. Mukesh Ambani and see his $1 billion home (called Antilia) and feel this hatred. They would curse him for all the problems that poor people in India face every day.

Honestly, that is a very socialist mindset. Mr. Mukesh Ambani took a great risk and, with his 'skill and vision', created great value for society. He took a small piece of the value he created. He is a capitalist and has the right to do what he deems fit with his post-tax money. People who have that kind of enterprise will add value to society in multiple ways. They will invest in new businesses, employ a large number of people, and do charity as necessary. As long as he pays his taxes (according to the laws of the land), people have no right to grumble.

Like I said, complainers will complain and continue to complain while taking their complaints to the grave. Champions will act and deliver, and in the process, create value for society. Instead of all the hate that average people have for people with wealth, champions would observe, learn from the best, and apply the secrets of how to create wealth for themselves and society.

As long as the wealthy create wealth by being clean and paying their dues, we should celebrate their success and ask them, 'How they did it?' We should try to learn from the stories of these champions and feel inspired to do the same.

To quote the Co-founder of Infosys, Mr. Narayana Murthy, "Wealth has to be created BEFORE it can be distributed."

There is a concept that says 'Increase the size of the Societal Pie'. I first read about it in the US, in one of their online newspapers. I believe it was the former President of the United States, Mr. Bill Clinton, who talked about increasing the size of the pie rather than fighting over the distribution of the existing pie. This was something that I quickly concurred with, having seen the crazy fight for pieces of societal resources back home.

It is only a mind that has imagination that can understand that concept. A 'limited mind' would only see a 'limited pie' that has to be fought over for a small piece. However, an 'imaginative mind' will think differently and ask, "Why not JUST increase the size of the pie?"

Time for a Joke.

In the 1970s, there was once an Arab gentleman who was flush with cash. These were the early days of the Oil Boom. The Arab gentleman was invited to see a football match. He had never seen one before, so he sat there and watched as the match played out.

He could not, however, make out 'what was going on'. Finally, he took out his checkbook and asked the person who brought him to the match if he could make a gift. He said he wanted to buy a ball for EACH of the 22 players on the field.

He just could not get his head around the fact that the players on the field were all fighting for a SINGLE ball!

Honestly, as a young boy, I watched India in the 1980s, crawl along economically. There was a fight for the "limited resources".

There was a fight for reservation in education and jobs, like during the *Mandal Commission* (a fight for reservations where people were immolating themselves in protest). Whether it was for the clamour for government jobs (secure jobs with assured pension), a complete lack of imagination in the education system (hard work ONLY mattered, obsession with mastering what was already there, an aversion to failure), a lack of the entrepreneurial spark (entrepreneurship was deemed inferior).

Entrepreneurship was only for those who were bad at studies or could not find a job. As for an entrepreneur looking for a 'bride', nobody wanted to touch a struggling entrepreneur.

As a country, we had developed a culture of dependence. We needed someone to give us a job and guarantee our retirement. Every problem was somebody else's problem. We were a country of argumentative complainers and whining losers. Adults sometimes behaved like children, while refusing to allow children to take responsibility, grow up, and become adults.

Society fought over caste, sub-castes, religion, language, economic divides, social divides, status-related issues, and a whole bunch of other economic-social issues one could possibly imagine. *Doordarshan* (India's Television Monopoly Channel), in the meanwhile, ran "Mile Sur Mera Tumara" (translates into "May your tune and mine meet and become one") campaigns in a hopeless cause.

Unfortunately, the imagination of this land was actually consumed in these petty issues, rather than being channeled into more productive channels leading to prosperity for all. The people were unable to grasp that they were all 'in the same boat'. Negative emotions and trying to 'outsmart the other' are just the equivalent of 'outsmarting oneself'.

One needs to have good role models and revel in their success. The need was to look at qualities that made successful people great and learn as much as possible from them, and then incorporate those qualities into one's lives.

Looking at the status symbols of success (cars, homes, boats, planes, etc.) and feeling greedy, angry, jealous, and anxious, and maybe all of them together at once, will NOT make one successful. It only makes one negative, bitter, and then finally a complainer. Honestly, beyond that, only God can help one.

One can choose to be a champ or a complainer. The fact is 'One HAS a choice', and the choice is in one's hands, as individuals and as a society.

The thing really is that the 'limited resources' people were fighting over were actually limited by their 'limited imagination'. This was something that would cross my mind for the first time and every time thereafter, from that moment when I heard on MTV, the group 'En Vogue' sing, "Free your mind and the rest will follow."

In the 1980s, once while exiting school, I happened to see a Tonga (a local horse and cart). Intuitively, as a fun game, I asked myself, "What if the cart was placed BEFORE the horse?" I had a hearty laugh. As a kid, I would use my imagination to have fun, just for fun.

I remember the first time I came across the concepts of capitalism and socialism (in the context of the then U.S.S.R and United States) during a history class. My initial reaction was 'Socialism was so noble', while 'Capitalism was exploitation'.

At some point in my life, I began to connect the 'Horse and the Cart' on one hand, and 'Capitalism and Socialism' on the other. But before we come to that, would it be possible to place the 'Cart before the Horse'? The answer is 'absolutely'. In fact, you can do whatever you please. But is it logical to expect the Cart to pull the Horse??

People with imagination and an understanding of Basic Economics 101 know intuitively that 'Capitalism is the Horse', and 'Socialism is the Cart'. You can't expect to place the 'Cart BEFORE the Horse' and expect it to gallop!!

That is what India was trying to do for the first 50 years of its existence. At least, it survived. Well, the U.S.S.R did NOT!

Socialism is definitely noble, no doubt, but 'too simplistic'. Just being benevolent and noble is NOT going to feed, clothe, and house all the common folk. That will require a meritocracy and NOT a government that runs the show like it is a charitable trust.

As a kid who was a misfit in India in the '90s, I was just waiting to catch a plane to the USA. Whenever I thought about the cart being BEFORE the horse, I couldn't stop laughing.

When I got the opportunity, I took off to the United States, laughing and then singing, imagining En Vogue singing, "Free your mind and the rest will follow!!"

In the 1990s, I did not imagine that when they said the "REST will follow", an EXODUS of the smartest of Indians to the United States would occur.

Soft Power... anybody??

CASTE DISCRIMINATION

"They have a saying in America, 'It does NOT matter where you came from, It matters WHERE you are going'."

– *Unknown*

"Never ever, UNDERESTIMATE the determination and capacity of the hungry and destitute."

– *Author*

The earliest written texts were inscribed on birch bark or palm leaves and later on parchment. Among these texts, The Vedas from India are considered the oldest, dating back over two millennia B.C. These knowledge books were vast compilations that reached their peak during periods spanning the mid-2nd and mid-1st millennia B.C. during the Iron and Bronze Ages.

The transmission of the Vedic texts was traditionally oral, with precision and accuracy maintained through elaborate mnemonic and chanting techniques. These texts were mostly in Sanskrit, widely regarded as the mother of languages, along with Tamil, which is considered the oldest living language in the world. Given the vastness of this body of knowledge and its consistent transmission over millennia, it is widely believed that the texts were transmitted in both oral and written forms.

The problem, however, with the ORAL tradition and limitations of HANDWRITTEN texts, was that this knowledge could NOT be widely disseminated. Since knowledge was transmitted orally, one needed to attend a *'Gurukula'* or school run by a *'Guru'* to partake in the dissemination of knowledge. This meant that knowledge did not spread easily and was confined to a smaller privileged group. This led to the 'caste system' in India, where knowledge was passed on from one generation to another. This then became an inheritance or birth-based system. While there were attempts to reach a larger audience with the establishment of universities in that era, it did not have the mass effect desired. The oldest of these universities were established at *Nalanda, Vikramshila,* and *Taxila* as early as the sixth century B.C. However, these did not help in breaking the monopoly over knowledge held by a few privileged people.

While the original objective of the caste system in India was to encourage specializations and prevent a SINGLE group from enjoying all privileges of society, namely 'Power', 'Knowledge', and 'Wealth', it led to major problems.

While one group was to enjoy 'Power', the second group was to enjoy 'Knowledge', and the third group was to enjoy 'Wealth', no assigned group was to enjoy ALL three and have a monopoly over society. While on the face of it, it seemed to be a system where ALL the societal advantages were NOT held by only ONE group of people, the system also led to the formation of groups that NEITHER enjoyed 'Power', 'Knowledge', nor 'Wealth' and were bereft as victims of oppression. Moreover, it failed to allow a person to choose his/her profession based on his/her natural proclivity and talents. This innately was a huge disservice to society, and in the long run, it did not allow society to harness the strengths of its inhabitants to the fullest extent.

For instance, the knowledge of metallurgy was confined to a closed group of blacksmiths and transmitted orally to the long line of blacksmiths in the family. There were three key problems that this created. The first was that the knowledge was easily lost over the centuries. The second was that without the ability to disseminate the knowledge, it was not 'built on' or furthered with the collective knowledge and wisdom of the larger population. The third was that if the knowledge was to be kept confined within a group, mass production of goods was not possible.

All these factors led to the demise of an amazing golden period in the history of the world where several inventions and innovations were created, and many of them perished due to the limitations brought on by social hierarchies.

Story of 'Zinc Extraction' from Zawar (Rajasthan, INDIA)

Zinc was first extracted in its purest form in INDIA, for over 6 millenniums, BEFORE the world learnt the art (six thousand years later!). 'Zinc by the distillation process' was known to the world only in the 12th Century B.C., while it was first discovered in the 6th Century B.C. in INDIA.

Unlike other usual metal suspects, Zinc had some unique characteristics that made its extraction in purest form challenging. Because of its low boiling point at 907°C, zinc is difficult to smelt, as it vaporizes quickly. Pure zinc could be produced only after the mastery of distillation techniques, which have been described in ancient INDIAN chemical treatises.

When heated, Zinc ore moves quickly from solid to vapor, without staying too long in a liquid state. Almost like sublimation, making it challenging to extract in the purest form.

In Zawar, (Rajasthan, INDIA), zinc was extracted by a method that can be best described as the 'Inverted Pot distillation Method'. Contrary to a normal distillation process, the distillation of Zinc can best be described as downward distillation.

The apparatus consists of two 'brinjal-shaped' retorts. While the upper furnace retort is held in an inverted configuration, the lower chamber served as the condenser. The upper inverted retort is stuffed with the pre-treated charge. The pre-treated charge included the zinc oxide ore, along with combustible charcoal, salt, borax (as a flux), cow dung, and water, which are suitably dried and converted to pellets.

The upper retort chamber acts as the furnace, where the pellets are stuffed. It is sealed with clay and affixed with a reed. This upper retort is then heated. When at about 600 degrees centigrade, the reed vaporizes and makes an opening. The zinc in the upper chamber first vaporizes and rises. It is captured within the INVERTED retort even as it rises, trying to escape. It collects there and fills the inverted upper chamber. Having filled the upper chamber, it then pushes through the opening at the bottom and collects in the lower condenser chamber as pure zinc.

The technology for zinc manufacture by reverse distillation was also described in several INDIAN alchemical works of the medieval period, including the Sanskrit treatise *Rasa Ratna Samuccaya*, compiled in the 13th-14th century. In Rasa Ratna Samuccaya, the Zinc distillation process is described with the term "*tirakpatnayantra*", which, when translated from the Sanskrit language, literally means "distillation by descending".

Various other Sanskrit texts such as *Rasarnavam Rastantram* (500-100 B.C.), *Rasratnakar* (2nd century A.D.), and *Rasprakash Sudhakar* (12th century A.D.) also describe the zinc-smelting processes.

The Story of the INDIAN origin of Wootz Steel (Damascus Steel)

The beginning of the 1st millennium B.C. saw extensive development in iron metallurgy in INDIA. The development of metallurgy during the Mauryas period (322—185 B.C.) was recorded by the Greek historian Herodotus (431—425 B.C.), marking the first western account of the use of iron in INDIA.

As early as 300 B.C., high-quality steel was being produced in Southern INDIA by a technique called the 'Crucible technique'. This involved mixing high-purity wrought iron, charcoal, and glass and heating it until the iron melted and imbibed the carbon.

The 'first crucible steel' was *Wootz Steel,* which originated in INDIA before the common era. Wootz derives from the Tamil term for steel, *urukku.* Indian Wootz Steel was the first high-quality steel that was produced.

Henry Yule quoted the 12th-century ***Arab Edrizi*** who wrote:

"The South Indians excel in the manufacture of iron, and in the preparations of those ingredients along with which it is fused to obtain that kind of soft iron which is usually styled Indian steel. They also have workshops wherein are forged the most famous sabres in the world....It is not possible to find anything to surpass the edge that you get from Indian steel (al-hadid al-Hindi)."

As early as the 17th century, Europeans knew of India's ability to make crucible steel from reports brought back by travelers who had observed the process at several places in southern India. Several attempts were made to import the process but failed because the exact technique remained a mystery.

Studies of Wootz were made in an attempt to understand its secrets, including a major effort by the famous scientist Michael Faraday, who was the son of a blacksmith. Working with a local cutlery manufacturer, he wrongly concluded that it was the addition of aluminum oxide and silica from the glass that gave Wootz its unique properties.

Will Durant wrote in **The Story of Civilization** I: Our Oriental Heritage:

"Something has been said about the chemical excellence of cast iron in ancient India, and about the high industrial development of the Gupta times when India was looked to, even by Imperial Rome, as the most skilled of the nations in such chemical industries as dyeing, tanning, soap-making, glass, and cement."

By the sixth century, the Hindus were far ahead of Europe in industrial chemistry; they were masters of calcinations, distillation, sublimation, steaming, fixation, the production of light without heat, the mixing of anesthetic and soporific powders, and the preparation of metallic salts, compounds, and alloys.

The tempering of steel was brought to perfection in ancient India, unknown in Europe until our own times; King Porus is said to have selected, as an especially valuable gift for Alexander, not gold or silver, but thirty pounds of steel. The Moslems took much of this Hindu chemical science and industry to the Near East and Europe; the secret of manufacturing "Damascus" blades, for example, was taken by the Arabs from the Persians, and by the Persians from India

The Famous 'Iron Pillar of Delhi'

The swords manufactured in INDIAN workshops find written mention in the works of *Muhammad al-Idrisi* (flourished 1154 A.D.). INDIAN Blades made of Damascus steel found their way into Persia. European scholars—during the 14th century—studied INDIAN casting and metallurgy technology.

INDIAN metallurgy under the *Mughal* emperor Akbar (1556 A.D. – 1605 A.D.) produced excellent small firearms. *Gommans* (2002) holds that *Mughal* hand-guns were probably stronger and more accurate than their European counterparts.

World famous Statues of *Nataraja* and that of *Vishnu* were cast during the reign of the imperial *Chola dynasty* (200 A.D. – 1279 A.D.) in the 9th century. The casting could involve a mixture of five metals: copper, zinc, tin, gold, and silver.

The world's first Iron Pillar, 'The Iron Pillar of Delhi', was erected during the times of of *Chandragupta II Vikramaditya* (375 A.D. – 413 A.D.). It still stands WITHOUT rusting away, lasting for almost 2 Millenniums. A marvel of metallurgy and often considered as one of the finest pieces of ancient metallurgy.

Despite being able to produce iron pillars that did not rust for a couple of millennia and being a world leader in metallurgy, societal constructs such as the caste system gradually corroded away the knowledge and ability to build upon, causing INDIAN society to slide down the slippery slope of decline.

While there are many evils in the caste system, this aspect alone is highlighted to illustrate how society limited its own progress and harmed itself. When the ability to transmit knowledge to the masses is hindered, it precludes the potential of the larger populace and its capacity to 'evolve and develop' a broader knowledge base for the advancement of humankind.

Education, by its nature, has to be disseminated to a larger group who can gain and later contribute to it. This is why the 'Printing Press' was a ground-breaking innovation that was as important as the 'invention of the wheel' or the 'discovery of fire'. It broke a major limitation that hindered the sharing of knowledge and laid the foundation for the further progress of humankind. This was a small step by humanity but a giant leap for humankind.

The first problem that the caste system created was that it never gave people a chance to choose a profession of their choice, a profession they could be passionate about and consequently excel in. It was a massive blot and disservice to individuals and society as a whole.

In that context, it does not surprise me that society lost its edge and gradually became more mediocre. In a way, the caste system was akin to socialism when considering how badly meritocracy was sacrificed at the altar of a defunct construct. With time, the caste system as a societal construct became fossilized and was later sanctioned by the likes of Manusmriti.

A

'Sanskrit Slokha'

On how karm (deeds) and NOT birth or belonging decide one's stature in society

नवनीतंघृतंदुग्धंदधितक्रंचपञ्चमम्।
सर्वमेककुलाज्जातामूल्यंसर्वस्यवैपृथक् ॥

navanītaṃ ghṛtaṃ dugdhaṃ dadhi takraṃ ca pañcamam ।
sarvamēkakulājjātā mūlyaṃ sarvasya vai pṛthak ॥

Meaning:

Milk, yogurt, butter, ghee and whey are all born in the same family, yet they all have different prices

(Superiority depends upon *karm* (deeds), irrespective of where you belong from).

With independence and a Constitution helmed by B.R. Ambedkar, INDIA did try to make a new beginning. They introduced reservation to correct past injustices heaped especially on the underprivileged and those at the bottom of the caste system. The reservations were meant to be a temporary measure, but they became a political rugby match from there on. With each group trying to get hold of the societal pie, represented by the rugby ball, it ended up being an unimaginative society that VIEWED the pie as being LIMITED.

We sure need more imaginative lawmakers and economic policymakers.

Ok, now, WHERE is THAT imaginative Arab fellow?

INDIA is READY to sign you a check!

Reverse Caste Discrimination

"True progress can be achieved only by planting meritocracy as being the central theme, with smart provisions to help the genuinely disadvantaged. Using socialism or reservation as bedrock of justice marshalled by slogans of social justice will just NOT cut it. Justice cannot be delivered on an empty stomach for the hungry, especially when your coffers are empty."

–Author

"Wealth has to be created, before it can be distributed."

***–Narayana Murthy**, Co-founder of Infosys*

There is nothing wrong with 'Reservation' or 'Socialism', for that matter. Both sound so noble on the face of it. But these are policies born out of an unimaginative mind that focuses on dividing an existing pie.

Once one's mind is freed, one will understand concepts like 'increasing the size of the pie', rather than focusing on grabbing or dividing what is there. Of course, 'Caste Discrimination' was unfortunate and embarrassingly stupid, I may add, but so is 'Reverse Caste Discrimination'. 'Two wrongs' DO NOT make a right. Either way, one is going down the pipe.

Smart people, whether entrepreneurs or those who are ready to work hard, should be given the best opportunity to lead, and in the process help everyone in society raise their socio-economic standards. This can't be achieved by socialism or reservation alone. Using socialism and reservation as THE bedrocks for social justice is like running hard on a treadmill and asking why one is at the same place.

Justice CANNOT be delivered to the hungry by a person on an empty stomach.

All Indians are familiar with the 'Crab story'. We Indians used to joke that once you put a number of Indian crabs in a jar, you don't need to cover it with a lid. The Indian crabs will make sure that none gets out. The moment a crab rises to get out of the jar, another will make sure it is pulled back.

There is a saying in the US, which is brash but true. It is simple and straightforward. It says, 'You either lead, follow, or get out of the way!'

(You can also have a nap if you so wish, I may add!)

In conclusion, 'neither was caste discrimination a good idea' nor 'is reverse caste discrimination a good idea'. The FOCUS of any society is to maximize the size of the pie by emphasizing merit and enabling the best, so that they can in turn enable the rest of society. The rising tide lifts ALL boats.

While 'MAINTAINING this FOCUS', provisions to enable the disadvantaged should be suitably provided, while keeping the story of the 'Horse and the Cart' in sight.

A

'Sanskrit Slokha'

<u>On How one's Greatness is decided by one's Qualities and NOT Birth</u>

ज्येष्ठत्वंजन्मनानैवगुणै: ज्येष्ठत्वम्उच्यते।
गुणात्गुरुत्वम्आयातिदुग्धंदधिघृतंक्रमात्।।

jyēṣṭhatvaṃ janmanā naiva guṇai: jyēṣṭhatvam ucyatē ।
guṇāt gurutvam āyāti dugdhaṃ dadhi ghṛtaṃ kramāt ।।

Meaning:

Greatness doesn't come by birth. Greatness is decided by the qualities of a person.

As the heaviness gets increased from milk to curd and from curd to ghee.

Time for some FUN

I will end this chapter here leaving you with **En Vogue's** hit song, **'Free Your Mind'** from their second album **'Funky Divas' (1992).** Enjoy!!

'Free Your Mind'

En Vogue, [Album **'Funky Divas' (1992)]**

SCAN above to see **YOUTUBE** ***Video of the Song***

Lyrics

[Free Your Mind]

(Prejudice, wrote a song about it)
(Like to hear it? Here it go!)

Free your mind
I wear tight clothing, high-heeled shoes
It doesn't mean that I'm a prostitute no, no
I like rap music, wear hip-hop clothes
That doesn't mean that I'm out sellin' dope, no, no, no
Oh my, forgive me for having straight hair, no
It doesn't mean there's another blood in my heir, yeah, yeah

I might date another race or colour
It doesn't mean I don't like my strong black brothers
(Ooh da-da, ooh da-da, ooh da-da, ooh da-da)
Why, oh why must it be this way?

(Oh, oh, oh, oh)
Before you can read me
You got to learn how to see me
I said

Free your mind
And the rest will follow
Be colour-blind
Don't be so shallow
Free your mind
And the rest will follow
Be colour-blind
Don't be so shallow
So I'm a sista
Buy things with cash
That really doesn't mean that all my credit's bad
Oh

So why dispute me and waste my time?
Because you really think the price is high for me
I can't look without being watched, no
You rang my buy before I made up my mind

Oww
Oh, now attitude
Why even bother?
I can't change your mind
You can't change my colour
(Ooh da-da, ooh da-da, ooh da-da, ooh da-da)
Why, oh why must it be this way?

(Oh, oh, oh, oh)
Before you can read me
You got to learn how to see me
I said

Free your mind
And the rest will follow
Be colour-blind
Don't be so shallow
Free your mind
And the rest will follow
Be colour-blind
Don't be so shallow
Free your mind
And the rest will follow
Be colour-blind
Don't be so shallow
Free your mind
And the rest will follow
Be colour-blind
Don't be so shallow
Free your mind

(Ooh da-da, ooh da-da, ooh da-da, ooh da-da)
Why, oh, why must it be this way?
Before you can read me
You got to learn how to see me
I said

Free your mind, and the rest will follow
Be colour-blind, don't be so shallow
Free your mind, and the rest will follow
Be colour-blind, don't be so shallow
Free your mind, and the rest will follow
Be colour-blind, don't be so shallow
Free your mind, and the rest will follow
Be colour-blind, don't be so shallow
Free your mind

<u>Part I</u>

Chapter 7.1

SERIOUSLY RICH, SERIOUSLY EXTINCT

When 'short-term needs' DEFEAT 'long-term wisdom'

"We are the first generation to feel the effect of climate change and the last generation who can do something about it."

– ***Barack Obama,*** *Former US President*

"Climate change is a terrible problem, and it absolutely needs to be solved. It deserves to be a huge priority."

– ***Bill Gates***

It is interesting to note the direction in which this world is moving. Most people and leaders are more concerned about a slowdown in the economy than the fact that we are fast nearing the point of NO RETURN on climate change. While the slowing down of the economy is worrisome, the silver lining is, if world GDP is slowing down, so is the consumption of oil and the consequent damage to the environment.

I have a small prediction at this point. Slower or faster, the GDP of the world will keep increasing. Ironically, when the GDP of the world reaches its peak and is at its pinnacle, humans will start racing down the slippery slope to mass extinction. Unless we make a course change and start caring for the environment as much as we care for our pockets, this prediction will come to fruition.

However, a course correction is not on our minds because caring for the environment is somebody else's problem, while our pockets are our immediate concern. Our 'short-term needs' override 'long-term wisdom'.

In the future, we may have a lot of money in the bank, but no food to buy, no water to drink, and no place to stay. By mid-century, the United States of America, China, the European Union, and India will be the richest economies of the world, or they COULD have been the richest and largest economic blocs in the world, because ironically, we may not be alive till then.

Reality versus Figment

"Climate change is the greatest threat to our existence in our short history on this planet. Nobody's going to buy their way out of its effects."

–***Mark Ruffalo,*** *Actor & Environmentalist*

"It is not that people fail to see it, it is just that they choose not to believe it."

–***Author***

As a race, we are delusional. We see the problem but choose to ignore it. Climate change is the inconvenient truth nobody wants to deal with because it is not an immediate existential threat. We do not want to face it because we think we will cross the bridge when we get there. The problem is, when we get there, it might be too late to cross over to the other side (of the problem). The bridge may have already been washed away a long time ago because of our lack of action and wisdom.

Boiling the Frog

"The natural tendency is to only react to what's immediate."

–***Author***

"Climate change is real. It is happening right now, it is the most urgent threat facing our entire species and we need to work collectively together and stop procrastinating."

–***Leonardo Di Caprio,*** *Actor & Environmentalist*

Humans have survived for thousands of years because, unlike other animals, humans could anticipate danger, think ahead, and plan. We humans avoided predators by taking precautions. We avoided starvation by planning for lean periods. Cattle rearing and agriculture came next, followed by an age of settlements, and then civilization as we know it.

But now, we only care about month-end, while big corporations care about the next quarterly results. Even our political leaders care only about the next election, leaving it to the helpless non-voting children to worry about their future and the future of this planet.

If we put a 'proverbial frog' in boiling water, it will immediately jump out. On the other hand, if the same frog is on a slow boil, it will stay in the water and slowly die from the increasing heat. It will slowly get cooked. The frog won't realize that the water is heating up. We are behaving in a similar fashion, where we, the human race, ARE the 'proverbial frog'.

Even as the planet slow-boils, we are too preoccupied with money matters, and our politicians with power projections and their egos. We are hardly taking notice of our changing climate. Ironically, unlike the frog, we are slow-boiling OURSELVES and are on our way to extinction.

The (not so) funniest part is we are dumber than the frog. At least, the frog was NOT boiling ITSELF. Humans on the other hand, are slow boiling themselves as they go about their lives unconcerned for the environment.

Sometimes, the most intelligent species can also be the most arrogant and consequently the most stupid.

Time for some FUN

Time for **Tamil** song ***'Enjoy Enjaami'*** **(2021)** written and sung by **Dhee** along with **Arivu.** Music composed by **Santhosh Narayanan** and the song is directed by **Amit Krishnan.** Enjoy!!

SONG

'Enjoy Enjaami'

Dhee Ft. Arivu, [Music Label **Maajja (2021)**]

SCAN above to see **YOUTUBE** ***Video of the Song***

Lyrics **['Enjoy Enjaami']**	*Translation* **['Have Fun My Dear']**
Cuckoo cuckoo Thatha thatha kala vetti	Cuckoo is the sound of cuckoo bird Grandpa weeding out the fields
Cuckoo cuckoo Pondhula yaru meen kothi	Who's in the trunk hole? It's the kingfisher
Cuckoo cuckoo Thanniyil odum thavalaikki	Cuckoo cuckoo Swimming frog in the water
Cuckoo cuckoo Kambali poochi thangachi	Cuckoo cuckoo Is sister of the caterpillar
Allimalar kodi angadhame Ottara ottara sandhaname	Lilly is making fun of me My adamant sweet sandalwood
Mullai malar kodi mutharame Engooru engooru kuthalame	My jasmine decked necklace With pearls Oh my native kutralamae
Surukku paiyamma Vethala mattaiyamma	My grandma's shrink bag With betel and nuts
Somandha kaiyamma Mathalam kottuyamma	The hands that carry them Play the parai drum
Thaiyamma thaiyamma Enna panna mayamma	Grandma grandma What magic did you do?

Valliamma perandi Sangadhiya kellendi	Valliyamal's grandson Tells me the story
Kannadiya kanamdi Indharra perandi	Where are my glasses? Take it my grandson
Annakkili annakkili Adi alamarakkela vannakkili	Parrot...Parrot.... Parrot sitting in the banyan tree
Nallapadi vazhacholli Indha manna koduthane poorvakudi	Blessing to lead a good life Our ancestors have Bequeathed us this soil
Kammankara kaniyellam Padith thirinjane adhikkudi	Across the river banks And on the fertile fields Our forefathers have sung Through their life
Nayi nari poonaikundhan Indha erikkolam kooda sondhammadi	The lakes and ponds belong To the dogs foxes and cats too
Enjoy enjami Vaango vaango onnagi Amma yi ambari Indha indha mummari (x2)	Enjoy my dear Come together as one Ride on the elephants shower In the rains (x2)
Cuckoo cuckoo Muttaiya podum kozhikku	Cuckoo cuckoo The hen is laying the egg
Cuckoo cuckoo Oppanai yaru maiyilukku	Cuckoo cuckoo Who dolled up the peacock

Cuckoo cuckoo Pacchaiya poosum pasikku	Cuckoo cuckoo Algae spreading its green
Cuckoo cuckoo Kucchiya adukkuna kootukku	Cuckoo cuckoo Nest arranged by tiny twigs
Padu patta makka Varappu mettukkara	The toiling farmer With his fertile fields
Vervathanni sokka Minukkum nattukkara	His sweat drenched shirt The glittering countryman
Akatti karuppatti Oodhangolu mannuchatti	The fire-kindling flute And the earthen pot
Athoram koodukatti Arambichcha nagareegam	Settling in the river banks is the Beginning of civilization
Jhan jhana jhanakku jhana makkale Jan jana janaku jana oh my people	Jhan jhana jhanakku jhana makkale Jan jana janaku jana oh my people
Uppuku chappu kottu Muttaikulla sathukottu	Tasting the salt yolk The source of all energy
Attaikku rathangkottu Kittipullu vettu vettu	Drip blood from leech bite Strike away the gilli danda
Nan anju maram valarthen Azhagana thottam vachchen	I planted five trees Nurtured a beautiful garden
Thottam sezhithalum En thonda nanaiyalaye	My garden is flourishing Yet my throat remains dry

En kadale, karaye, vaname, saname Nelame, kolame, edame, thadame	My sea bank, forest, people Lands, clan, place, and track
Enjoy en jami Vaango Vaango onnagi Amma yi ambari Indha indha mummari (x2)	Enjoy my dear Come together as one Ride on the elephants shower In the rains (x2)
Pattan poottan katha boomi Atam pottu kattum sami	My ancestors guarded the land The devotee that dances
Ratinandha suthi Vandha seva koovuchu	As the earth rotates Around the rooster crows
Adhu pottu vachcha Echamdhane kada marichu	Its excretions Fertilized the forests
Namma nada marichu Indha veeda marichu	It turned into our country Then our home too
Enna kora enna kora	What's the matter What's the matter my dear?
En seeni karumbukku enna kora	What's the matter my sugarcane? What's the matter
Enna kora enna kora	What's the matter What's the matter my dear?
En chella perandikku enna kora	My darling grandson What's the matter?

Pandhalulla pavarka Pandhalulla pavarka	Bitter gourd in my canopy Bitter gourd in my canopy
Vedhakallu vitturukku Vedhakallu vitturukku	It has given us seeds Given us seeds
Appan atha vittadhungo Appan atha vittandhungo	Left by our mom and dad Left by our mom and dad
Enjoy enjami Vaango Vaango onnagi Ride on the elephants Shower in the rains (x5)	Have fun my dear Come together as a team Ride on the elephants Shower in the rains (x5)
En kadale, karaye, vaname, saname Nelame, kolame, edame, thadame	My sea bank, forest, people Lands, clan, place, and track
Cuckoo cuckoo	Cuckoo cuckoo

' Enjoy Enjaami **(Dhee Ft. Arivu)** [**Moana Version**] '

SCAN above to see **YOUTUBE** ***Video of the Song***

<u>Part I</u>

Chapter 7.2

THE EARTH OUR HOME

A Ode to Our ONLY Home 'The EARTH'

"Sooner or later, we will have to recognise that the Earth has rights, too, to live without pollution. What mankind must know is that human beings cannot live without Mother Earth, but the planet can live without humans."

– ***Evo Morales***

"By polluting the oceans, not mitigating CO_2 emissions and destroying our biodiversity, we are killing our planet. Let us face it, there is no planet B."

– ***Emmanuel Macron,*** *President of France*

POEM

'The Earth Our Home'

BOOK

'HopScotch'

(Poetry for All Reasons)

SCAN above to see **YOUTUBE** ***<u>Lyrical Video of the Poem</u>***

Lyrics

[The Earth Our Home]

Billions of stars tickle our skies
Trillions more hidden from our eyes
There are many planets in the Universe
But only one like our beloved Earth

A stunning August ball of blue n white
Floating in space n basking in the sun's light
Clocking its rounds with precision around the sun
Spinning on its axis like a ballerina having fun

Love and respect is what our earth deserves
It has that magic called life that it preserves
Step by step.. Hand in hand.. We will fight
For our climate... Our children... n what is right

We may be divided by nations n artificial lines
But our fate is as fragile as a turn of a dime
Our future lies in our actions n in our hands
We need to look beyond and understand

We may have differing views which are subjective
Science does provide answers being objective
Together we will stand tall and keep alive
Divided, our children may find it hard to survive

Love and respect is what our earth deserves
It has that magic called life that it preserves
Step by step.. Hand in hand.. We will fight
For our climate... Our children...n What is right

Climate change is happening this very moment
As a trailer of Forest fires and Storms torment
The earth is like a fragile n tender new born
The atmosphere being its soft blanket worn

This is not the time for us to procrastinate
Doors are closing on us, even as we vacillate
Climate change is real and current
Denying it would be trouble we knowingly invent

Love and respect is what our earth deserves
It has that magic called life that it preserves
Step by step.. Hand in hand.. We will fight
For our climate... Our children... n what is right

God has adorned the vast universe
With a crown jewel that we call earth
We can continue to relax... and into its lap we can snuggle
But only if... we promise to keep it out of trouble

Every person needs to act now to prevent doom
Big or small actions taken will be earth's boon
Our ONE n ONLY abode is... our nice n cozy Earth
What NOW do you think... it is ultimately WORTH?

Part I

Chapter 8

'LAUGHING YOUR WAY TO THE BANK'

May Your Bank Deposits (Memories & Happiness) Grow with Each Passing Day

"It is silliness to live when to live is torment; and then have we a prescription to die when death is our physician."

– ***Shakespeare*** *(Othello, Act 1, Scene 3)*

"Doing something you don't particularly enjoy, for something else, that you think you may need or enjoy, does NOT sound like a great strategy for happiness."

– ***Author***

Success and happiness are not some destination to be reached, where then, magically, one becomes happy. A miserable person with a million dollars is going to be an even more miserable person with a billion. If fundamentally one is unhappy or bitter, then seeking happiness from the outside is still a bad strategy. If one is miserable, then one needs to look inward BEFORE one looks outward and asks oneself a few tough questions.

'Happiness is THE journey', and 'Success is IN the Journey'. Of course, the 'fruits of success' are like the 'golden pot at the end of the rainbow'. However, if along the way on one's journey, if one 'doesn't smell the roses' and 'appreciate the colours of the rainbow' then that journey is unlikely to be a fun and happy one.

There is a saying, "One would have to make great sacrifices to succeed. The greater the sacrifices made, the greater the success." I can't help but just laugh at that statement. I do not know 'how or whoever' came up with that.

First of all, doing something you DON'T particularly enjoy to obtain something else that you think you MAY enjoy, does NOT sound like a great strategy to me. This is because, if you are NOT enjoying the journey, you are NOT making those fun memories and relationships. Ultimately, at the end of the day, those memories and relationships are your treasures. No number in your bank statement, no matter how big, can be a substitute.

The Richie Rich Cartoon

"Being carefree and living without burdening yourself with what others may think or say, is the first step to happiness."

–Author

"True Wealth is more than just hard cash. Your health, your family & friends, your learning & wisdom, happy memories and experiences are your TRUE wealth."

–Author

There is a Richie Rich cartoon in which a bunch of thugs decide to rob Richie Rich's parents. It so happens that Richie Rich's parents have a massive safe that is highly protected. The gang of thugs come to know of it and then try really hard to locate and break it open. The thugs fail in breaking open the massive vault and hence, kidnap the parents and take them to this massive vault.

They then threaten the parents of Richie Rich to disclose the combinations to the massive vault. The parents tell them anyway. So the thugs begin turning the dials one by one according to the numbers told to them. The dials are turned one by one, and finally the last dial is turned. The thugs manage to get the combination right and unlock the vault.

The gang of thugs are super excited and jump for joy. They then hurriedly and greedily enter the vault. The gang of thugs imagined unlimited bundles of cash, gold, diamonds, and jewellery would be in the vault. However, much to their dismay, the vault had nothing of that sort.

The vault was filled with "worthless" memorabilia from travel trips, photos, travel postcards, birthday cards, love letters, and heart-shaped cushions, much to the consternation of the bunch of thugs.

The leader of the gang then asks the parents of Richie Rich, "Where are the ACTUAL wealth and treasures?" Richie Rich's parents look surprised and confused and say, "THESE are our treasures and THIS is OUR wealth."

This is just a cute cartoon. However, it does illustrate how misguided we are. We have brought up our children in a world in which money, fame, and power are sold as the central themes at the core of happiness. It is just unfortunate because it is so misleading and leaves our children going down a path that only leads them to suffer unnecessary unhappiness and misery.

Someone once said, "We need to teach our children the VALUE of things and NOT the PRICE on the label."

I hope the media and society would talk about the 'VALUE of things rather than PRICE'. Rather than talk about billionaires and the obsession with their planes, cars, boats, and how many billions they are worth, let us talk about how self-made billionaires succeeded: their work ethic, their enterprise, their drive, their motivation, the amount of time and effort they put in, their passion, their intensity, their endurance, their patience, their perseverance, their persistence, their struggles, their never-say-die qualities, their intelligence, their wisdom, their education, their experience, their smarts, their sociable traits, their empathy, their humility, their leadership, their ability to laugh at themselves, the fun they had along the way, and finally their love for humanity.

The billions in equity shares, the boats, the planes, cars, the homes, their expensive vacations, their expensive watches, and their expensive jewelry are just, in two words, "Entrepreneurial Porn". It is in other words, misleading.

The founder of OYO in INDIA, who was one of INDIA's youngest billionaires, once said that every start-up entrepreneur you suddenly hear of in the papers has a backstory spanning a minimum of 5 years. I say, why 5 years? Backstories can be as long as 5, 10, 15, 20, even 40 years.

My professor of Management and Entrepreneurship at ISU (Iowa State University), Mr. Sam DeMarie, was giving a lecture and began to explain the process of metamorphosis of a butterfly. The butterfly actually starts out as a caterpillar; it eats and devours the leaves of plants. This goes on for a while. It then spins a cocoon around itself. It stays in the cocoon that it had wrapped around itself for a long time. It gestates and grows in the cocoon, invisible and unknown to us.

While neither the caterpillar nor the cocoon is particularly pretty, what happens next is so beautiful. While the whole process takes time and effort on the part of the caterpillar, at some point the result breaks out of the cocoon. It is a beautiful butterfly that takes to the skies. It is to be noted that this takes time. The butterfly breaking out and taking flight is NOT instant, as we may want to believe; it takes time.

In one moment of time, the butterfly breaks out. In an instant, it takes to its wings in unparalleled beauty. However, creating that beauty takes time and effort. While looking at the butterfly break out and admiring how beautiful it is, we should not forget that this is not an instant or easy process. Often, good and beautiful things take time to reveal themselves.

Success is never instant; it takes time. The media feeds us with stuff that makes us think success is instant and easy. It is NOT that easy or QUICK. However, one does NOT need to suffer to get there. You CAN and SHOULD enjoy the journey in anything you may do.

Again, "Happiness is IN the journey, savor it. Success IS the journey." Enjoy the journey, and honestly, you don't have to suffer or sacrifice or feel pain to get there. You need to pick your passion (use IKIGAI Principles as a guide), then go on, 'Enjoy the ride!!'

Life is an adventure, LIVE it like one.

One big component of the wealth you accumulate in your journey is the time you spend with your friends and family. Those memories, those moments of interaction, those moments of giving, the smiles on the faces of people you cherish, the flutter of your heart when you see the object of your love, the warmth you radiate and feel when you interact with people, the joy you get in celebrating the success of others, the gratitude you feel deep in your heart for the sacrifices (love shown) by people who care about you, and finally, your ability to love and embrace people of the world—irrespective of how different people may be from you, irrespective of their color, creed, religion, race, nation, social status, sexual orientation, gender, height, weight, opinions, age, etc.—is 'WHAT Success and Happiness is all about'.

So, **go ahead** and **embrace your journey!!**

Time for some FUN

Time for a fun **Hindi** song! Let us run-riot with **Ranbir Kapoor** in the song ***'Badtameez Dil'*** from the movie ***'Yeh Jawani Hai Deewani'* (2013)** starring **Ranbir Kapoor** and **Deepika Padukone**. The Movie is directed by **Ayan Mukerji** and produced by **Karan Johar.**

The songwriter is **Amitabh Bhattacharya.** The music is composed by **Pritam** and the song is sung by **Benny Dayal and Shefali Alvares.** Enjoy!!

SONG

'Badtameez Dil'

MOVIE

***'Yeh Jawaani Hai Deewani'* (2013)**

SCAN above to see **YOUTUBE** ***Video of the Song***

Lyrics **['Badtameez Dil']**	*Translation* **['Naughty Heart']**
Badtameezee ek bimari hai Ek aisi bimari Jo dheere dheere waqt ke saath Budhaape mein badal jaati hai Main kehta hoon jab tak budhaapa nahi aata Thodi badtameezee hi kar lete hai	The Naughty heart is a virus It is such virus which slowly with time wears down into old age I am saying until the time we get old We may as well be a little naughty

Paan main pudeena dekha Naak ka nageena dekha Chikni chameli dekhi Chikna kameena dekha Chaand ne cheater hoke cheat kiya toh Saare taare bole gilli gilli akhaa	I have seen the mint in the betel leaf I have seen the gem on your nose ring I have seen a beautiful girl and a handsome rascal too A Moon became a cheater and cheated So all the stars said gilli gilli akhaa
Pa para para...(x3) Pa ra ra para ra ra	Pa para para...(x3) Pa ra ra para ra ra
Pa para para...(x3) Pa ra ra para ra ra	Pa para para...(x3) Pa ra ra para ra ra
Meri baat, teri baat Zyada baatein boori baat Thaali mein katora leke Aaloo bhat, Muri bhat Mere peeche kisi ne repeat kiya toh Saala maine tere muh pe maara mukka	My words, your words Too much words and talk is a bad habit Take a bowl on the plate with potato rice and fried rice bread If anyone repeats with me behind my back I'll punch that rascal on the face
Pa para para...(x3) Pa ra ra para ra ra	Pa para para...(x3) Pa ra ra para ra ra
Pa para para...(x3) Pa ra ra para ra ra	Pa para para...(x3) Pa ra ra para ra ra
Ispe bhoot koi chadha hai The Tharna jaane naa Ab toh kya buraa kyaa bhalaa hai Fark pehchaane naa Zidd pakad ke khadaa hai kambakht Chhodna jaane naa	Some Spirit has taken over And it does not know how to stop Now it can't tell the difference between What is good and what is bad Sticking to its stubbornness It just refuses to let go

Badtameez dil, batameez dil, batamiz dil Maane na, maane na	This Naughty heart, This Naughty heart, This Naughty Heart Just does not listen, Just does not listen
Yeh jo haal hai, sawaal hai, kamaal hai Jaane na jaane na Badtameez dil, battameez dil badtameez dil Maane naa..	This condition is questionable as it is fantastic it does not know, does not know This Naughty heart, This Naughty heart, This Naughty Heart Just does not listen
Hawa mein Havana dekha Dhimka falaana dekha Seeng ka Singhara khaake Sher ka ghuraana dekha Poori duniya ka gol gol chakkar leke Maine duniya ko maara dhakka	I have seen Havana from the air I have seen this and that After having eaten the water caltrop of a lion I have seen the lion roar I have roamed around the world and I have pushed away the world
Pa para para...(x3) Pa ra ra para ra ra	Pa para para...(x3) Pa ra ra para ra ra
Pa para para...(x3) Pa ra ra para ra ra	Pa para para...(x3) Pa ra ra para ra ra
Hey Bollywood Hollywood very very jolly good Raayi ke pahaad par teen futa liliput Mere peeche kisi ne repeat kiya toh Saala maine tere muh pe maara mukka	Hey Bollywood or Hollywood, very very Jolly good On the mountain of black mustard seeds I have seen a 3 Foot Liliputian If anyone repeats with me behind my back I'll punch that rascal on the face

Ayaashi ke one way se khudko Modna jaane naa Kambal bewajah sharam ka Odhna jaane naa Zidd pakad ke khadha hai kambakht Chodhna jaane na… Haha..	It does not know how to turn away from the one way road of carefree living Without any reason, it does not know how to put cover itself a blanket of shame Stuck to its stubbornness it just refuses to let go
Badtameez dil, batameez dil, batamiz dil Maane na, maane na (x2)	This Naughty heart, This Naughty heart, This Naughty Heart Just does not listen, just does not listen (x2)
Aaj saare, chaand taare Bann gaye hai disco lights Jal ke, bujha ke humko bula ke Keh rahe hai, party all night	Today all the stars and the moon Have become disco lights After having burnt and extinguished, and having called us They are saying, party all night
Naata betuki dillagi se, todna jaane na Aane wale kal ki fikar se, judna jaane na Zidd pakad ke khada hai kambakht Chodhna jaane na… Haha..	It does not know how to break the relationship with useless love It does not know how to attach itself with the worries of tomorrow Stuck to its stubbornness it just refuses to let go
Badtameez dil, batameez dil, batamiz dil Maane na, maane na (x2)	This Naughty heart, This Naughty heart, This Naughty Heart Just does not listen, just does not listen (x2)

Yeh jo haal hai, sawaal hai, kamaal hai Jaane na jaane na Badtameez dil, battameez dil badtameez dil Maane naa..	This condition is questionable as it is fantastic it does not know, does not know This Naughty heart, This Naughty heart, This Naughty Heart Does not listen..

Part I

Chapter 9.1

WHY 'HAPPINESS AND SUCCESS' IS A JOURNEY AND NOT A DESTINATION

Enjoy the journey because 'Success and Happiness' is right there for the taking

"The truth is, money CAN't and WON't buy you happiness. It buys you OPTIONS. What you do with THOSE options, would determine how happy your life would become."

–Author

"Do not put your Happiness in other people's hands. Take control of your life and happiness. Live life on YOUR terms."

–Author

My two sisters and I had a lot of fun in our childhood. However, it was a different childhood from what children and teenagers have these days. The truth is, we had only ONE channel on television (which later generously became two, when Doordarshan [the 'Local Government Channel' in INDIA then] launched another!). The channel ran only in the evenings, from 5 p.m. until 10 or 11 p.m. On Sundays, the channel had programs that included a morning session.

As children, we did not have cable, internet, or mobile phones, let alone smartphones. My friends and I played in the sun, carefree and without bother. Concerns about getting tanned or sweating were never issues. We just 'did not care'. Issues of tan or sweat, etc., are issues that current society unnecessarily 'sweats' about.

I had a childhood buddy who also happened to be my neighbor. We would hang out and cycle around. We played street cricket with other friends using tennis balls (we also used open plots and grounds to play, wherever we found one) and played table tennis often (we used a really nice sponge table-tennis ball and flat bats. My Dad had gotten that for me from Germany. It was really cool because it didn't make a sound when bouncing, so we didn't have to worry about waking up my mother or grandparents from their respective afternoon siestas).

One of the most fun things we did as children was when my two sisters, my neighbor, and I played the game of *Monopoly.* Afternoon hours would go by as we played and played. The things we would do to win were just hilarious. We would jockey for sitting positions (on the floor) around the board. We would fight to sit close to the Monopoly's bank, where the cash was. I would never allow my neighbor to sit next to where the bank was (where the cash was kept), and he would never let me sit close to it, either. We would watch like hawks as money was being deposited or taken out from the bank.

The most fun part would be when someone landed on my neighbor's property on the board, and my neighbor had his chance to collect rent. Before the moment the die was rolled, he would be praying hard, looking at the sky, just for the right number to turn up—a number he arrived at after pre-counting squares on the board. He would pause the rolling of the die until he got the count of squares right and said his prayers.

The moments before the die was rolled, he would literally be wishing, hoping, and talking to the dice. The moment it landed and if his wish came true, he would leap and make those hilarious hand gestures and start demanding his rent. The person paying the rent would be completely distraught, while the rest at the board would just enjoy the hilarity of the interactions.

In case my neighbor landed on one of my sisters' or my property, he would ask how much, and then say, "Pichai kasu" (beggar's alms) and throw the money for the rent in a huff. The comedy was simply in the expressions and the fun arguments. The reactions that each would have to the roll of the die, to the situation, and to each other were just hilarious!

Going back in time, I sometimes remember my Paternal Grandfather. My Paternal Grandfather was an extremely calm person (much to the annoyance of his wife, I may add!). He rarely reacted to anything. My father was once advised by my Paternal Grandfather. When my dad started earning, my Paternal Grandfather calmly told him (in Tamil), "If you cannot learn to be happy with Rs 100, you will never be happy with even Rs 10,000."

The point he was trying to make was that money was not central to happiness. Nowadays, there is a societal obsession with money and fame. Maybe it has always been that way; I don't know. But the truth is, money CAN'T buy happiness. It buys one OPTIONS. What one does with THOSE options determines HOW happy one will be.

For instance, one can choose to 'buy time' by 'paying money'. I used to joke with my Father that, "The previous generation in their time spent 30 minutes to save Rs 500, but now the next generation would rather spend the Rs 500 to save 30 minutes." The dynamics of time and money have changed in the last 2-3 decades (at least in INDIA).

The truth is, for a wise man, "The MORE money he has, the LESS he will value it." In fact, money will STOP being a factor once a certain threshold is crossed. This threshold will be reached much EARLIER ON for a wiser man than for most others. This is because he will quickly figure out how much he needs to be happy and stay within that circle. It will be a circle he is comfortable with, one he does not have to sweat about. This will then allow him to concentrate on other aspects of his life that give him true happiness.

Again, I would be the first to admit that 'money is like oxygen'. One would gasp and struggle if one does not have the MINIMUM. So, I am NOT saying or implying that one needs to be a saint or fakir to be happy. I understand that people have requirements for the minimums according to their chosen lifestyle. All I am saying is it's important to live your life on your terms and determine, 'what are the things that give you TRUE HAPPINESS'.

In this context, it's important to lead ONE'S life, NOT according to what one thinks would please or create jealousy in others. "Keeping up with the Joneses", one's neighbors, or other people one wants to impress, is a poor and very outward-looking approach.

The key to happiness is to look inward, ask, and contemplate, "What is true happiness to one?" The more honest and deep one's questions are, the more happiness one will be able to derive from one's contemplations.

Always keep in mind that Success and Happiness are 80% 'IN the JOURNEY'. While reaching the destination would definitely be a high, if one misses smelling the roses along the way, one would have missed 80% of the happiness due to one. One would also have potentially burned a lot of bridges and relationships along the way. It would make one's journey an unpleasant one where one would endure UNNECESSARY pain and stress.

Even if, and when, one reaches one's destination, one would arrive alone at an expensive "Ivory Tower". Expensive NOT because of its cost, but because of the PRICE ONE PAID to get there. It would leave one without anyone to share one's happiness and success with.

The private island and large mansion one would have bought at that point in time would actually make one feel EVEN MORE lonely and unhappy!

Time for some FUN

Time for the **Hindi** song titled ***'Tere Bina'*** from the movie ***'Guru'* (2007)** starring **Aishwarya Rai** and **Abhishek Bachchan.** The Movie was directed by **Mani Ratnam.**

Music was composed by **A.R.Rahman** and the songwriter was **Gulzar**. The song was performed by **A.R.Rahman, Murtuza Khan, Quadir Khan** and **Chinmayi**. Enjoy!!

SONG

'Tere Bina'

MOVIE

***'Guru'* (2007)**

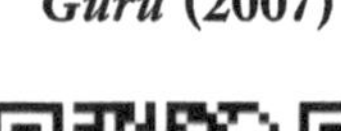

SCAN above to see **YOUTUBE** ***Video of the Song***

Lyrics **['Tere Bina']**	*Translation* **['Without You']**
	(Indian music beats)
Dum dara dum dara mast mast dara	Dum dara dum dara mast mast dara
Dum dara dum dara mast mast dara	Dum dara dum dara mast mast dara
Dum dara dum dum	Dum dara dum dum
Oh hum dum bin tere kya jeena	Oh beloved, there is no life without you
	(Indian music beats)
Dum dara dum dara mast mast dara	Dum dara dum dara mast mast dara
Dum dara dum dara mast mast dara	Dum dara dum dara mast mast dara
Dum dara dum dum	Dum dara dum dum
Oh hum dum bin tere kya jeena	Oh beloved, there is no life without you
Tere bina beswaadi beswaadi ratiyan	The nights are tasteless without you
Oh sajna	Oh beloved
Tere bina beswaadi beswaadi ratiyan	The nights are tasteless without you
Oh sajna	Oh beloved
Rookhi re oh rookhi re	They are dry and withered
Kaaturc kaatc kate na	They don't pass by easily
Tere bina beswaadi beswaadi ratiyan	The nights are tasteless without you
Oh sajna	Oh beloved
Tere bina beswaadi beswaadi ratiyan	The nights are tasteless without you
Oh sajna	Oh beloved
	(Indian music beats)
Dum dara dum dara mast mast dara	Dum dara dum dara mast mast dara
Dum dara dum dara mast mast dara	Dum dara dum dara mast mast dara
Dum dara dum dum	Dum dara dum dum
Oh hum dum bin tere kya jeena	Oh beloved, there is no life without you

	(Indian music beats)
Dum dara dum dara mast mast dara	Dum dara dum dara mast mast dara
Dum dara dum dara mast mast dara	Dum dara dum dara mast mast dara
Dum dara dum dum	Dum dara dum dum
Oh hum dum bin tere kya jeena	Oh beloved, there is no life without you
(Sargam)	*(Sargam)*
Oh o ho ho ho... oh o ho ho ho	Oh o ho ho ho... oh o ho ho ho
Na jaa chakri ke maare	Don't go away by giving reasons of work
Na jaa souten pukaare	Don't go away by saying my sister wife is calling
Saawan aayega toh poochega na jaa re	If the rains come, they will ask me
Pheeki pheeki beswaadi yeh ratiyan	The nights are tasteless and dull
Kaature kaate na kate na	They don't pass by easily
Ab tere bina sajna sajna kaate kate na	My beloved, it doesn't pass without you
Katena katena tere bina	They don't pass by without you
Tere bina beswaadi beswaadi ratiyan	The nights are tasteless without you
Oh sajna	Oh beloved
	(Indian music beats)
Dum dara dum dara mast mast dara	Dum dara dum dara mast mast dara
Dum dara dum dara mast mast dara	Dum dara dum dara mast mast dara
Dum dara dum dum	Dum dara dum dum
Oh hum dum bin tere kya jeena	Oh beloved, there is no life without you
Oh o ho ho ho... tere bina	Oh o ho ho ho... without you
Tere bina chaand ka sona khota re	Without you the moon's shine is fake
Peeli peeli dhool udaawe jhoota re	It just seems like flowing yellow sand
Tere bina sona peetal	Without you gold seems like copper
Tere sang kikar peepal	Without you the kikar seems like a fig
Aaja katena ratiyan	Come the nights are not passing by

	(Indian music beats)
Dum dara dum dara mast mast dara	Dum dara dum dara mast mast dara
Dum dara dum dara mast mast dara	Dum dara dum dara mast mast dara
Dum dara dum dum	Dum dara dum dum
Oh hum dum bin tere kya jeena	Oh beloved, there is no life without you
Tere bina beswaadi beswaadi ratiyan	The nights are tasteless without you
Oh sajna	Oh beloved
Tere bina beswaadi beswaadi ratiyan	The nights are tasteless without you
Oh sajna	Oh beloved
Rookhi re oh rookhi re	They are dry and withered
Kaature kaate kate na	They don't pass by easily
	(Indian music beats)
Dum dara dum dara mast mast dara	Dum dara dum dara mast mast dara
Dum dara dum dara mast mast dara	Dum dara dum dara mast mast dara
Dum dara dum dum	Dum dara dum dum
Oh hum dum bin tere kya jeena	Oh beloved, there is no life without you
	(Indian music beats)
Dum dara dum dara mast mast dara	Dum dara dum dara mast mast dara
Dum dara dum dara mast mast dara	Dum dara dum dara mast mast dara
Dum dara dum dum	Dum dara dum dum
Oh hum dum bin tere kya jeena.	Oh beloved, there is no life without you.

<u>Part I</u>

Chapter 9.2

HAPPINESS IS...

Finding the Happiness in Small Things

"Sometimes the smallest things take up the most room in our heart".

– Winnie The Pooh

"While it may seem small, the ripple effects of small things is extraordinary".

– Matt Bevin

Why Happiness Comes in Small Packages

Sharon Draper says that it's the little things that make happy moments, not just grand events. She describes 'Perfect Happiness' as being found in a beautiful sunset, the giggle of a grandchild, and in the beauty of the first snowfall.

To quote Sharon Draper, "Joy comes in sips, not gulps."

So let us sit back and take a sip with the poem titled, **'Happiness is'**, from my FIRST poetry and song book, "FACETS (Poetry for All Seasons)".

POEM

'Happiness is'

BOOK

'FACETS'

(Poetry for All Seasons)

SCAN above to see **YOUTUBE** ***Lyrical Video of the Poem***

LYRICS

[Happiness Is]

HAPPINESS IS..

When after a long and dreary wintery phase
The warm spring rays of the sun kisses your face

When you, your spouse and children are in a tight embrace
As the spontaneous laughter of your children lights up your space

When a white blanket of snow is created by many a flake
Announcing the joys of Christmas day in its wake

When you are back home after a vacation tired as a log
And you are leaped at, greeted and licked by your dog

When excited children are waiting to try your wonderful cake
Even as the waft from the oven permeates from your bake

HAPPINESS IS..

When after a day's work, drained and tired you come home
As your excited children rush to hug you in affection shown

When you passionately practice singing love songs in the shower
Even as you are being secretly overheard by your lover

When you play sport hard with your father and taste success
Unknown to you, he let you win so that you could impress

When after a tough game fought hard, sweat pours down your brow
And a handy bottle of cool water quenches your thirst as you begin to pour

When the first monsoon showers replace the long anticipation with delight
Quenching the parched earth and helping the farmers in their fight

HAPPINESS IS..

When after a hard work out your body radiates that heat
And the burst of a cool shower, cools you from head to feet

When your daughter looks up to you and still counts you as a superhero
Even when the world treats you as a mere statistic and values you at zero

When it is time to sleep and you are tucked in neatly by your mother
Caring for you with love n tenderness as she would treat a beautiful flower

When the setting sun dials down the sky from orange to red in colour
Even as you sit there in wistful admiration, hand in hand with your lover

When at the end of a long day the school bell rings
Children rush out embracing their joy and giving it wings

Hence...

As simple as it is, most HAPPINESS IS actually free of charge
It can't be bought but can be multiplied by a big n embracing heart

Part I

Chapter 10

WHY DOES A CHILD NOT LISTEN TO HIS PARENTS?

(Parents & Children)

The reason why your children don't listen to you is because they are smarter than you think!

"Love is not obedience."

– *Humble the Poet*

"Children are precious. When you love them, don't love them as if their love lacks. Love them as if their love is already full.

When you teach them, don't teach them as if ignorance defines them. Teach them as if their soul is already full."

– *Hendrith Vanlon Smith Jr,*

(The Wealth Reference Guide: An American Classic)

One lazy Sunday afternoon, I was on the couch reading one article after another on the mobile version of *The Economic Times*. My young daughter (about 4 years old) was on my wife's mobile phone, watching one episode after another of the *Peppa Pig* cartoon.

As I watched through the corner of my eye, my young daughter was enjoying the cartoon. I continued with my scrolling even as I quietly disapproved of my daughter's excessive screen time. Intermittently, I managed to admonish her multiple times to put the mobile phone down. My daughter did not even bother to heed any of that. She just nonchalantly continued watching the cartoon, while ignoring anything I had to say.

It had been more than an hour, and I continued reading one newspaper after another, even as I kept an eye on my daughter. Intermittently, I continued to let out admonishments at regular intervals and then returned to my readings.

At some point, I was almost finished. It had been more than 2 hours. My daughter, on the other hand, was still completely glued to the mobile. By now, I was exasperated. I called out her name and told her that she needed to stop watching Peppa Pig. My daughter ignored me and did not even acknowledge my "command". By then, I was losing it. I walked across to her, took the mobile out of her hand, and gave her a scolding.

My daughter was now very upset and angry. She stormed out of the room crying loudly and went straight to her mother. My wife then came out of the adjoining room. She was angry, and I, in turn, got a piece of my wife's angry mind. Soon, my wife and I were in a heated argument. My wife was like, "She is just a child. You can't be so harsh". By now, I was defensive. I was like, "I was only telling her to stop watching cartoons for so long. She has been watching cartoons non-stop for more than 2 hours".

So my wife and I were in a continuing and escalating argument. Soon, my Dad and Mom entered the picture. Our loud arguments drew them into the war zone (if you want to call it that). Each had their own views on the situation. By now, all four of us had completely forgotten what the whole discussion was originally about!

As for my daughter, well, she was back. Back on the sofa, happily watching the next episode of Peppa Pig!!

Children are MUCH smarter than YOU give them CREDIT for

"Let your child see you doing a good deed instead of you telling him or her to do it, and the little child shall one day grow up to become a real kind human being."

– Abhijit Naskar,

Human Making is Our Mission: A Treatise on Parenting

"The Parenting Sonnet

Anybody can make a baby, that's no glory, To raise a true being, that's a glorious thing.

It takes less than a minute to make a baby, But more than a decade to make a being.

So if you choose to have baby someday, Focus on their character, not just sustenance.

And make sure to keep luxury away from them, For luxury is curse for character development.

Pass on the tradition of compassion to them, Be a living example of the possibility of humanity.

Teach them the belief of non-discrimination, Demonstrate to them a never-before seen sanity.

Be the person you want the kids to grow up to be. The best kind of parenting is that of exemplarity."

– Abhijit Naskar,

('Honor He Wrote' : 100 Sonnets For Humans Not Vegetables)

Children are much smarter than we give them credit for. My daughter knows she has a total of about 7 cards she can play (or buttons she can push). For instance, if I scold her, she would go to her mom. If going to her mother didn't work, she has two grandfathers, two grandmothers, and then my wife's brother she could go to. My in-laws just happened to live 7 houses down the street at that time. I must say, this arrangement was so convenient for my daughter!

My daughter had incisive intelligence (unadulterated by "education") and understood the complete family dynamics just by observation. She knew instantly "what buttons to push" and "what reactions" she could expect from each one of us. Through just acute observation and application, she had gathered the complete family dynamics.

When this was enhanced by unlimited imagination, she had the power to set any of the family members against each other, as and where, and as and when, she chose to. Having lit the match as necessary, my young daughter would then continue her business, coolly and calmly, right in the middle of the war zone. The adults (or should I say children) on the other hand, slugged it out as if in some imaginary gladiator fight.

My daughter may have been only 4 years old then, but the application of her intelligence, (and OUR lack of it, you may add,) worked perfectly to her advantage.

She would happily set one family member against the other and continue with what she was doing, even as we so-called adults would continue arguing like children!!

Why Setting an Example is MORE effective than Words

"Your child is a mirror of your behaviour and the culture of your home"

–Jignesh Ahalgama

"Sometimes we forget that parenting, like love, is a verb."

–Jessica Joelle Alexander

['The Danish Way of Parenting': What the Happiest People in the World Know About Raising Confident, Capable Kids]

Smart people, for instance, never buy too much into what you have to say. They look at what you do. Even better, they look to see if 'what you say' and 'what you do' are consistent. Words are 'easy and cheap', and children 'know that better than us'. Children are much smarter than we give them credit for and are NOT likely to listen to what one just says.

It is actually simplistic thinking on our part to assume children will just take our words as sacrosanct. Children observe and often mimic their parents. So it is what YOU DO that matters, and NOT what YOU SAY. This is true no matter how logical, right, or well-meaning one's words are.

Ultimately in life, it does NOT matter 'what you say'. It matters 'what you do'. Smart people look at what you do and don't give too much weight to what you say in isolation. Your actions should be consistent with your words for them to be credible from a child's point of view. Children have unadulterated 'intelligence' and 'smarts'. They are going to mimic and do exactly what they see you do, rather than do what you say. Children are fully well aware that words are cheap and that it is the actions that count.

Instead of telling my daughter to put down the mobile, I should have first put down mine and set an example. Children learn by example. One can't keep telling children that too much mobile is bad for them, while one continues to do the opposite. Children will easily pick up on the inconsistency in our words and actions.

My Dad, for instance, never ever told me that smoking, drinking, or drugs were bad. These were conversations that never really happened in the family. None of my Dad's three children ever took to any of the three. My parents just set that example and never said a word about them. We as children just followed the example. All five (my Dad, Mom and my two Sisters, and myself) in the family have strong personalities and strong independent streaks. Of course, we had minds of our own and made independent decisions. However, an example was set, and we saw merit in it. From that point on, it was easier for us to make those independent decisions to keep our physical and mental health in order.

It was the same with physical exercise. First thing in the morning, my Dad would set off on his hour-long morning walk. He saw health as an important component of his wealth. This just percolated to his children. We as children saw merit in those actions and incorporated that health consciousness into our lives.

There was one particular incident I would like to highlight. I was in my 20s and watching television at about 7 p.m. in the evening. The room was dark without the lights switched on. My Dad was passing by. He told me not to watch TV in the dark (as the contrast of a bright TV and the dark room was tough on the eyes and bad for them). I then told him the tube light was NOT working. He told me that the connection was loose and I needed to make a few twists and turns of the tube light in its holder to get it to work.

So, I got up and pulled a chair from the dining room nearby. I then stood on it and reached for the tube. I tried turning and twisting it for about 10-15 minutes. The tube light flickered but flattered to deceive. It never lit up, as though teasing me. My shoulders started to feel it. I got fed up and gave up. I had been trying for about 15 minutes. My arms, up in that position, had begun to ache badly. I decided to quit and put the chair back in the dining room.

I went back to the sofa and continued watching. My Dad was again passing by the room and asked me what happened. I told him that I tried, but it was no good. He did not say anything and went on his way. About 5 minutes later, he came back and pulled the chair from the dining room and said, "Let me see". I smiled as if to say, "be my guest".

My Dad was at it for about 10 minutes. I could see his hand begin to ache as it came down from the raised position. I smiled and continued watching television. Another 10 minutes went by, and my Dad continued trying. I was by now like, "I told you so". My Dad, however, was still at it, and another 5 minutes went by. It was now 25 minutes, and yet my Dad never gave up. At that point, the flickering suddenly gave way to bright light, as light filled the room.

My Dad got down and put the chair back in the dining room. I was completely dumbfounded. Without saying a single word, my Dad had taught me one of my life's greatest lessons.

[80% effort = 0 Result] but **[120% = 100% Results]**

From then on, **the choice in life** was clear to me and **'I had made my choice'.**

Time for some FUN

Time for the song **'Glory of Love'** by **American** singer, songwriter, bassist, and producer, **Peter Cetera.** The song is from his album **Solitude/Solitaire (1986)** and was produced by **Michael Omartian.**

Songwriters for the song included **Peter Cetera, David Foster**, and **Diane Nini.** The song was also featured in the movie soundtrack of **Karate Kid II (1986).** Enjoy!!

'Glory of Love'

Peter Cetera, [Album **'Solitude/Solitaire' (1986)**]

SCAN above to see **YOUTUBE** ***Video of the Song***

Lyrics

[Glory of Love]

Tonight it's very clear
As we're both lyin' here
There's so many things I wanna say
I will always love you
I would never leave you alone

Sometimes, I just forget
Say things I might regret
It breaks my heart to see you crying
I don't wanna lose you
I could never make it alone

I am a man who will fight for your honor
I'll be the hero you're dreaming of
We'll live forever
Knowing together that we
Did it all for the glory of love

You keep me standing tall
You help me through it all
I'm always strong when you're beside me
I have always needed you
I could never make it alone

I am a man who will fight for your honor
I'll be the hero you've been dreaming of
We'll live forever
Knowing together that we
Did it all for the glory of love

Just like a knight in shining armor
From a long time ago
Just in time, I will save the day
Take you to my castle far away

I am a man who will fight for your honor
I'll be the hero that you're dreamin' of
We're gonna live forever
Knowing together that we
Did it all for the glory of love

We'll live forever (we'll live forever)
Knowing together that we (knowing together)
Did it all for the glory of love
Ooh, we did it all for love
We did it all for love
We did it all for love
We did it all for love

Part I

Chapter 11

GENERATIONAL CONFLICTS (PARENTS & YOUNGSTERS)

Why the Parent and the Youngster are BOTH Right?

"Parents rarely let go of their children, so children let go of them. They move on. They move away.

The moments that used to define them are covered by moments of their own accomplishments.

It is not until much later, that children understand; their stories and all their accomplishments, sit atop the stories of their mothers and fathers, stones upon stones, beneath the water of their lives."

– Paul Coelho

"That's an impossible thing for sons to grasp, and a source of shame for fathers to have to admit: that we don't want our children to pursue their own dreams or walk in our footsteps. We want to walk in their footsteps while they pursue our dreams."

– Fredrik Backman, *Anxious People*

I used to joke to my Father that, "The previous generation, in their time, spent 30 minutes to save Rs 500, but now the next generation would rather spend the Rs 500 and save 30 minutes". This is because the dynamics of time and money have changed in the last 2-3 decades in INDIA and continue to change.

Across generations, perspectives often clash. Honestly, this is to be expected. While in INDIA, things have been changing since liberalization, parents who grew up in a time of scarcity still hold on to their value systems, which made them successful then. Thrift is definitely a virtue, alright, but there is a difference between 'being thrifty' and 'being miserly'. The latest generation have an abundant mindset. They don't try to save every penny as the previous generation did. Both, however, are right in their own ways.

For example, let us take this statement:

Statement 1: "The previous generation, in their time, spent 30 minutes to save Rs 500, but now the next generation would rather spend the Rs 500 and save 30 minutes".

Let me reframe the 'concern and grouse' that the two generations have against each other. Let us take this statement to an enhanced explanatory state.

Statement 2: "If the previous generation INVESTED the Rs 500 and made it work for them, and if the next generation USED the 30 minutes they saved productively, then aren't both right in their own ways?"

It is a matter of perspective, isn't it?

Let me enhance that statement EVEN further.

Statement 3: "Let us say, for argument's sake, the previous generation is retired and the next generation are busy students. Wouldn't it make sense both ways? The retired generation VALUE the 'cash to time', while the next generation, who want to achieve big and are under time pressure, value the 'time to cash'."

Each is doing 'a swap' of 'time and money' ACCORDING to their circumstances. Both are right in their own ways. Both the parents and children may actually be doing the optimum thing from their perspectives. While both are right from their perspectives, the REASON for the grievance is that they DO NOT see it from the other's perspective.

If the parents and the youngsters both REFUSE to LISTEN to each other, then they are likely to complain and feel let down. The parent is likely to label the youngster as 'entitled', and the child is likely to refer to his parents as 'old and outdated'.

All this is actually unnecessary if BOTH sides can communicate with 'empathy and patience' and make an effort to understand the other's point of view. That is ALL that is needed. They will both realize that they are right in their circumstances and may not necessarily be right if they projected their views onto the other.

The thing to note is, depending on circumstances, people can be right in their own ways. The important thing here is, for BOTH the parents and the youngsters, to have the empathy to understand the other's point of view and NOT project THEIR thinking and beliefs onto the other.

For instance, I often have had differing views with my Dad with respect to investments. These are not uncommon. Some people would call it the 'generation gap'. For instance, in the simplest terms, the differences in investment styles may arise due to their differing 'investment horizons'. We have differing investment horizons we subconsciously perceive based on our age. We anchor to those investment horizons in our respective minds. My Dad would obviously be 'overweight on bonds', and I would put my 'weight on equities'. Both are right, BUT from THEIR respective perspectives.

An older person would NOT want to 'take on the volatility' of the stock market at his/her age. He/she would prefer the security and steady cash flows that bonds provide. A younger person would be right in investing in equities, as 'his focus would be on growth'. He/she is more likely to accept the volatility and ride it, considering he/she has more time on his/her hands to ride it out.

Often, in family-run businesses, generational clash is not uncommon. We often see the next generation approaching the business differently. This, more often than not, sets off alarm bells in the older folks. For instance, the younger generation may want to expand the business aggressively, as he may be willing to put in the time and effort while taking on the risk. The older generation may prefer stability rather than risking expansion. These differing thought processes have, and will always exist. They can only be resolved via communication, active listening, and understanding.

Like all children in their teens, I had differences with my parents. My parents came from an old-school style of parenting and had a simple approach to parent-child conflict: 'They were right, period'. This was because they were older and supposedly wiser. Hence, I had to respect and follow what they said without questioning. They were older and hence had much more 'wisdom and experience'. I was younger and did not have the experience, and hence was immature.

The problem was that the experience they were talking about was from their perspective and from their unique situations. The fact is that things had changed since their time, and just maybe, things that worked then were less effective in the current time.

How the Conflict gets Seeded

"Give people room to be what God created them to be. Don't force them to fit into your own mold."

– ***Bernard Kelvin Clive***

"We're taught to expect unconditional love from our parents, but I think it is more the gift our children give us. It's they who love us helplessly, no matter what or who we are."

– ***Kathryn Harrison,*** *The Kiss*

"In parenting patience is the greatest virtue."

– ***Abhijit Naskar,*** *Human Making is Our Mission: A Treatise on Parenting*

Differences of opinion with parents are expected to occur and do occur often. In my case, if and when I did flag an issue (even if in a soft tone), my parents would respond by saying, "Don't raise your voice".

I initially found this perplexing. Even if I said something in a very soft and low voice, even if I said the same in a calm manner, the response I got was, "Do not raise your voice". When I sat back and dissected that interaction, I began to realize what the problem was. It had nothing to do with the tone or delivery. When my parents said, "Do not raise your voice", what they were actually saying is that, irrespective of tone or words, "You are being disrespectful".

Now, having a better handle on the problem, I began to explain to my parents that while I had great respect for them, there WAS a difference BETWEEN 'disagreeing' with someone and being 'disrespectful'. While I was just 'disagreeing' with them on issues, my respect for them was still intact and will always be.

The difference we had was a 'difference of opinion' born out of 'differing experiences and situations'. What was needed was the understanding that, when making decisions pertaining to myself, an understanding of my position was important. My approach was born out of present-day scenarios and cannot be understood through the prism of the scenarios my parents had faced back then. The references from their time and experiences needed to factor in the fact that times have changed. Approaches based on what worked in the past 'may' or 'may not' apply in current scenarios.

Also, comparing their successful 'approaches of the past' versus what was being proposed now was akin to comparing 'apples to oranges'. While both approaches have their merit, they have merit only within the CONTEXT of their respective times. Also, a current approach needs ground-up thinking based on current times and unique current scenarios. The context needs to be the current time and place.

The ability to 'talk AND listen', explain each other's positions, and have the empathy to understand the other person's 'WHY' before doing or recommending something would go a long way toward a successful 'parent–child' relationship. Maintaining a respectful style of communication and approaching the problem empathically would open the door to the way forward.

Maintaining cordiality and active listening, leading to a better understanding of perspectives, is central. This would go a long way for the happiness, productivity, harmony, and peace of both parties involved.

Hence, an approach based on empathy and grounded in current reality, while keeping things practical, would help to achieve optimum results. This would eliminate the unnecessary misunderstanding and consequent conflict.

Time for some FUN

Time for the song **'MMMBop'** by the **American** pop rock band **Hanson.** The song is their lead single from their first full length album **'Middle of Nowhere' (1997).** Enjoy!!

'MMMBop'

Hanson, [Album **'Middle of nowhere' (1997)]**

SCAN above to see **YOUTUBE** ***Video of the Song***

Lyrics

[MMMBop]

Oh
Oh, oh
Oh, oh
Oh, yeah

You have so many relationships in this life
Only one or two will last
You go through all the pain and strife
Then you turn your back and they're gone so fast
Ooh yeah
And they're gone so fast, yeah

Oh, so hold on to the ones who really care
In the end they'll be the only ones there
When you get old and start losing your hair
Can you tell me who will still care?
Can you tell me who will still care?
Oh, will care

Mmmbop, ba duba dop
Ba du bop, ba duba dop
Ba du bop, ba duba dop ba du
Yeah
Mmm bop, ba duba dop
Ba du bop, ba du dop, yeah
Said oh yeah
In an mmmbop they're gone
Yeah, yeah

Plant a seed, plant a flower, plant a rose
You can plant any one of those
Keep planting to find out which one grows
It's a secret no one knows
It's a secret no one knows
No one knows

Mmmbop, ba duba dop
Ba du bop, ba duba dop ba du
Yeah
Mmmbop, ba duba dop
Ba du bop, ba duba dop ba du
Yeah

In an mmmbop they're gone
In an mmmbop they're not there
In an mmmbop they're gone
In an mmmbop they're not there
Until you lose your hair, ooh
But you don't care, yeah

Mmmbop, ba duba dop
Ba du bop, ba duba dop ba du, yeah
Mmmbop, ba duba dop
Ba du bop, ba duba dop ba du
Yeah

Can you tell me?
No you can't, no you don't know
Can you tell me? Oh yeah
You say you can but you don't know
Can you tell me? (Which flower's going to grow)
No you can't, no you don't know

Can you tell me? (If it's going to be a daisy or a rose)
You say you can but you don't know
Can you tell me? (Which flower's going to grow)
No you can't, no you don't know
Can you tell me? (If it's going to be a daisy or a rose)
You say you can but you don't know
Say you can but you don't know
You don't know
You don't know

Mmmbop
Duba
Duba
Du
Yeah

Mmmbop
Duba
Duba
Du
Yeah

Mmmbop, ba duba dop
Ba du bop, ba duba dop ba du, yeah
Mmmbop, ba duba dop
Ba du bop, ba duba dop ba du
Oh

Mmmbop, ba duba dop
Ba du bop, ba duba dop ba du, yeah
Mmmbop, ba duba dop
Ba du bop, ba duba dop ba du
Oh yeah, yeah

Can you tell me?
No you can't, no you don't know
Can you tell me?
You say you can but you don't know
You say you can but you don't know
Don't

<u>Part I</u>

Chapter 12

DRESSED FOR SUCCESS

While Optics Matter, Substance is 'More Substantial'

"If we think we ALONE are responsible for OUR success, we are really going to end up ALONE!"

–Author

"Unknown to us we are victims of our own biases. Already having formed a conclusion with our closed minds, we then look for evidence to support and buttress our hypothesis."

–Author

I was in the 8th grade and was listening to my Hindi teacher, Ms. Shanta Sharma, in her class. She would often regale us with a lot of fun stories. I enjoyed her passion for storytelling and the fun way she would tell them, often narrating stories and embodying them with her expressions and hand gestures.

One such story that stuck was about a famous writer/philosopher who was invited as the guest of honor to a dinner. The dinner was to be hosted by a very wealthy and influential man at his mansion.

On the appointed day, the writer/philosopher arrived on foot at the grand mansion's gates, only to be stopped by the security guards. Dressed in an unremarkable and average, plain kurta (an ethnic Indian dress) and in sandals, he seemed like a wanderer who had lost his way to the security at the gate.

The guards shooed him to the side, even as they were busy checking and passing the other guests arriving in expensive luxury cars. The writer/

philosopher tried to plead his case, but the guards were in no mood to listen. Finding the situation hopeless, the writer/philosopher returned home.

Having reached home, he then took off his clothes and took out his finest suit and boots. He looked in the mirror as he adjusted his expensive tie. He then rode, seated in the back seat of his chauffeur-driven car, as he headed back to the mansion.

When he arrived at the mansion, the security guards, without any fuss, opened the gates and let him in. The writer/philosopher then got out of the car at the entrance and entered the mansion. He was greeted by the guests, who were patiently and eagerly awaiting his arrival. He apologized for being late and then gave a fine speech.

The writer/philosopher was then introduced to each of the distinguished guests. Finally, it was time for dinner. All the guests sat down at the table. The head of the table was reserved for the writer/philosopher, who was the guest of honor. A toast was raised in his honor, and dinner commenced.

The writer/philosopher took food from his plate with a spoon in his right hand and pleaded with his suit to eat it! He pulled his jacket forward with his left hand and gestured with his right hand, like one would do when feeding a baby.

At this point, all the guests stopped eating and conversing, and the room became quiet. All of them were transfixed on what the writer/philosopher was trying to do. The host and all the guests were totally perplexed. They were trying to make sense of what was happening. The writer/philosopher kept telling his suit, "Eat... Eat... Eat". These words filled the room, which by now was screaming in its pin-drop silence.

The wealthy host then politely leaned toward the writer/philosopher and asked, "Are things okay? Do you need anything?" The writer/philosopher put his spoon down, sighed, and said, "I was just trying to GET the 'guest of honor' to eat".

Even as the bewildered guests listened in, the writer/philosopher innocently asked, "Who is the 'guest of honor'?" The host responded, "You are the esteemed 'guest of honor', of course". "Why the doubt?" continued the host, completely baffled.

The **writer/philosopher** smiled, and then **narrated the story** on **'WHY he was late!'.**

How easily we Judge people

As we go through our lives, we humans develop OUR heuristics or shortcuts to form impressions of people. We quickly and easily judge people by their appearances. We treat people based on deductions drawn from shortcomings in our own minds and simplistic approaches. These shortcuts or heuristics about our impressions of groups or people then get imprinted in our minds.

We easily judge people according to these preconceived ideas and notions. We judge people if they dress differently, if they talk differently, if they eat differently, etc. Worse still, we refuse to see them as individuals with their own situations and compulsions. We group these heterogeneous people into a homogeneous group and label them in twisted ways. This often germinates in us as misunderstanding and contempt, leading on to hate.

These heuristics can even extend beyond just differences in race, color, religion, gender, or other identity markers. Even WITHIN the same race or any other such identity markers, people can be stereotyped.

A fat person is rejected the moment he walks into an interview because he is already lazy in our minds. A quiet person may be very bright but can end up being labeled as dumb because he speaks less. A thin person is a pushover even though, unseen to us, he has a mind that is 'tough as nails'. A big, muscular person is seen as tough and would be laughed at if he happens to feel low or cry. Short people can't make leaders and need to be looked down upon. Fairer people are more right, while darker people are evil. A person who is not fluent in a language is not smart because he can't put together a sentence articulately.

Actually, ultimately, these are OUR own shortcomings as individuals and as a society. These are NOT the shortcomings of the individual. Sometimes, even unknown to us, WE are victims of our own biases. The fault is in OUR preconceived perceptions.

Having already "formed a conclusion" with our closed minds, we then look for selective evidence to support and buttress our conclusions. We revel in our own ignorance and rush to conclusions, even as we puff out our chests and pat ourselves on the back for being so "intelligent and smart".

Hmm... 'Ignorance is bliss'.

Just a Thought

EVERY individual has God-given 'potential and capability'. The individual's failure is not JUST his/her failure ALONE. It is sometimes our failure as a society and as a community of nations to harness these individual gems. It is for us as a society to help every individual attain their potential and maximize our potential as a human race.

Success is not JUST for a privileged few. Success is for everyone. While it is the responsibility of society to empower everyone, it is also our responsibility, as empowered individuals, to strive, work hard, and make use of opportunities given to us. It is also necessary to understand and recognize that when we succeed, it is because of teamwork and not our genius ALONE. Having succeeded, we should then have the gratitude to give back. It then becomes OUR duty to help OTHERS realize THEIR dreams. Success is, and never has been, a zero-sum game. We are in it together. While society helps us, it is our duty to give back so that the cycle of good continues.

I will end this chapter with a thought. "If we think we ALONE are responsible for OUR successes, we are really going to end up ALONE!"

As the saying goes, "If you want to go FAST, go ALONE, but if you want to go FAR, walk TOGETHER".

Time for some FUN

Below is '**Dressed for Success**', from Album '**Look Sharp**' **(1988),** by the **Swedish** pop rock duo **Roxette**. Enjoy!!

'Dressed for Success'

Roxette, [Album **'Look Sharp' (1988)**]

SCAN above to see **YOUTUBE** ***Video of the Song***

Lyrics

[Dressed for Success]

Tried to make it little by little
Tried to make it bit by bit on my own.
Quit the job, the grey believers
Another town where I get close to the bone.

Whatcha gonna tell your brother?
Oh oh oh
Whatcha gonna tell your father?
Oh I don't know!
Whatcha gonna tell your mother?
Let me go … O OO Oh.

I'm gonna get dressed for success
Shaping me up for the big time, baby.
Get dressed for success
Shaping it up for your love yea yea yea.

I'm not afraid
A trembling flower
I'll feed your heart
And blow the dust from your eyes and
In the dark things happen faster.
I love the way you sway your hips next to mine.

Whatcha gonna tell your brother?
Oh oh oh
Whatcha gonna tell your father?
Oh I don't know!
Whatcha gonna tell your mother?
Let me go..O OO Oh.

I'm gonna get dressed for success
Shaping me up for the big time, baby.
Get dressed for success
Shaping it up for your love

Whatcha gonna tell your brother?
Oh oh oh
Whatcha gonna tell your father?
Oh I don't know!
Whatcha gonna tell your mother?
Let me go..O OO Oh.

Dressed for success
Hmm…I'm gonna get dressed for success
I'm gonna get dressed for success
Hitting a spot for the big time, baby.
Get dressed for success
Shaping it up for your love

For your love..…yea yea yea
For your love…..yea yea yea
For your love…..yea yea yea
For your love….yea yea yea

<u>Part I</u>

Chapter 13

LOVE WHAT YOU DO

If One's situation is such, One Can't 'Do what one Loves', then, One can STILL 'Love what one Does'

"Teams that show up to work with passion and a zest for what they do prioritize quality and excellence in their work. They feel more connected to the work they're doing and this correlates directly to how your customer feels about your product or service. Simply state, happy employees who love what they do lead to happy customers who keep coming back."

– Warren Buffett

"Yes, we live in uncertain and stressful times. But people who do work they love, with people they love, never feel the need to bow to the shrine of problems. They focus on the future, set ambitious targets, have the courage to consider the obstacles, and remember to rejoice with arms stretched to the sky when they conquer them."

– Warren Buffett

While some are lucky to be able to live life on their terms and 'Do what they love', others CAN still learn to 'Love what they do'. The latter is something I learned just by observing my Dad. No matter how 'big or small' the task at hand was, no matter how 'interesting or mundane', no matter 'how big or small the incentive', my Dad simply did the work with equal love, enthusiasm, and dedication. He simply 'Loved what he did'.

Whether it was leading the charge in building a multi-billion-dollar township or just fixing a plumbing issue at home, my Dad supervised it with equal dedication. He so simply taught me that, at times, EVEN if you do not have the luxury of 'Doing what you love', you CAN still 'Love what you do'.

Many young people will call that old-school or outdated thinking. Many a time, I would mock the likes of my Dad and call them the World War II generation. However, certain principles and approaches NEVER go out of fashion. Many young people have the 'luxury of choice' BECAUSE the previous generations made that sacrifice with their dedication to providing a better life for their children. The older generation most of the time did NOT have the 'luxury of choice', and yet, they seem to be in a happier space than most of those who followed.

Dad, the Scooter and the British Gentleman

My Dad's first job was with a British paint company in Bombay (Mumbai). The office was far away, so my Dad decided to cycle to work. He had to cycle long distances to get to work on time. My Dad's first boss was a kind British gentleman. One morning, having noticed my Dad arriving at the office on a bicycle, he called my Dad and told him that the company would provide him with a *Lambretta* scooter. He also added that the company would pay the installments for it.

One day the scooter arrived, and my Dad was given its keys. My Dad didn't have a license, so he pushed the scooter along the curb all the way home. Once he got his license, he rode the scooter to the office every day.

At the company, my Dad did his job with complete dedication. After a year, he got another offer from an upcoming oil company and made the decision to leave. Having resigned, he thanked his boss and handed him back the key to the scooter.

His boss, who by then was impressed with my Dad's work ethic, told him to keep the scooter as a gift from the company for the work he had done. That is how Dad got his first vehicle!

Loving what you Do

Having joined the oil industry, my Dad's first assignment was to supervise the laying of lamp posts—mile after mile of just lamp posts. As mundane and boring as one may think it is, my Dad, who was a junior engineer then, would do the supervision and guide the construction workers with complete love and dedication.

Whether it was the laying of lamp-posts or working on bridges, building highways, or constructing huge oil storage facilities, his dedication and enthusiasm for the task at hand was COMPLETE. He was quickly promoted and rose up the ranks.

On one occasion, his boss handed him a promotion letter, making him a Class-I officer. However, there was a murmur and then a protest in the ranks. There was a company policy that specified a minimum age requirement to be appointed a Class-I officer. That minimum age at the time was around 27 years. His boss was forced to take back the promotion letter. However, the boss kept it in his drawer and waited.

On my Father's 27th birthday, first thing in the morning, his boss called him into his office and handed him the appointment letter!

When you CAN still 'Love what You Do', that is what happens!!

After completing my Master's in Engineering, I took up a job in Dallas, TX in the late 1990s. My Dad came to visit. I had taken a single-bedroom furnished apartment (with Spartan furniture) and a small TV. My Dad came to visit me and stayed for a few months. I had no cable, no computer, or internet. I had just started my career, and the future of a person on a work visa was uncertain, so I tried keeping to the minimum. Every morning, when I took the car and went to work, I worried about what my Dad was going to do the whole day alone in the apartment. While the apartment was in a gated community, my Dad knew no one and was alone. I thought he was going to be really bored and lonely.

However, my Dad not only kept himself busy but was always in good spirits and happy. He just knew how to be happy. He simply would do even the most mundane tasks with total dedication, love, and enthusiasm. He cooked lunch, at other times he would dust the apartment, he went for walks and befriended all the Mexicans who were mowing the lawn in the complex, or he would sit and watch PBS channel (free channel) like a child soaking in the world's wonders. No matter what the situation, he was always in good spirits and happy.

As I write this and think about my Dad, the words of Warren Buffett come to mind: "The happiest people do not necessarily have the best of things. They simply appreciate the things they have, the best".

Time for some FUN

Time for the **Hindi** song *'Suraj Hua Maddham'*, starring **Shahrukh Khan** and **Kajol**, from the movie **K3G** a.k.a **'*Kabhi Khushi Kabhi Gham*' (2001).** The film was directed by **Karan Johar** and produced by **Yash Johar.**

Music was composed by **Sandesh Shandilya**, and the songwriter was **Anil Pandey**. Playback singers were **Sonu Nigam** (male) and **Alka Yagnik** (female). Enjoy!!

SONG

'Suraj Hua Maddham'

MOVIE

'Kabhi Khushi Kabhi Gham' **(2001)**

(Sometimes Happiness, Sometimes Sadness)

SCAN above to see **YOUTUBE** *Video of the Song*

Lyrics **['Suraj Hua Maddham']**	*Translation* **['The Sun Went Dark']**
--MALE-- Suraj hua maddham, chaand jalne laga Aasmaan yeh haai kyoon pighalne laga? Main thehra raha, zameen chalne lagi Dhadka yeh dil, saans thamne lagi Oh, kya yeh mera pehla pehla pyaar hai Sajna, kya yeh mera pehla pehla pyaar hai **--FEMALE--** Ho oh oh, oh oh oh oh oh, aa aa aa aa aa aa Suraj hua maddham, chaand jalne laga Aasmaan yeh haai kyoon pighalne laga Main thehri rahi, zameen chalne lagi Dhadka yeh dil, saans thamne lagi Haan, kya yeh mera pehla pehla pyaar hai Sajna, kya yeh mera pehla pehla pyaar hai **--MALE--** Hai khoobsurat yeh pal, sab kuch raha hai badal Sapne haqeeqat mein jo dhal rahe hai Kya sadiyon se puraana hai rishtaa yeh hamaara Ke jis tarha tumse hum mil rahe hai	**--MALE--** The sun was darkened, and the moon was kindled The sky, oh, why did it seem to melt? I stood still even as the ground seemed to move As my heart beats faster, I began to gasp Oh, is this my first love? My dear, is this my first love? **--FEMALE--** Ho oh oh, oh oh oh oh oh, aa aa aa aa aa aa The sun was darkened, and the moon was kindled The sky, oh, why did it seem to melt? I stood still even as the ground seemed to move As my heart beats faster, I began to gasp Oh, is this my first love? Honey, is this my first love? **--MALE--** This moment is beautiful, even as everything is changing My dreams are coming true Has my relationship with you been for centuries? It so seems for you and I, as we find ourselves

--FEMALE-- Yunhi rahe har dam pyaar ka mausam Yunhi milo humse tum janam janam	**--FEMALE--** Let it be like this always. Like the season of love Let us meet, life after life
--MALE-- Main thehra raha, zameen chalne lagi	**--MALE--** I stood still even as the ground seemed to move
--MALE-- Dhadka yeh dil, saans thamne lagi	**--MALE--** As my heart beats faster, I began to gasp
--FEMALE-- Haan, kya yeh mera pehla pehla pyaar hai Sajna, kya yeh mera pehla pehla pyaar hai	**--FEMALE--** Ah, is this my first love? My dear, is this my first love?
Tere hi rang se yun main to rangeen hoon sanam Paake tujhe khud se hi kho rahi hoon sanam O maahiya, ve tere ishq mein Haan doobke paar main ho rahi hoon sanam	It is only by your colour that I have became colourful Even as I gained you, I began to lose myself, my love, Oh, darling, I crossed the river bank, even as I drowned in your love
--MALE-- Saagar hua pyaasa, raat jagne lagi Sholo ke dil mein bhi aag jalne lagi	**--MALE--** Even the oceans became thirsty, Even the depths of the night began to wake up Even the heart of the flames were lit by the bigger fire as they began to burn

--FEMALE-- Main thehri lagi, zameen chalne lagi Dhadka yeh dil, saans thamne lagi	**--FEMALE--** I stood still even as the ground seemed to move As my heart beats faster, I began to gasp
--MALE-- Kya yeh mera pehla pehla pyaar hai	**--MALE--** Ah, is this my first love?
--FEMALE-- Sajna	**--FEMALE--** My dear,
--BOTH-- Kya yeh mera pehla pehla pyaar hai	**--BOTH--** Is this my first love?
--MALE-- Suraj hua maddham	**--MALE--** The sun was darkened
--BOTH-- Chaand jalne laga	**--BOTH--** and the moon was kindled
--MALE-- Aasmaan yeh haai	**--MALE--** The sky, oh,
--BOTH-- Kyoon pighalne laga	**--BOTH--** Why did it melt?
--MALE-- Sajna, kya yeh mera pehla pehla pyaar hai	**--MALE--** Honey, is this my first love?

<u>Part I</u>

Chapter 14

JUST WHEN WE THINK 'WE ARE BETTER'

Just When We Think We are Better, We May Meet Our Match!

"Always keep your ego in check and not be afraid to listen. Listening is a great art form."

– Clint Eastwood

"If your pride is bigger than your ego, which is bigger than your head, grow up or you will be alone for life!"

– Warren Buffett

Like any son would, my Dad was my benchmark. Often, my Dad liked to 'center himself'. He did this by sitting in the pooja room (prayer room) and reciting Sanskrit Slokhas (Sanskrit Verses). So as I passed him one day, I thought to myself,

1. He knows ***Sanskrit,*** well, so do I. Check!
2. He knows ***English***, well, so do I. Check!
3. He knows ***Hindi***, well, so do I. Check!
4. He knows ***Tamil****, well, so do I. Check!

[*Let us ignore the details (in the last one) especially! As they say, "The Devil is in the details"]

So that is, 4 on 4, I thought as I puffed my chest, and strutted past the *Pooja* room.

My Paternal Grandmother had passed away in the year 1990. She left her one and only one-bedroom *Chawl* in Dadar, in Mumbai (Bombay), to her only two sons. Neither of her sons, however, had a use for it. They had moved out after marriage.

My Paternal Grandmother was particularly proud of her home in Mumbai. She was sentimentally attached to that house and had left instructions to NOT sell that home, even after she had passed away. So, it stayed locked for over a decade after her death.

At some point, my Father's younger brother pressed my Dad to sell, as he was in urgent need of money. My Dad initially tried to reason against the sale but finally agreed.

It was the year 2000, and my Dad needed to go to Mumbai to complete the formalities of the sale. My Dad's younger brother was staying in Gujarat and had to come too to complete the sale. My Dad asked me to come along, and I gladly agreed. We were to take a train from Chennai to Mumbai.

We planned to stay in Mumbai for a day or two, and so did not have much luggage. To get to the railway station, we hailed an auto-rickshaw and got into it. My Dad then instructed the auto-rickshaw driver in *Tamil* (the local language in the State of 'Tamil-Nadu'. Chennai is the Capital of Tamil-Nadu) to take us to the railway station.

Having reached the station, we located our train and compartment and got in. It so happened that as we settled down into our seats, a family entered and took their seats facing us. The family happened to be a *Gujarati* family, with a particularly beautiful daughter.

Thanking my stars and fancying my chances, I adjusted my shirt and collar and sat back, waiting for the appropriate moment to break the ice. That fantasy balloon quickly popped, as the father of the girl started his small talk with a quick ice-breaker. He pointed at my Father and myself and asked, "Are the two of you BROTHERS?"

For me, it was not an 'ice-breaker'; it was a 'heartbreaker'! My Dad, on the other hand, was in seventh heaven. Suitably deflated, I did a quick retreat and left the stage to my Father. Always in good spirits and now in even better spirits, my Dad started to engage the father of the girl in a conversation in Tanglish (a mix of the Tamil and English language).

That was only until my Father realized his counterpart was of Gujarati origin. I was still recovering from my fainting spell and almost dead at that point when my Father started conversing in fluent *Gujarati* (the local language of the state of 'Gujarat'). I was shocked enough and woke up as if after a kick-start from a defibrillator.

I looked at my Father in awe and thought, "Oh, NOW my Father knows Gujarati!"

On the train and having had 36 hours for me to recover from my shock, we landed in Mumbai. We needed a taxi to reach our pit stop, which was our relative's place. We hailed a taxi and took our seats. As the taxi driver spoke, it became apparent to me that the taxi driver was a person from U.P. (the state of 'Uttar Pradesh', a state where chaste Hindi was spoken).

Now, my Dad instructed the taxi driver in chaste *Hindi* (pure and perfect Hindi), guiding him on how to get to our destination. Still recovering, I was in complete awe of my Dad's linguistic skills.

Finally, we reached our pit-stop. After having a bath and breakfast, we headed out to complete the formalities to register the sale. My Father's younger brother joined us, and we completed the sale registration. Having then completed the sale registration, we made a trip to my Grandmother's home for the handover of the flat. After completing the handover, my Dad decided to pop into the adjacent neighbor's house.

The neighbor was an old Marathi lady (whom we affectionately called Ms. Lila Thai) with two grown sons. As neighbors, she had seen my Dad grow up during those early years. My Dad and the Marathi lady sat down to have a conversation over tea and biscuits.

My Dad now started talking to the Marathi Lady in chaste *Marathi* (the local language of the State of 'Maharashtra', whose capital is Mumbai). Still recovering, I was by now in complete and total shock. I did not have the slightest inkling until this trip that my Dad could speak so MANY languages.

As we finally headed to our relative's house in the evening in a taxi, I turned to my Dad and asked him in a really low voice, "Just how many MORE languages do you know?"

As he started the list, "Assamese and....", I pretty much fainted!

From then on, I was careful about WHO I chose to benchmark myself against!

When my Maternal Grandmother found HER Match in my Mother

While my Paternal Grandmother was particularly fond of her younger son, she was particularly proud of her elder son, until...

One day, my Mother went to my Paternal Grandmother (her mother-in-law) with some good news. My Mother informed my Paternal Grandmother that my sister (my immediate sister) had topped the Matriculation Board Exams and had come FIRST.

To my Paternal Grandmother, HER son was the best. She responded by saying, "What is so great about that, MY son stood FIRST in his school too!" My Mother tried explaining the difference between 'topping the school' and 'topping the state', but to no avail.

The MAGNITUDE of that achievement "dawned" on my Paternal Grandmother only when a whole horde of press reporters invaded our residence. My Paternal Grandmother was in complete shock at the tsunami of cameramen and press reporters!

To her credit, however, she quickly recovered and took pole position as the photographers started clicking pictures of my Sister and Mother together. It was super funny to see her invade the photo session and pose with HER granddaughter.

Up to the task, the photographers decided to make the most of it and started instructing her to give her GrandDaughter a kiss on the cheek, and then pose 'like this', and then 'like that'. I looked at my Mother and pointed out in amusement how my Grandmother had kick-started her 'modeling career'!

My Paternal Grandmother subscribed to a particular Tamil News Daily for herself. The next morning, in that same paper, there was a big article along with a huge photo of my Mother kissing her daughter on the cheek.

My Paternal Grandmother then went around showing the newspaper article to anybody and everybody, telling them that HER granddaughter had stood 'First in the State'. She emphasized 'State' and took pains to EXPLAIN the 'difference' between 'School' and 'State'.

At that point, my Dad was a long-forgotten entity, and my intermediate elder sister had taken center stage!!

Time for some FUN

Time for the song **'You Gotta Be'** from the album **'I Ain't Movin' (1994)** by the **British singer and songwriter 'Des'ree'.** Enjoy!!

'You Gotta Be'

Des'ree, [Album **'I Ain't Movin' (1994)**]

SCAN above to see **YOUTUBE** ***Video of the Song***

Lyrics

[You Gotta Be]

Listen as your day unfolds
Challenge what the future holds
Try and keep your head up to the sky
Lovers, they may cause you tears
Go ahead release your fears
Stand up and be counted
Don't be ashamed to cry

You Gotta Be
You Gotta Be bad, You Gotta Be bold, You Gotta Be wiser
You Gotta Be hard, You Gotta Be tough, You Gotta Be stronger
You Gotta Be cool, You Gotta Be calm, You gotta stay together
All I know, all I know
Love will save the day

Herald what your mother said
Read the books your father read
Try to solve the puzzles in your own sweet time
Some may have more cash than you
Others take a different view
My oh my, yeah, eh, eh

You Gotta Be bad, You Gotta Be bold, You Gotta Be wiser
You Gotta Be hard, You Gotta Be tough, You Gotta Be stronger
You Gotta Be cool, You Gotta Be calm, You gotta stay together
All I know, all I know
Love will save the day

Time ask no questions, it goes on without you
Leaving you behind if you can't stand the pace
The world keeps on spinning
Can't stop it, if you tried to
The best part is danger staring you in the face

Remember listen as your day unfolds
Challenge what the future holds
Try to keep your head up to the sky
Lovers, they may cause you tears
Go ahead release your fears
My oh my, eh, eh, eh

You Gotta Be bad, You Gotta Be bold, You Gotta Be wiser
You Gotta Be hard, You Gotta Be tough, You Gotta Be stronger
You Gotta Be cool, You Gotta Be calm, You gotta stay together
All I know, all I know
Love will save the day
Yeah, yeah, yeah

You Gotta Be bad, You Gotta Be bold, You Gotta Be wiser
You Gotta Be hard, You Gotta Be tough, You Gotta Be stronger
You Gotta Be cool, You Gotta Be calm, You gotta stay together
All I know, all I know
Love will save the day
Yeah, yeah

Got to be bold
Got to be bad
Got to be wise
Do what others say
Got to be hard
Not too, too hard
All I know is love will save the day

You Gotta Be bad, You Gotta Be bold, You Gotta Be wiser
You Gotta Be hard, You Gotta Be tough, You Gotta Be stronger
You Gotta Be cool, You Gotta Be calm, You gotta stay together
Yeah!
You Gotta Be bad, You Gotta Be bold, You Gotta Be wiser
You Gotta Be hard, You Gotta Be tough, You Gotta Be stronger
You Gotta Be cool, You Gotta Be calm, You gotta stay together

Part I

Chapter 15

WHEN ONE GETS STUCK IN THE QUICK SANDS OF TIME

Why Blindly following Culture can be a Problem?

"Traditions are the guideposts driven deep in our subconscious minds. The most powerful ones are those we can't even describe, aren't even aware of."

– Ellen Goodman

"If we are to preserve culture, we must continue to create it."

– Johan Huizinga

More than a decade ago when I was working in the management of a construction company, I would often sit down with the sales team during product launches and observe customers.

Often, the first question a customer would pose would be related to the price of the product. That was completely understandable as a customer would want to consider if the product offered fitted his budget.

The second question asked, though, was surprising to me. The customer would ask if the product was *Vaastu** Compliant. The most immediate question reflected the concern and priority of the customer. (**Vaastu Shastra* is an ancient text dealing with the construction of homes).

The second question rarely, if ever, pertained to the layout of the home, the quality of construction, the track record of the builder, delivery times, the stage of construction, the down payment, financing, the design of the building, amenities, features, or even discounts on offer.

The most important question that the majority of the customers had was whether the product was Vaastu compliant.

I have nothing for or against Vaastu Shastra; the truth is that Vaastu Shastra has a scientific basis. However, the whole point is not whether Vaastu Shastra is a science or tradition or mumbo jumbo; the point is WHETHER Vaastu Shastra is applicable DIRECTLY in a 'lock, stock, and barrel' approach to TODAY's time and age.

There is no doubt Vaastu Shastra has a scientific basis, but whether it can be DIRECTLY applied to the situation currently at hand is to be ascertained before BLIND application. The times have changed, and so has the way homes are being built. The technology and modern housing designs are completely different from the time when Vaastu Shastra was formulated as a guideline.

In any case, Vaastu Shastra, or for that matter any other such ancient treatise, was written in its time and in another era. While there is no doubting its' intelligent and applicative recommendations for the construction of homes, one would need to understand its recommendations in the context of when and the times during which they were written.

For instance, Vaastu Shastra recommends the Kitchen to be in the South-East corner of the home. The reason for such a recommendation, for instance, could be that the sun rises in the east, and early morning rays act as a disinfectant. It is also located in the south, which is to keep it quiet and private. So locating it in the South-East is a reasonable recommendation.

Similarly, Vaastu Shastra takes into consideration the direction of the prevailing winds. For instance, it recommends keeping the bathrooms in a manner that the wind direction carries any odours away from the living quarters.

However, modern homes have exhaust fans, chimneys, while modern living provides us with disinfectants and deodorizers. Moreover, Vaastu Shastra was primarily meant for independent homes in vast spaces nestled in rural settings. They were not designed for apartments or buildings in tight spaces as in modern cities.

As a person who went through plans, I began to realize that as long as a plan was Vaastu compliant, customers would prefer vastly inferior plans and suboptimal designs VERSUS an efficient and well-laid-out plan.

An architect, when constrained by Vaastu's rules, would never be able to give a plan that is optimal. This is because when taken out of context, Vaastu would tie down one's ability to apply current knowledge to a contemporary situation in an unconstrained manner.

Rigidly and blindly applying rules meant for another context and another time to today's context and age is just blind ignorance. Also, one can't ignore the growth and development of construction design and technology since those times.

So, the point is you could choose to apply anything. Whether concepts or rules were from ancient times or contemporary times, understanding WHY one had those rules in the first place would help to reduce conflict between the ancient and the modern. This would help us to use the knowledge of the ancient texts in ways that can enhance our present-day applications.

So, do read ancient texts and literature. However, rather than applying them blindly, ASK WHY they were applied 'then', and then, having understood the context and reason they were used, apply those learnings WITHIN the contemporary context.

Such problems are NOT unique to INDIA; if you look around the world, you would find many such instances where RULES which may have HAD context in the past have been handed down over generations and STILL applied centuries later WITHOUT any QUESTIONING or REASONING.

The Story* of Railroads and Horse's Ass

(*Anonymous Source)

The US standard railroad gauge (distance between the rails) is 4 feet, 8.5 inches. That's an exceedingly odd number.

Q.1) Why was that gauge used?

Ans 1) Well, because that's the way they built them in England, and English engineers designed the first US railroads.

Q2) Why did the English build them like that?
Ans 2) Because the first rail lines were built by the same people who built the wagon tramways, and that's the gauge they used.

Q3) So, Why did 'they' use that gauge then?
Ans 3) Because the people who built the tramways used the same jigs and tools that they had used for building wagons, which used the same wheel spacing.

Q4) Why did the wagons have that particular odd wheel spacing?
Ans 4) Well, if they tried to use any other spacing, the wagon wheels would break more often on some of the old, long distance roads in England. You see, that's the spacing of the wheel ruts.

Q5) So who built those old rutted roads?
Ans 5) Imperial Rome built the first long distance roads in Europe (including England) for their legions. Those roads have been used ever since.

Q6) And what about the ruts in the roads?
Ans 6) Roman war chariots formed the initial ruts, which everyone else had to match or run the risk of destroying their wagon wheels. Since the chariots were made for Imperial Rome, they were all alike in the matter of wheel spacing.

THEREFORE the United States standard railroad gauge of 4 feet, 8.5 inches is derived from the original specifications for an Imperial Roman war chariot. Bureaucracies live forever.

So, the next time you are handed specifications/processes/procedures and you begin to wonder, 'Who the horse's ass came up with this?' you maybe exactly right.
Imperial Roman army chariots were made just wide enough to accommodate the rear ends of two war horses. (Two horse's asses.)

Twist to the Story

Now, the twist to the story: When you see a *Space Shuttle* sitting on its launch pad, there are two big booster rockets attached to the sides of the main fuel tank. These are solid rocket boosters, or SRBs. The SRBs are made by *Thiokol* at their factory in Utah.

The engineers who designed the SRBs would have preferred to make them a bit fatter, but the SRBs had to be shipped by train from the factory to the launch site. The railroad line from the factory happens to run through a tunnel in the mountains, and the SRBs had to fit through that tunnel.

The tunnel is slightly wider than the railroad track, and the railroad track, as you now know, is about as wide as two horses' behinds. So, a major Space Shuttle design feature of what is arguably the world's most advanced transportation system was determined over two thousand years ago by the width of a horse's ass.

And you thought a horse's ass wasn't important? Ancient horses' asses control almost everything!

Time for some FUN

Time for the song **'Freedom! '90 '** by the **British** singer-songwriter **George Michael** from his album **'Listen without Prejudice Vol.1' (1990).** Enjoy!!

' Freedom! '90 '

George Michael, [Album **'Listen without Prejudice Vol 1'. (1990)**]

SCAN above to see **YOUTUBE** ***Video of the Song***

Lyrics

[Freedom! '90]

I won't let you down
I will not give you up
Gotta have some faith in the sound
It's the one good thing that I've got

I won't let you down
So please don't give me up
'Cause I would really, really
Love to stick around, oh yeah

Heaven knows
I was just a young boy
Didn't know what
I wanted to be
Didn't know what

I wanted to be
I was every little hungry
Schoolgirl's pride and joy
And I guess it was enough for me
To win the race?
A prettier face!

Brand new clothes and
A big fat place
On your rock and roll TV
But today the way
I play the game is not the same
No way
Think I'm gonna get myself happy

I think there's
Something you
Should know
I think it's time
I told you so

There's something
Deep inside of me
There's someone
Else I've got to be
Take back your
Picture in a frame

Take back your
Singing in the rain
I just hope you understand
Sometimes the clothes
Do not make the man

All we have to do now
Is take these lies and
Make them true somehow
All we have to see
Is that I don't belong to you
And you don't
Belong to me yeah, yeah

Freedom
Freedom
Freedom
You've gotta give
For what you take

Freedom
Freedom
Freedom
You've gotta give
For what you take

Heaven knows we sure
Had some fun boy
What a kick just a buddy and me
What a kick just a buddy and me
We had every big shot

Good-time band on the run boy
We were living in a fantasy
We won the race
Got out of the place
I went back home got a

Brand new face
For the boys on MTV
But today the way
I play the game has got to change
Oh yeah
Now I'm gonna get myself happy

I think there's something
You should know
I think it's time I stopped the show
There's something deep inside of me
There's someone I forgot to be
Take back your picture in a frame
Don't think that I'll be back again
I just hope you understand
Sometimes the clothes
Do not make the man

All we have to do now
Is take these lies and
Make them true somehow
All we have to see
Is that I don't belong to you
And you don't belong
To me, yea yea
Freedom (I won't let you down)
Freedom (I will not give you up)
Freedom
(Gotta have some faith in the sound)
You've gotta give for what you take
(It's the one good thing that I've got)
Freedom

(I won't let you down)
Freedom
(So please don't give me up)
Freedom
('Cause I would really, really love to stick around)
You've gotta give for what you take

Well it looks like the road to heaven
But it feels like the road to hell
When I knew which
Side my bread was buttered
I took the knife as well

Posing for another picture
Everybody's got to sell
But when you shake your ass
They notice fast
And some mistakes were built to last

That's what you get, that's what you get
That's what you get, I said that's what you get
That's what you get, for changing your mind
That's what you get, for changing your mind
That's what you get, that's what you get

And after all this time
I just hope you understand
Sometimes the clothes
Do not make the man, do not make the man

All we have to do now
Is take these lies and
Make them true somehow
All we have to see
Is that I don't belong to you
And you don't belong
To me, yea yea

Freedom, oh
Freedom
Freedom
You've got to give for what you take

Freedom (hold onto my)
Freedom
Freedom
You've got to give for what you take
You've got to give for what you take

Yeah, you've got to give for
What you, give for what you give
May not be what you want from me
Just the way it's got to be
Lose the face now
I've got to live I've got to live

<u>Part I</u>

Chapter 16

HOW DOES ONE MULTIPLY ONE'S SUCCESS?

May Your Happiness Multiply, while Your Sorrows Divide

"O gentlemen, the time of life is short!
To spend that shortness basely were too long,
If life did ride upon a dial's point,
Still ending at the arrival of an hour."

– ***Shakespeare*** *(Henry IV, Act 5, Scene 2)*

"Living in the moment brings you a sense of reverence for all of life's blessings."

– Oprah Winfrey

<u>Why your FAMILY & FRIENDS are important</u>

HAPPINESS and SORROW, DON'T listen to or follow the rules of mathematics.

<u>Happiness</u> MULTIPLIES when you DIVIDE it

&

<u>Sorrow</u> DIVIDES when you MULTIPLY it.

Now one CAN'T multiply happiness or divide sorrow when all alone. One needs people around us who would love and cherish us, to be able to spread our joy and dissolve our sorrow.

Greed and self-interest, therefore, would NOT allow us to maximize our joy in times of success, nor would it allow us to dissolve our grief in times of distress. Having good relations with loved ones and nurturing those relationships is definitely a win-win and happy situation.

An African Proverb crisply conveys the importance of taking people along in your journey of Success and Happiness. It states :

"If you want to go QUICKLY, go ALONE.
If you want to go FAR, go TOGETHER".

While Family, Friends, and well-wishers are important, one also needs to maintain the right outlook to be able to find success and happiness. Living in the moment is an important pillar of germinating success and happiness.

Living in the Moment

"The secret of health for both mind and body is not to mourn for the past, not to worry about the future, or not to anticipate troubles, but to live in the present moment wisely and earnestly."

– Buddha

"Doing the best at this moment puts you in the best place for the next moment."

– Oprah Winfrey

By focusing one's energy on the moment, one gets multiple benefits. It helps one conserve one's physical and emotional energies and direct them toward the moment. It prevents us from scattering our energies and efforts without any helpful outcomes.

One stops wasting one's time and energy on worrying about past events that cannot be undone. Worrying about something is NOT going to change the outcomes of the past.

Also, by focusing on the current moment, we can block out the anxieties that would limit our ability to perform at the moment. Sometimes, rather than worrying about making the right decision, we may be better off being decisive and making that decision right.

Time for some FUN

Time for the song titled *'Adiyae Kolludhey'* (Girl, If Looks Could Kill), from the soundtrack of the **Tamil** language romance-drama film ***'Vaaranam Aayiram'* (2008)** (Thousand elephants).

The song features **Suriya** (male lead) and **Sameera Reddy** (female lead). The movie is written and directed by **Gautham Vasudev Menon** and produced by **V. Ravichandran** of *Aascar Films.*

The song was penned by **Thamarai** and sung by **Benny Dayal, Krish and Shruti Haasan.** The music was composed by **Harris Jayaraj.** Enjoy!!

SONG

'Adiyae Kolludhey'

(Girl, If Looks Could Kill)

TAMIL MOVIE

***'Vaaranam Aayiram'* (2008)**

(Thousand Elephants)

SCAN above to see **YOUTUBE** ***Video of the Song***

Lyrics **['Adiyae Kolludhey']**	*Translation* **['Girl, If Looks Could Kill']**
Adiyae Kolludhae Azhago Alludhae Ulagam Surungudhae Iruvaril Adangudhae	Girl, if looks could kill Your looks vacuum my heart The world seems so small in comparison Can be contained in the two of us
Unnodu Nadakum Ovvoru Nodikum Arthangal Sernthidudhae	As I will walk with you for every moment of time It begins to make sense
En Kaalai Neram En Maalai Vaanam Nee Indri Kaainthidudhae	My morning moments My evening moments under the sky Are dry without you
Adiyae Kolludhae Azhago Alludhae Ulagam Surungudhae Iruvaril Adangudhae	Girl, if looks could kill Your looks vacuum the heart The world seems so small in comparison Can be contained in the palm of the hands
Unnodu Nadakum Ovvoru Nodikum Arthangal Sernthidudhae	As I will walk with you for every moment of time It begins to make sense
En Kaalai Neram En Maalai Vaanam Nee Indri Kaainthidudhae	My morning moments My evening moments under the sky Are dry without you
Iravum Pagalum Un Mugam Irayai Polae Thurathuvadhum Yeno	Morning or night Why does your face chase me like I were a prey

Mudhalum Mudivum Neeyena Therintha Pinbu Thayanguvathum Veeno	Knowing that the beginning and then end Is you What is the point in wavering (hesitating)
Vaadai Kaatrinil Oru Naal Oru Vaasam Vanthadhae Un Nesam Endradhae	One day even in the chill winds Came an aroma which said Your affection for me was true love
Unthan Kangalil Yedho Minsaram Ulladhae En Meedhu Paainthadhae	In your eyes there was something electric which struck and captured me
Mazhai Kaalathil Sariyum Man Tharai Polavae Manamum Unai Kandathum Sariya Kandenae	Like in the winter/rainy season One slips in the slippery rain/snow My heart has slipped me As I took notice of you
Adiyae Kolludhae Azhago Alludhae Ulagam Surungudhae Iruvaril Adangudhae	Girl, if looks could kill Your looks vacuum heart The world seems so small in comparison Can be contained in the two of us
Unnodu Nadakum Ovvoru Nodikum Arthangal Sernthidudhae	As I will walk with you for every moment of time It begins to make sense
En Kaalai Neram En Maalai Vaanam Nee Indri Kaainthidudhae	My morning moments My evening moments under the sky Are dry without you

Azhagin Sigaram Neeyadi Konjam Adhanaal Thalli Nadapenae	You constitute the peak of what is beautiful For that reason I stay cautious as I keep a distance When I walk beside you.
Oru Sol Oru Sol Solladi Indha Kanamae Unnai Manapenae	Just say that one word I will marry you this very moment
Sollaa Vaarthaiyin Sugamae Mayil Thogai Polavae En Meethu Oorudhae	The joy of the word even when unspoken caresses me softly like the feathers of a peacock
Ella Vaanamum Neelam Sila Neram Maathiram Senthooram Aagudhae	The sky is always blue but Sometimes it turns vermilion
Enakaagavae Vanthaai En Nizhal Polavae Nindraai Unnai Thotru Nee Ennai Vendraayae	You came just for me and stayed like a shadow You have won me over by dissolving yourself in me
Adiyae Kolludhae Azhago Alludhae Ulagam Surungudhae Iruvaril Adangudhae	Girl, if looks could kill Your looks vacuum heart The world seems so small in comparison Can be contained in the two of us
Unnodu Nadakum Ovvoru Nodikum Arthangal Sernthidudhae	As I will walk with you for every moment of time It begins to make sense
En Kaalai Neram En Maalai Vaanam Nee Indri Kaainthidudhae	My morning moments My evening moments under the sky Are dry without you

PART II

HAPPINESS seen through The PRISM of MONEY

Part II

Chapter 1

ESSENTIALS

Know the most basic building blocks of happiness

"Three grand essentials to happiness in this life are something to do, something to love, and something to hope for."

*–**Joseph Addison** (English writer 1672-1719)*

"The First Essentials is of course to know what you want."

*–**Robert Colliner** (American Author 1885-1950)*

It was the first day of the fall semester final exams. The year was 2004, and I was in the U.S., pursuing my M.B.A. course. The first exam was for a one-credit course, meant to be a general introduction to the M.B.A. program. It was a three-hour exam, and the students were informed of the exam question in advance. The question was open-ended and repeated year after year, albeit with slight twists. We all came well-prepared for the question, just in case there was a slight twist that year. We were allowed to carry anything into the exam hall, and I was all set.

As I entered the corridor, the professor of the course smiled at me and said, "You're looking relaxed and ready". I answered in the affirmative and pointed at the large bag that I was wheeling into the exam hall. I stated that I was confident and well-equipped, no matter what twist would be thrown at me.

I took my seat, and the exam began. The question was written on the board and was simple. It read, "What are the essentials you need to complete your course successfully? Justify". I understood that by "justify", it meant I was to attach proof. The professor then informed us that this was an open-ended question and that there was no one correct answer.

So, I gathered the entire stack of papers and photos of the 'essentials' that I had previously taken a snapshot of and laid them out on the table. There was a huge pile on the table and in front of me. I had previously completed my M.S. in engineering in the U.S. and had been quite clear about what I needed when I landed at the University to do my full-time M.B.A.

I called it the '5Cs' essentials. In fact, I maintained a folder called the '5Cs'. It had subfolders which were the '5Cs'. The Car, Computer (laptop), Cell (mobile phone), Camera (we did not have smartphones then), and Credit Card. Within the '5Cs' subfolders, I had maintained excel worksheets and other statements relating to fuel expenses, phone bills, credit card statements, and photos.

So I began my exam with the list that I had named as the '5 essentials'. These were the key 'essentials' I had zeroed in on even before I had landed in the U.S. Then, I set out to add other things to the list and went on to attach photos wherever I could. I thought, "Hey, the winter coat was very important", "I definitely required heating", "How about books, writing pads, stationery including pens, stapler, stapler pins, glue?", "How about a stereo system to listen to some music in my room?", "How about an ice maker, because I loved ice in my lemon ice tea come summer or winter?" and so on. I began to lose direction before I began to pull back.

Then, I thought 'health' is most important. My mind began to ramble further, and I thought water is essential. To avoid unhealthy pop, I needed to carry my own water. Hence, I needed a sturdy metal water bottle to lug around. I thought my answer was getting smarter. For maintaining my health, the fundamental tripod; Sleep, Exercise, and Healthy Food was essential. So I thought I needed a comfortable mattress and pillow to maintain good sleep hygiene. I would need to eat an apple every day (to keep the doctor away). I would have to measure the calories burnt in the gym, and so an electronic strap-on device (equipment of those days) to track the calories I burned was necessary. Additionally, I would need my gym gloves (for weights), a towel, a gym water bottle, cross-training shoes, workout pants, and t-shirts, and the list went on.

While I surmised that good health was essential, I wondered about the other intangibles. As I deliberated on these, my answers were tending to get more open-ended. How about 'motivation', 'passion for the subjects', 'discipline' as essentials? I kept feeling like I was getting smarter and smarter with my answers, and I began to think harder.

Suddenly, my stack of notes and photos were missing; they weren't in front of me or anywhere on my desk. I got up and went in search of them. I was told they were in the room down the hall and had been transferred there because they were occupying too much space. I searched for a while until I found the room. They were stacked in the room alongside material brought in by the other candidates. By the time I sorted them out and returned to the exam hall, my time was up, and I wasn't able to complete my exam.

I refused to hand in the exam paper and told the proctor that I had not written the answers to my satisfaction and would rather take the exam again next semester. This was an important question, and I wanted to answer it after a lot of thought. The proctor said that unless I finished this one-credit course, I could not proceed with my other coursework. We had a debate, and there was a heated exchange of words. Suddenly, the question on the classroom board got reframed as "What are the essentials of life?" I was so shocked that I finally woke up.

Being Awake and Alive

It was 2 a.m., and I had awakened from a strange dream that also stirred something within me. This dream seemed to have its roots in memories from about a decade ago. The actual one-credit course I took in the 1st semester of my M.B.A. program was on 'Strategy'. In my dream, I had somehow reframed the question and had reimagined the scenario. So I sat up and began to re-analyze my dream and rephrased the question; "What is most important to me in LIFE?"

The flowing mix of the logical and illogical in my dream world made for a strange combination of answers. However, while I lay awake and consciously pondered on this question, my answers were almost predictable. I moved to the computer and began to type in my thoughts. Understandably, my list began with family - my wife, my kids, my parents, and then my siblings, as well as other family and friends.

A

'Sanskrit Slokha'

Describing the source of happiness and peace

शान्तितुल्यंतपोनास्तिनसन्तोषात्परंसुखम्।
नतृष्णायाःपरोव्याधिःनचधर्मोदयापरः।। - चाणक्यनीतिः

śāntitulyaṃ tapō nāsti na santōṣāt paraṃ sukham ।
na tṛṣṇāyāḥ parō vyādhiḥ na ca dharmō dayāparaḥ ॥

Meaning:

There is no penance like peace, no happiness like contentment,
No disease like lust and there is no dharma like kindness.

Then, at once, I moved on to health, as 'Health is wealth'. The same health list involving essentials for good sleep and exercise formed part of my list. My subconscious self that wrote dreamy notes was in sync. I couldn't stress more on the importance of sleep, exercise, and healthy food; the fundamental tripod. This tripod forms the foundation for a good life and stands ahead of every other essential. If family and friends are like one's flesh and blood, one's good health would form the very bones in this body of life. To be able to function independently without being a burden or an outcast, one needs the wealth of good health. In fact, these would form the backbone of life ahead of anything else.

'Family & Friends' are the flesh and blood without which there is no life to the body. However, we still do need the bone structure to stand up and function without being a burden to others. 'Family & Friends' and 'Good Health' are two of the three most essential components for a good life.

What could then be the **third** essential? What else did one need? As I pondered, I keyed in a list that came to my mind. In most cases people would like to have:

i. Work life balance
ii. More leisure time

iii. Time with family
iv. Time to pursue one's passions
v. Job satisfaction or should I reframe it as 'Life Satisfaction'
vi. Ability to live in the moment without worrying about the past or future

A closer examination of the list revealed a single thread that may be common for all. To have more 'free' time or to be engaged in work that one enjoyed, rather than to be consumed by work that is thrust upon them, there was one other need. People would definitely like more free time and would like to be engaged in work that they chose, rather than being obliged to work. This is where I would like to introduce the concept of finance. This sense of stress-free time in the pursuit of happiness and life satisfaction is achieved by a certain something that would maintain the stability of an individual's life. From the prism of finance, it has a name. It is called 'FINANCIAL FREEDOM'.

'Financial freedom' would help one achieve this list. Money does make this list possible. If one had financial freedom, one could have more free time and leisure. One could choose a job with more work-life balance, one could pursue one's passions, and one could take care of one's family and health.

Moreover, when we do follow our passion, "work" would no longer feel like work, and it would be transformed into something fun. It wouldn't become a daily drudgery but instead become something one looked forward to. If one had 'FINANCIAL FREEDOM', a lot of what I had said above would fall into place automatically. 'Financial freedom' is when one has the bandwidth to stop worrying about money and start living life to one's fullest potential and desires. It is not necessarily a huge amount of money, but it is the point where money stops being a factor, and it is different for different people. However, one could calibrate that point by understanding and adjusting one's needs, desires, and focusing on what one would really need to do to achieve the goal of being happy.

So to begin with, the **THREE ESSENTIALS** of a happy life are:

i. 'HEALTH',
ii. 'FAMILY & FRIENDS' and
iii. 'FINANCIAL FREEDOM'.

Let us delve into it a little more as we go along in this book.

Time for some FUN

Now it's time for **Australian** pop duo **Darren Hayes** and **Daniel Jones** with their group **'Savage Garden'** to give us more love with **'Truly Madly Deeply'** from their debut album '**Savage Garden' (1997)**. Enjoy!!

'Truly Madly Deeply'

Savage Garden, [Album **'Savage Garden' (1997)]**

SCAN above to see **YOUTUBE** ***Video of the Song***

Lyrics

[Truly Madly Deeply]

I'll be your dream, I'll be your wish, I'll be your fantasy
I'll be your hope, I'll be your love, be everything that you need
I love you more with every breath truly, madly, deeply do
I will be strong, I will be faithful 'cause I'm counting on
A new beginnin'
A reason for livin'
A deeper meaning, yeah

I wanna stand with you on a mountain
I wanna bathe with you in the sea
I wanna lay like this forever
Until the sky falls down on me

And when the stars are shining brightly in the velvet sky
I'll make a wish, send it to heaven and make you want to cry
The tears of joy for all the pleasure and the certainty
That we're surrounded by the comfort and protection
Of the highest powers
In lonely hours
The tears devour you

An' I wanna stand with you on a mountain
I wanna bathe with you in the sea
I wanna lay like this forever
Until the sky falls down on me
Oh, can you see it, baby?
You don't have to close your eyes
It's standin' right before you
All that you need will surely come

Ooh, yeah

I'll be your dream, I'll be your wish, I'll be your fantasy
I'll be your hope, I'll be your love, be everything that you need
I'll love you more with every breath truly, madly, deeply do

I wanna stand with you on a mountain
I wanna bathe with you in the sea
I wanna lay like this forever
Until the sky falls down on me

I wanna stand with you on a mountain
I wanna bathe with you in the sea
I want to live like this forever
Until the sky falls down on me

Part II

Chapter 2

HOW MUCH DO YOU NEED TO BE HAPPY?

Why the definition of happiness is in your own hands and how best to define it

"The real measure of your wealth is how much you'd be worth if you lost all your money."

– Anonymous

"It is not the man who has too little, but the man who craves more, that is poor."

– Lucius Annaeus Seneca

There was once a billionaire who was staying in a penthouse with his wife and young child. His home was lavish with an indoor pool, an indoor personal home theater, and all other trappings of a billionaire's lifestyle. The home was a spacious penthouse with a massive flowing hall, eight large bedrooms, a private bar, a private study, and a private elevator to get to the top of the skyscraper.

The billionaire's son was spoiled as he was accustomed to all the luxuries. The young boy often threw tantrums, much to the vexation of the billionaire father. The son was always glued to the mobile phone, television, or computer, playing games and wasting precious time by mindlessly watching videos. The wealthy father wanted the child to understand the value of things and hence decided to take the child on a three-day trip to his simple native village where the inhabitants lived frugally.

He wanted the child to see his simple beginnings. He wanted his child to appreciate how far he had come and how happy and grateful they needed to be to have such a rich and comfortable lifestyle. He desired that his child would realize and see the hardships that he had endured before he became who he was now. He wanted his son to witness the trials and tribulations of life, the struggles and subsequent challenges, the sorrows and difficulties that a common person goes through in his/her life.

Hence, one day, they drove hundreds of miles out of the city, deeper and deeper into the countryside. Once they had reached their village,the billionaire and his son got off their vehicle and decided to camp on the outskirts of the village. They spent three grueling days during which the son spent his time meeting the villagers and living their life. He would walk with them and help draw water from the well. He spent time in the fields assisting with the harvest of crops and vegetables. He learned how to milk the cows. He immersed himself in the chores and games of the village kids. After sundown, like birds, the children would return to their nests. As they sat down on the floor for their early dinner, they would hear village elder's fascinating stories mixed with rustic songs. They then retired outside on their rope cot beds or simple mats spread in the courtyard. The billionaire father watched all of this with satisfaction.

On the fourth day, they packed up their belongings and began their drive back home. As they drove back, the billionaire asked his son how his experience was and what he thought of the difficult and poor lives of the villagers. The son looked perplexed and responded by saying that the villagers lived luxurious lives. This mystified the billionaire. "How is that?" he asked, amused.

The son began to list a few things. He said he would miss sleeping under the open sky, watching out for shooting stars, and breathing in the gentle grass-touched breeze. He said his air-conditioning in the penthouse wasn't as 'cool'.

He said the milk was fresh, and he enjoyed the fresh vegetables that he plucked. He loved its taste more than what he ate in the city or at fancy restaurants. His father then thought that the food was indeed fresh, and the fruits and vegetables were organic. On the other hand, he thought they ate processed foods and drank soft drinks from cans, plastic packaging, and pet bottles. He also thought that, as city dwellers, they drank water and carbonated drinks from pet bottles, while the villagers found use for every small thing, recycling or down-cycling even simple clothes that would be used until they were rags for cleaning or wiping. This took care of the environment too, unlike the waste and trash that cities generated and found difficult to dispose.

His thoughts were interrupted as the child spoke animatedly about bathing in the streams and swimming in the lake. He said it was not at all like the private indoor swimming pool they had. The indoor pool had water that was stagnant and smelled of chemicals, while the lake was expansive, and the streams were crystal clear and flowing. His father understood that the child was referring to the chlorine in the pools when he said "chemicals".

The villagers lived amongst the green and with nature in a serene atmosphere surrounded by mountains, streams, and fresh air. In contrast, they lived in a polluted city, pigeonholed into their penthouse. The villagers spent time playing board games, and the children had simple toys made of readily available materials, which allowed them to use their imagination. They spent a lot of time outdoors in the sun and the open without their fancy playstations and multiple gadgets.

The child then mentioned the stories he had heard and asked why he didn't get as much time with adults and neighbors. He liked that all the villagers lived as a community and spent time together every evening. He loved the stories, music, and chalk-drawn games played with little stones. As the child spoke, his father thought how this was again in stark contrast to their own lives where one only interacted on social media and did not even know one's neighbor. The child's delight expressed a yearning for time together, with family as a community; something that we miss in our hurried lives spent chasing the next million dollars.

The billionaire was completely taken aback by his son's answers. He had brought him to teach him something about the 'real' world. The child, in his unbiased manner, had made unconditioned factual observations that astounded him and taught him something in return. The billionaire had to admit that it is NOT money alone that makes one wealthy. He learned a lot from the experiences of his child.

A

'Sanskrit Slokha'

Describing that one can learn from anybody including a child

बालादपिग्रहीतव्यंयुक्तमुक्तंमनीषिभिः।
रवेरविषयेकिंनप्रदीपस्यप्रकाशनम्॥

bālādapi grahītavyaṃ yuktamuktaṃ manīṣibhiḥ ।
ravēraviṣayē kiṃ na pradīpasya prakāśanam ॥

Meaning:

Sensible words, if coming even from a child, should be received by mankind. Doesn't a lamp illuminate where the sun cannot?

This story only illustrates the many different dimensions of wealth and happiness. While we are conditioned and bombarded with images of success, happiness, and methods of celebration advertised and projected by both media and society, we forget to experience or think of some of the simple pleasures in our lives. We are conditioned by the media and society to believe that we cannot be happy without all the trappings of modern living and that we cannot be happy until we achieve billionaire status and own that private jet. This is far from the truth.

One actually defines one's happiness. The story is to make one realize that we could decide how much we want and what could make us actually happy. Happiness lies within our definition of our needs, and this could be anything or nothing. Then, when we do define these needs, the question that would then arise is, "What are we giving up in pursuit of these 'needs'?"

The intention is neither to sound philosophical nor to say that one needs to live like a villager. That is unnecessary, impractical, and also impossible for all of us. The story only seeks to differentiate between needs, wants, and luxuries. We need to first make a list of what we would consider as our 'needs', what we would define as our 'wants', and what would fall under the category of 'luxuries'.

This would then help us categorize, reduce, and eliminate those that fall under luxuries, maybe cancel a few wants only to lead happier lives in pursuit firstly of our needs. This would also make us take cognizance of what we would be 'giving up' in exchange for each of our 'needs', 'wants', and 'luxuries'. To illustrate, let's look at examples of some 'needs' and see if they are actual 'needs'. For instance, do we ask if five bedrooms are truly necessary? Could we do well with a two or three-bedroom home? Do we all really care about changing cars every three years? Do we really need that luxury car and private pool? Do we need to put in overtime and trade it for our leisure and time with family? Do we actually need those 'things' we buy with all the extra earnings from over-time? Even if we could afford all these trappings, do these really add to our happiness? These are pertinent questions to ask. More money does NOT necessarily equate to more happiness.

Now, everyone is different and will have a different answer. Some may live within $30,000 per year, some need $10,000,000 per year. Are we trading our happiness for more money? Are we trading our leisure? Are we trading our time with family and friends? Are we too preoccupied to set aside time for our health and fitness? While we do compromise and make sacrifices, are we forced to let go of our old hobbies, interests, and other pursuits? Are we slowly forgetting our passions and life goals? If the answers to these questions are YES, then do we need to cut down on our luxuries to lead happier and holistic lives? We need to answer these questions and answer them honestly to ascertain where our happiness equation and equilibrium stand.

It is necessary for us to understand that there are MANY dimensions to wealth and MANY kinds of wealth. Dimensions like Money, Status, Time, Family, Friends, and Health are individual pillars in their own right. The question is, "Are we sacrificing the last four (Time, Family, Friends, and Health) while we seek to achieve the first two (Money and Status)?" and can we find a balance to maximize our happiness?

We need to know OUR happiness formula, where we add and/or subtract 'needs', 'wants', and 'luxuries' to multiply our sense of contentment and happiness. The definition of wealth is limited when we choose to use only money and status as the measures. Pleasure, satisfaction, contentment, and happiness are all nuanced emotions that we are driven to achieve through a multi-pronged approach.

The nuances of money and status have many projected trappings, faces, notions that are sometimes make-believe and pretty. They are "states" that one hopes to achieve and are beautifully crafted to seem just out of reach, such that one ends up constantly chasing them like a mirage.

We see it daily on different screens promoted by our media, society, and peer group. They slowly seep into our mind and eat away our imagination. We need to unlearn these and de-condition ourselves, only to ascertain what OUR own formula is, so that we could make our own path in pursuit of HAPPINESS.

It is not necessary to expand one's possessions at the expense of the other pillars of our lives to achieve happiness. Happiness sometimes lies in balancing ambition with contentment. As Epictetus once stated, "As wealth consists not in having great possessions, but in having few wants".

Time for some FUN

Now time for the song **'Have You Ever Seen the Rain?'** by the **American** rock band **Creedence Clearwater Revival** from their debut album **'Pendulum' (1970).** The song was written by **John Fogerty** and released in **1971.** Enjoy!!

'Have You Ever Seen the Rain?'

Creedence Clearwater Revival , [Album **'Pendulum' (1970)**]

SCAN above to see **YOUTUBE** ***Video of the Song***

Lyrics

[Have You Ever Seen The Rain?]

Someone told me long ago
There's a calm before the storm
I know, it's been comin' for some time
When it's over, so they say
It'll rain on a sunny day
I know, shining down like water

I wanna know, have you ever seen the rain?
I wanna know, have you ever seen the rain
Comin' down on a sunny day?

Yesterday and days before
Sun is cold and rain is hard
I know, been that way for all my time
'Til forever on it goes
Through the circle, fast and slow
I know, it can't stop, I wonder

I wanna know, have you ever seen the rain?
I wanna know, have you ever seen the rain
Comin' down on a sunny day?

Yeah!
I wanna know, have you ever seen the rain?
I wanna know, have you ever seen the rain
Comin' down on a sunny day?

Part II

Chapter 3

QUANTUM OF HAPPINESS

Know the real secret to happiness in the modern world and how a change in outlook could make you happy

"The happiest people in the world are NOT those who have the best of things, but those who know how to appreciate the things they have the best."

– Warren Buffett

"Happiness is a choice, not a result. Nothing will make you happy until you choose to be happy, No person will make you happy unless you decide to be happy. Your happiness will not come to you. It can only come from you."

– Ralph Harslon

I was working in a management position for a company during one of my stints. I happened to have had a very capable junior colleague working for me. He was a top performer, young, and on a handsome salary for his age group. He was treated very well. Yet, one day he came into my cabin and began to pour out his frustrations to me.

He said that he was very unhappy with his life and felt very dissatisfied despite having all the material goodies. I asked him if his salary was the reason. He replied in the negative and said that he did not have a clear understanding of why he was unhappy. He had been given a raise of more than 30% year on year for the past three years. He had all the material trappings a young man in his twenties would desire. He had a nice car, the latest mobile phones, a home theatre system, a nice apartment that was well-furnished, etc. I inquired about his lifestyle. He ate out, hung out with friends, went to movies, and played many console games like any other young person of his age. Yet, he felt incomplete and amiss. He said nothing seemed to interest him, and he felt low.

David Foster Wallace put this outlook in perspective when he said, "In this country (U.S.A), we're unprecedentedly safe, comfortable, and well-fed, with more and better venues for stimulation. And yet if you were asked, 'Is this a happy or unhappy country?' you'd check the 'unhappy' box. We're living in an era of emotional poverty, which is something that serious drug addicts feel most keenly."

We belong to a generation that could achieve instant gratification on an impulse. We are part of that age, and it is easy to feel dissatisfied, and nothing seems to make us feel sufficiently satiated. Our highs and excitement are short-lived; it was consumed yesterday, and we look forward to the next one immediately. It isn't easy to appreciate what we have, and we often get bored too soon.

I felt I needed to step back to analyze and re-evaluate his and my state of things. I then went on to tell him about how good his life actually was. He needed to, and well, we all needed to understand why we should appreciate our lives better.

In this modern era, our lives and lifestyles are actually way better than the lifestyles of the rich and powerful kings who reigned in our lands just a few hundred years ago. Kings and emperors who built lavish castles and reigned supreme over several kingdoms wouldn't have had the comforts that we have today. Today, our lifestyle is rich, comfortable, and adventurous (without risk), and it is filled with the choicest of options and variety that NO king or queen could have commanded. This young colleague was both intrigued and skeptical, yet he asked me to explain more. I began to explain each scenario.

When the kings of yore wanted to listen to music, what were the ways they could get what they wanted? Musicians would need to be pre-arranged, and at the appointed time, they would arrive and play music. On the other hand, nowadays, one could listen to music of any kind at the touch of a screen. Music from around the world, all genres from pop, classical, hip-hop, blues, jazz, melody, and so on are all at one's disposal. We could go encore, stop, start, skip, switch in a jiffy. We could also choose to hear it on headphones or stereos if we wished, at the prescribed volume, and even adjust the acoustics with greater bass or more treble, without even moving from our chair. Even today's live performances and 'shows' offer limitless entertainment with visual effects, laser light shows, while the experience of yesteryear kings would seem 'poor' with their highly limited options.

Similarly, think of any other kind of entertainment, like dance, theatre, or the court jesters of old times – they have all been replaced and are now made available in better, larger-than-life formats. It was previously limited to the king and his courts. We live lives filled with entertainment that could be obtained, consumed, and enjoyed so easily by all, at a flick of a switch.

If we were to travel like the way the kings traveled before, it would probably take a lot of motivation and possibly a lot of strength and stamina. The kings traveled miles across plains and mountains on horseback, chariot-drawn vehicles, or caravans which were extremely bumpy rides. Traveling kings were exposed to the elements, enduring heat and cold on horsebacks, leaving them with sore behinds. They would either get sunbaked or be cold and stiff depending on the weather. Today, travel is a leisure activity, not a tough workout (unless we choose to go hiking or cycling). In the modern era, it is pleasurable to travel for work or a holiday. We can sit on a comfortable car seat and drive smoothly in an air-conditioned car equipped with shock absorbers that ply on smooth bitumen-layered roads. To add to our royal travel, we can easily listen to the finest choice of music from our personal collection or simply turn on the radio while we travel. In this manner, we can easily cover great distances in style with little fatigue. The king's travel experience actually pales in comparison to this.

Having an appetite and being a king still had limitations. Pre-arranged menus, the search for ingredients, and the seasonal availability of fruits, vegetables, and spices would remain as constraints. Nowadays, we have food ordering applications and food guides that can cater to us on the spur of the moment. They provide us with food from the choicest of restaurants. Cuisines and variety that were unheard of are available to us, allowing us to be as finicky as a royal. We can choose from Chinese, Italian, Mexican, Indian, Thai, and other cuisines from around the world. We can cherry-pick and have either fast food, gourmet fare, or a healthy mix anytime of the day.

Legend has it that Philippides or Pheidippides, the Greek messenger, was sent to Athens to announce the defeat of the Persians. Athens was about 42.195 Kms. away from his destination. He ran the whole distance to say his famous last words, "Niki! Niki!"(Victory! Victory!), before he collapsed to his death, thus sharing the news of the Grecian victory in the Battle of Marathon. That's how kings got their news. Expensive and sometimes life-threatening. For information and entertainment in the modern era, we get alerts delivered directly onto our handsets, or we could seek them out easily on the web. We have several options and several screens, including televisions, tablets, and e-readers. We can order online and read e-versions or order them to be delivered to our doorsteps. The king, on the other hand, depended on foot soldiers, horseback messengers, ships, boatmen, and spies to deliver information that may have taken days to pass on.

Singapore's founding father, Mr. Lee Kuan Yew, believed that the single biggest secret reason for Singapore's success was the invention of air-conditioning. It changed the nature of civilization by making development possible in the tropics. Apart from comfort and increased efficiency at work, air conditioning allowed people to migrate and live in inhospitable climates. Inventions like refrigeration allowed one to enjoy the choicest fruits and vegetables brought from far-off lands. Additionally, we could easily store food in refrigerators and cabinets to be eaten as desired. Even simple pleasures like a glass of cold water or a cup of ice cream would have been a luxury for the kings of those days. Even not so far back as a hundred years ago, the only way royals could enjoy an iced drink in the tropics was by constructing an 'ice-house' and transporting ice from afar to be stored and retrieved from this ice house. Those days and times were truly difficult, and it was genuinely challenging to enjoy these simple pleasures that we now take for granted.

Entertainment would either be adrenaline-driven wars or hunting campaigns. Of course, the Romans used gladiators to fight each other, and we have truly come a long way from those barbaric times. Nowadays, if one needed to be entertained, one could go to amusement parks, catch a movie in a theater, organize game nights with *PlayStations,* and so on. War games, virtual reality, augmented reality games amuse and entertain us and cause little harm to our fellow beings, while we get the same rush without having to nurse deep wounds in the aftermath.

Kings and Queens would send explorers and scientists to research and view the world through their eyes. Long-distance travel by both ship and horseback was tough. One was exposed to difficult conditions, the elements of nature, and attacks by wild animals. Nowadays, we could jet around the world in a fraction of the time and choose to stay in different types of accommodations such as hotels, lodges, homestays, etc.

We wear the choicest clothing and footwear, not to mention the wide range of accessories available in malls and bazaars. We can even shop from our couch while browsing online and order merchandise to be home delivered.

In every facet, technologies have increased our comfort and conveniences by many folds in our lives. When we compare the kind of medical care and preventive medicine available to us today with what was available for the kings and queens of yesteryears, we are far more privileged and blessed.

We can also learn arts, music, dance, martial art forms, do aerobics, learn yoga at our convenience, or even online. All these are made possible in convenient and affordable ways.

If we were to just get down to the basics, even a good bath under a decent shower and flush toilets were a luxury in those days. Whether it is learning music, gathering knowledge, accessing books, information, travel, food, healthcare, or entertainment, WE ARE TRULY LIVING LIKE KINGS AND QUEENS!!!

These words and scenarios made my junior colleague's eyes light up. I could see he was re-evaluating his life. The possessions and advantages DIDN'T change and were always there, but the change that was necessary was in his attitude and approach, which was what was required.

Over the next few days, I could see that change in the way he was; he didn't get despondent. To be happy, 'we really need to first be happy with what we have' BEFORE 'we crave for more'.

As Warren Buffett once famously said, "The happiest people in the world are NOT those who have the best of things, but those who know how to appreciate the things they have the best."

We have come a long way from what our forefathers were and the kind of lifestyles they led. I don't denigrate the lives of kings and queens, but only bring up those scenarios to show how royally advantaged we are. We benefit from the work and progress made by several generations. They have made us what we are today, yet when we don't understand or appreciate how far we have come, where we were, and where we now are, it would be difficult for us to further the progress. Many cultures teach us to respect and appreciate what we are given. Almost every culture teaches us to say a prayer of thanks before we eat, a practice widely prevalent in many religions.

Festivals giving thanks are celebrated worldwide, as either harvest festivals, Thanksgiving, or festivals that offer gratitude. They all help us realize and appreciate every bounty in our lives, from agricultural produce and our families to animals, books, tools of work, etc.

A variety of cultures practice these customs to instill a sense of gratitude in us, helping us realize how fortunate we are for receiving such bounties. It is not necessarily just to praise GOD, but as introspection to make us look within and find happiness. Those who are thankful understand the true value of what they have and are the happiest people. Gratitude before seeking more and more is one step toward a happier life.

We need to incorporate these notions into our lives, where we introspect to first respect and cherish what we have before becoming despondent about what we don't have. Therein lies the secret to happiness. We need to find that sense of contentment first, and then happiness will follow automatically. This certainly doesn't mean we should stifle our ambitions. We just shouldn't let ambition and greed get in the way of our present happiness.

While finance is an essential component of happiness, it does not guarantee happiness. Our attitude will determine how happy we are or will be. This is why blind materialism does NOT lead to happiness, because materialism is an endless chasm, and we would sacrifice our present happiness in pursuit of something we think will make us happy and complete tomorrow. That never happens because it is in our nature to desire and crave for more.

As a wise man once said, "Now and then, it is better to pause in our pursuit of happiness and just be happy." Happiness is a function of your approach and attitude, and finance has a limited role to play in it. So, while finance is important, our approach to life is more important. Having the right attitude and practicing gratitude are the two keys to happiness.

Time for some FUN

Now time for **American** Pop Singer **Vanessa Carlton** with her debut single **'A Thousand Miles'** (originally titled 'interlude') from their debut album **'Be Not Nobody' (2002)**. Enjoy!!

'A Thousand Miles'

Vanessa Carlton, [Album **'Be Not Nobody' (2002)**]

SCAN above to see **YOUTUBE** ***Video of the Song***

Lyrics

[A Thousand Miles]

Making my way downtown walking fast
Faces pass and I'm home bound
Staring blankly ahead just making my way
Making a way through the crowd

And I need you
And I miss you
And now I wonder

If I could fall into the sky
Do you think time would pass me by?
'Cause you know I'd walk a thousand miles
If I could just see you tonight

It's always times like these when I think of you
And I wonder if you ever think of me
'Cause everything's so wrong and I don't belong
Living in your precious memories

'Cause I'll need you
And I'll miss you
And now I wonder

If I could fall into the sky
Do you think time would pass me by?
'Cause you know I'd walk a thousand miles
If I could just see you tonight

And I, I don't want to let you know
I, I drown in your memory
I, I don't want to let this go
I, I don't

Making my way downtown walking fast
Faces pass and I'm home bound
Staring blankly ahead just making my way
Making a way through the crowd

And I still need you
And I still miss you
And now I wonder

If I could fall into the sky
Do you think time would pass us by?
'Cause you know I'd walk a thousand miles
If I could just see you

If I could fall into the sky
Do you think time would pass me by?
'Cause you know I'd walk a thousand miles
If I could just see you, if I could just hold you tonight

Part II

Chapter 4

LIVING WITHIN YOUR MEANS

How to categorise and define your spending to put yourself on the road to 'Financial Freedom'

"If you buy things you do not need, soon you will have to sell things you need."

– *Warren Buffett*

"How rich you are is NOT defined by HOW MUCH you spend, but by HOW MUCH you save."

– *Author*

Middle-class parents around the world have advised their children on the dangers of overspending and living beyond their means. While this is sound advice, one really needs to dissect and define what this means. One also needs to present it in a fashion that the young spenders would understand and adopt. Children of such parents often hit back or rebel when advised about their spending. They see it as an infringement on their right to happiness that the material things could bring.

Hence, there is a need to help children define and understand that some money is to be spent for immediate needs and happiness, while some needs to be saved and invested for the future. It's a balance. Delayed gratification can sometimes have benefits as the invested money can grow manifold and provide stability and hence happiness.

Before one ventures out into investments, one first needs to save. One also needs to save to gradually build a 'Reserve', which would serve as a cushion in bad times. It would also help to build a 'Nest Egg' that would ensure that there is a perpetual inflow of money in the form of 'Passive income'. When this 'Passive income' is sufficiently high, it would lead to financial liberation and what I call 'Financial Freedom'. To be able to save, however, one needs to understand how one spends his/her money. Spending has to be dissected to understand whether its contribution to happiness is commensurate.

Handling your Expense Account

"We lost our way and allowed greed and excess to become the twin pillars of too much of the financial culture. We became a society utterly absorbed in consumption and dismissive of moderation."

– *Tom Brokaw*

"I'd like to live as a poor man with lots of money."

- *Pablo Picasso*

The first advice to any one handling or budgeting for an expense account is to divide one's expenses into one of the three categories:

- Needs
- Wants
- Luxuries

The names are pretty descriptive. 'Needs' are essentially those items in our expense account which are needed for basic living. One needs to pay rent or mortgage. One needs to pay the utility and fuel bills. One needs food, clothing, etc.

'Wants' are those things that one desires that could make one happier but are those things that one probably could do without. So basically, one may want to change a car every three years, but one really doesn't NEED to. One may want to drive a bigger SUV but one really doesn't need it. If one does make the purchase, then one would probably end up paying higher insurance and have higher fuel bills. One may want a bigger five-bedroom house, but one may actually be single and one could do with a two-bedroom house that one could share with a roommate. Actually, one's 'need' is accomplished by a two-bedroom house but one desires or 'wants' a five-bedroom house. Now, with a five-bedroom house one could end up paying higher property taxes, higher utility bills, and one may have to work harder to maintain the home, etc.

One's 'needs' are what one NEEDs, while one's 'wants' are what one DESIREs. Desires are something that would be nice to have. Not all 'wants' are necessary and could be eliminated depending on whether it makes sense, and if it really contributes to one's happiness. Often, 'wants' should be treated as items of delayed gratification and should only be procured or attained after a long wait. It should be treated as a reward for one's hard work. The wait would increase our desire and happiness when one ultimately acquires or experiences one's reward.

'Luxuries' are those that one shouldn't try to acquire if it stretches one's budget or if one has to sacrifice something else like leisure or one has to work much harder to obtain. For example, one may commit to buying a luxury vehicle but may end up having to work harder for the next 5-7 years trying to pay off a depreciating asset. Another example is first-class travel or international holidays. Generally, unless my passive income is paying off such luxuries, these are just that 'luxuries'. If one had to draw from one's active income (income from working) to pay for them, then one would rather forego them. It makes very little sense to pay for these via active income or pay for the same by committing to a heavy monthly EMI.

Another example is expensive jewelry. Weddings and engagements are truly once-in-a-lifetime celebrations (at least that's our belief and hope). However, if that big-ticket themed wedding with the large diamond engagement ring is truly out of one's spending capacity, one should not fall into debt just for it. This is particularly true if it is going to chain us to our work and cut down on any possibility to save for the future. Rather than extravagant spending, one could let weddings also be occasions where one sows the seeds for financial growth. Love should grow with the people one is in love with. Impressing the fiancée by buying that BIG diamond may be great. However, one needs to ask oneself if it is a need, want, or luxury in an objective manner. There is an interesting study that says that the bigger the engagement ring and the more money spent on the wedding; on average, the shorter the marriage. It is not some paradox, it is actually logical. Marriages that start out with larger debts are often financially strained and hence, are more likely to end badly.

A

'Sanskrit Slokha'

<u>That conveys the power of simple living</u>

सुखंशेतेसत्यवक्तासुखंशेतेमितव्ययी ।
हितभुक्मितभुक्चैवतथैवविजितेन्द्रियः ॥ - चरकसंहिता

sukhaṃ śētē satyavaktā sukhaṃ śētē mitavyayī ।
hitabhuk mitabhuk caiva tathaiva vijitēndriya: ॥

Meaning:

One who speaks truth sleeps well, one who spends less sleeps well.

One who eats nutritious food in limited quantity and one who has control over the mind and senses also gets peaceful sleep.

The objective of this piece is not to tell people to spend less. That is hardly what this is all about. Everyone's situation is unique, and each one of us operates from different financial backgrounds. It is important to be aware of the divisions between needs, wants, and luxuries for us individually, from our own standpoints. The danger is an oft-repeated 'question'. We often choose to act only based on that constant question that stays on our minds; "What will others say?" It is better to spend only when we can afford to. It is not advisable to spend only to impress others. When in doubt, we need to ask ourselves if that spending would truly contribute to our long-term happiness and well-being.

The media and our peer group would often make us feel incomplete. There is constant bombardment by corporations and media. They seem to tell us why we need to do this and how it could make us feel happy and complete. I don't blame them; that's their job and they do it beautifully, but we must be aware that it is just pure marketing. They want us to feel incomplete so that they could sell us more and more things that we actually don't need. So before one buys a product or service, one needs to ask oneself some honest questions.

- Do I **really need** to buy this? Will I **really use** it?
- Will it really **make me happy** in the **long term,** or is it an impulse?
- Am I **giving up more** than I **gain**?

Before signing a check for $100 or more, my dad often advised me to pause and calmly ponder if I really needed it. The idea was to pay attention to the dollars and pounds and NOT be 'penny-wise and pound-foolish'. We need to pay more attention to big-ticket items like renting, buying a house or car, buying jewelry, electronics or appliances, or paying for education, etc. Smaller items that add up could be weighed against what they give us in return. We definitely should not buy stuff on impulse for the sake of it, especially those things which we barely use.

My American officemate went on a sabbatical to a third-world country. She came back happier with a better perspective on life. Just after her return, she sold half the things that she had in her house. After her trip, she had come to the realization that she did not need most of the things that she thought she could not do without. They were just adding to the clutter in her house. As she disposed of them, she felt lighter and mentally happier. Her experience is an example to highlight the fact that most people often buy or acquire things they really do not need. They then have to work harder and longer to pay for their spending 'sins'. This greatly delays or postpones indefinitely their arrival at the milestone of 'Financial Freedom' and liberation.

So let me spell out a few rules that could help.

- Divide spending into 'needs', 'wants', and 'luxuries'.
- Eliminate the 'luxuries' unless they can be paid for by 'passive income' (income coming from returns on investments for which we do not have to put in active work).
- Prune the 'wants' to things that really give one 'Value for the Money' or 'Bang for the Buck'. Avoid impulsive purchases of wants to avoid randomly splurging on things we really don't need. Do spend on a *few* wants that really make you happy. It is best when wants are delayed and treated as items of delayed gratification. It should often be a reward for things well done. The wait and final acquisition would be truly rewarding and would make one happier than the short-lived pleasure derived from an impulsive purchase.

When one does follow these rules, one could balance one's happiness with one's savings. Savings should be invested to grow the 'Passive income' that could be earned from it. 'Passive income' would further ease our financial position and take us closer to 'Financial Freedom'. This is one good way to lay out a practical and effective financial plan.

Time for some FUN

Time for the song titled ***'Hosanna'*** from the **Tamil** movie ***'Vinnaithaandi Varuvaayaa'*** **(2010),** starring **STR** a.k.a **Silambarasan** and **Trisha Krishnan.** The Movie was directed by **Gautham Vasudev Menon**.

The playback singers for this song were **Vijay Prakash**, **Suzanne D'Mello**, and **Blaaze**. Music was composed by **A R Rahman**, and the songwriters were **Thamarai** and **Blaaze**. Enjoy!!

SONG

'Hosanna'

MOVIE

'Vinnaithaandi Varuvaayaa' **(2010)**

(Will you cross the skies for me?)

SCAN above to see **YOUTUBE** ***Video of the Song***

Lyrics **['Hosanna']**	*Translation* **['Hosanna']**
Yennn idhayam... Udaiythaai norunggavey... Yennn maru idhayam... Tharuvaen nee udaikavey... [FEMALE] Ohhh Ooooh.. Hosanna Hosanna.. Ohhh Ooooh.. Hosanna Hosanna.. [MALE] Andha neram andhi neram, Kann paarthu kandhalaagi pona neram Yedho aachu... Oh vaanam theendi vandhachu Appavin veetti yellam kaatrodu Poye pochu... Hosanna...En vaasal thaandi ponaaley.. Hosanna..Veyr-ondrum seiyamaley.. Naan aadi pogiren, Sukku nool-aaghiren, Aval pona pinbu yendhan nenjai, Thaedi pogiren... Hosanna...Vaazhvukum pakkam vandhaen, Hosanna...Saavukkum pakkam nindren, Hosanna...Yen endral kadhal yenbaen, Hosanna...	Why did you shatter my heart into pieces? I'll give you my other heart to break. [FEMALE] Ohhh Ooooh.. Hosanna Hosanna.. Ohhh Ooooh.. Hosanna Hosanna.. [MALE] That moment...one evening, the time our eyes met, the time I lost myself... Something happened. Touched by the sky, Dad's chiding words vanished with the wind. Hosanna, she just crossed my doorstep. Hosanna, that's all she did. I am getting shaken, I am falling to pieces. After she left, I went in search of my heart. Hosanna...I came close to life. Hosanna...I came close to death too. Hosanna...because I'll say it's love. Hosanna...

[RAP] Everybody wanna know what'd be lika feel lika, I really wanna be here with you… It's not enough to say that we are made for each other, It's love that is Hosanna true…	[RAP] Everybody want to know I feel like? I feel like I really want to be here with you. It's not enough to say that we are made for each other... It's love that is Hosanna true.
Hosana…be there when you're callin' out me name… Hosana…feeling like me whole life has changed… I never wanna be the same… It's time we rearrange… I take a step, you take a step, Im here callin out to you...u...	Hosanna…be there when you are calling out me name. Hosanna…feeling like my whole life has changed. I never want to be the same. It's time we rearrange. I take a step, you take a step, I'm here calling out to you..u..
Hello…Halloo…… Hallooooo…Yo…Hosanna..	Hello…Halloo... Hallooooo…Yo…Hosanna...
[FEMALE] Hosanna Hooooohhhh.. Hosanna Hooooohhhh…	[FEMALE] Hosanna Hooooohhhh.. Hosanna Hooooohhhh…
[MALE] Vanna vanna pattu poochi, Poo thaedi poo thaedi, Angum ingum alaighindradhe.. Oh sottu sottaiy, Thotu poga megam ondru megam ondru, Yeng-engo nagargin-dradhey..	[MALE] Butterflies flutter here and there in search of flowers. A cloud... a single cloud moves here and there to caress me softly drop by drop.

Hosanna..pattu poochi vandhacha.. Hosanna..megam unnai thottacha.. Kilinjal aagirai-naan, Kuzhandhai aaghiraen, Naan unnai alli kaiyil vaithu pothi kolghiraen..	Hosanna...is the butterfly here? Hosanna...has the cloud touched you? You become a shell. I become a child. I'll clasp you in the palm of my hand.
Hallo…Halloo……Hallooooooo…Yo… Hosanna Hosanna…yen meedhu anbu kozha.. Hosanna…yennodu serndhu sella.. Hosanna…Hmm yendru sollu podhum.. Hosanna…	Hallo…Halloo……Hallooooooo…Yo… Hosanna Hosanna...to shower love on me. Hosanna…to walk along with me. Hosanna...it's enough if you just say okay. Hosanna...
[MUSIC] Yennn idhayam… Udaiythaai norunggavey… Yennn maru idhayam… Tharuvaen nee udaikavey… Yennn idhayam… Udaiythaai norunggavey… Yennn maru idhayam… Tharuvaen nee udaikavey…	[MUSIC] Why did you shatter my heart into pieces? I'll give you my other heart to break. Why did you shatter my heart into pieces? I'll give you my other heart to break.

Part II

Chapter 5

WHY A 'FINANCIAL CUSHION' IS IMPORTANT

Know why keeping a 'Financial Cushion' is a necessity to safeguard your financial future

"Do not leave yourself or your family unprotected against financial storms... Build up savings."

– Ezra Taft Benson

"Planning is bringing the future into the present, so that you can do something about it now."

– Alan Lakein

People in desperation make bad choices. Often, choices presented to one in life are a direct function of the strength of one's financial position. When one is in a position of financial strength, one is presented with better choices; when one isn't, one is limited by one's financial constraints, and hence one's options are poorer. One bad decision leads to another, pulling one notch lower, step by step. The next time around, one may end up being presented with options that are worse than before, and this could go on until one finds oneself at rock bottom. On the other hand, when one makes decisions from a position of strength, one ends up with better choices, which would put one in a stronger position, and so on. One moves on from strength to strength.

Let me explain with an example. I had landed in the US to do my Master's in engineering. One year later, I got an internship with a big automotive manufacturing giant. I needed to buy a car, as there was really no other way I could report to work at their site. Hence, I bought a twelve-year-old used car for about $1400, as that was the number that kept me within my assumed budget and capacity. As luck would have it, the car broke down on three separate occasions for the same problem over a period of four months. Apart from going through enormous stress and agony, the vehicle's constant need for repair cost me another $1400. Furthermore, the money I spent on repairs really did NOT add to the book value of my car. Additionally, I ended up spending on towing charges and on car rentals. So, one bad decision led to another, and I was bleeding financially.

When I finally graduated from university and got a job, I ended up disposing of the car for $400 to a car dealer. Net on net on what was spent, I was down $2400 on the transaction over a period of a year. Also, for the number of times the car broke down and needed repair, I ended up spending an additional $540 on towing and rentals.

After moving to a new city to take up my new job, I bought a three-year-old vehicle as my next car. I chose a three-year-old car because I calculated that most of the financial depreciation of a car occurs in the first three years. This time around, as I was in a better position, my options were better, so I purchased a relatively new car for $12,500. I kept and enjoyed driving it without any trouble for about two years, finally selling it for $9,900. Over a two-year period, I was net-on net down by only about $2,600. During this time, I had the pleasure of driving a relatively new car. In contrast, when I purchased my first car with a constrained budget, I incurred a net loss greater than I should have, and I also faced car troubles. I went through enormous stress and difficulties while trying to ensure that my car would hold up. It was a tough experience, and my spending was higher. This small example illustrates that when we are strapped for finances, we are forced into making damaging and challenging decisions. Having a little more money and cushion allows us to make better decisions from a position of strength. This saves us a lot of stress and protects us from the financial damage that would otherwise accompany a constrained decision.

Another example is credit card debt. Credit card debt can also put us in a tight spot. When we swipe a large amount, we may end up paying and servicing an ever-increasing interest burden. This would make us move lower and lower on the financial scale, often requiring us to work harder and harder to pay it off. Most people don't choose to be burdened with credit card debt. They find themselves in a position where they desperately need to use their card for an emergency. Unforeseen emergencies like car repairs or healthcare costs could often set us back. This setback could cause a lot of financial strain as we need to keep working harder and harder to try and pay back this high-interest debt.

I would, therefore, emphasize the importance of maintaining a 'financial cushion' to protect one's credit history and avoid high-cost debt. High-cost debt can be very damaging. Additionally, failing to pay our dues on time can result in downgrades to our credit history. This, in turn, would increase the cost of any future borrowings and force us to work harder to pay them off. To illustrate, if we were to compare two individuals attempting to borrow the same amount of money, the one with a poor credit rating and credit history would have to pay larger and larger amounts and borrow at a higher interest rate than the one with a good credit rating. Many people borrow at times when they can least afford the debt, which can push them further into bad debts and financial hardships. The root causes are usually emergencies and urgent needs, and these factors lead many people to fall into bad debts and become entangled in debt traps.

What Research says

"Most people don't plan to fail, they fail to plan."

–John L. Beckley

"Think ahead. Don't let day-to-day planning drive out planning."

– Donald Rumsfeld

When people are preoccupied with the present, they often compromise the future. For instance, research and data have shown that farmers in distress tend to make poor choices. When in distress, individuals are both psychologically and circumstantially prone to making unfavorable decisions. In times of financial distress, one's mental capacity to deal with life's challenges is limited, and this can lead to poor financial decisions. This isn't necessarily due to stupidity but rather because people in distress are often not in a position to make sound choices. Their distress focuses their attention on immediate needs, diverting their thoughts away from long-term planning.

A study conducted by Princeton University, published in the 'Journal of Science', explores the impact of financial woes on decision-making. When individuals have a surplus of cash, they worry less and are consequently better equipped to make rational decisions. Conversely, when individuals are trapped in financial difficulties, their energies are consumed by the pursuit of what they lack, leading to suboptimal decision-making.

This cycle is why many people seem to remain trapped in a vicious cycle of poverty. The report from Princeton University conducted two experiments to test this theory—one among mall-goers in New Jersey and the other among sugarcane farmers in India.

The New Jersey shoppers were given a series of problem-solving tests. For instance, they were asked how they would handle a 5% salary cut, a 15% salary cut, or an emergency car repair that would cost $150 or $1500. With that on their minds, they were asked to focus and concentrate on solving a set of problems. While some of the New Jersey shoppers made an average sum of $20,000 a year, a few of them made sums as high as $70,000 a year. Hence, as far as the tests were concerned, the shoppers performed more or less equally, as there were only minor financial issues at the back of their minds. However, when the car repair was more expensive or when the salary cut was higher, the lower earners did significantly worse on the tests than higher earners.

The study concluded that while individuals are distracted by their problems, it could take their attention away from their problem-solving capacities, thus causing them to make poorer decisions. Poorer folks may be just as smart when the car repair is cheaper, but they begin to make dumber decisions when faced with a financially taxing situation. It is really what is at the back of the mind that changes that.

A similar test carried out in real-world situations in India yielded similar results. The test found that sugarcane farmers in India made better decisions just after harvest and made worse decisions the month before harvest when they were broke for money. Just after harvest, the farmers were flush with money and were found to make fewer bad decisions. However, poor actions like pawning one's jewellery or borrowing at high-interest rates were most prevalent during the months preceding harvest when the farmers were low and hard-strapped for money. These findings could not be explained by differences in time available, nutrition, and work effort. Instead, it appeared that poverty itself diminished cognitive capacity.

Often, when one is out of money, one makes poor decisions. For example, scenarios leading to poor preventive healthcare decisions, inability to keep appointments, being less attentive parents, being less productive workers, and being worse managers of finance, etc., are all directly related to a lack of financial wherewithal. Hence, poor people make bad decisions NOT because of lower IQ but because of diminished cognitive ability brought on by poverty.

These issues are particularly troubling because they deepen poverty and push one into a debt trap. Having to worry about money is a huge distraction that causes one to make poor decisions. Moreover, when one is in a poor financial position, one is often only presented with inferior options compared to when one is in a position of financial strength.

One way to tackle the problem is to ALWAYS keep a 'Financial Cushion'. I always recommend that people need to FIRST save up for a 'Financial Cushion' BEFORE spending on non-necessities. The 'Financial Cushion' will save us enormous grief, especially when one is faced with emergencies. Emergencies that are very difficult or too prolonged to get out of could often push one into making bad choices.

As Ben Bernanke put it, "Smart financial planning - such as budgeting, saving for emergencies, and preparing for retirement - can help households enjoy better lives while weathering financial shocks. Financial education can play a key role in achieving these outcomes.". Smart financial planning, which includes saving up for emergencies, can help millions from sliding into the trap of poverty and future deprivation.

Hence, it is absolutely necessary that one works towards a 'Financial Cushion'. One needs a 'Financial Cushion' at all times to guard against emergency healthcare, job losses, acts of nature, and expenses such as expensive repairs. One could further bolster this cushion by taking appropriate insurances such as life insurance, health insurance, job loss insurance, home, and car insurance. These insurances, along with a financial cushion, are a must to help secure one's financial stability so that it doesn't erode one's ability to make better decisions. A 'Financial Cushion' is essential for financial health and, consequently, happiness. It safeguards one's journey towards 'Financial Freedom'. Make sure you plan for one according to your needs today!

Time for some FUN

Here is The **Canadian** songwriter-singer **Alanis Morissette** with her song **'Ironic'** from her third studio album **'Jagged Little Pill' (1996).** The song was written by **Alanis Morissette** and **Glen Ballard.** Enjoy!!

'Ironic'

Alanis Morissette, [Album **'Jagged Little Pill' (1996)**]

SCAN above to see **YOUTUBE** ***Video of the Song***

Lyrics

[Ironic]

An old man turned 98
He won the lottery and died the next day
It's a black fly in your Chardonnay
It's a death row pardon two minutes too late
And isn't it ironic, don't you think?

It's like rain on your wedding day
It's a free ride when you've already paid
It's the good advice that you just didn't take
And who would've thought, it figures

Mr. Play It Safe was afraid to fly
He packed his suitcase and kissed his kids goodbye
He waited his whole damn life to take that flight
And as the plane crashed down, he thought
"Well, isn't this nice?"
And isn't it ironic, don't you think?

It's like rain on your wedding day
It's a free ride when you've already paid
It's the good advice that you just didn't take
And who would've thought, it figures

Well, life has a funny way of sneaking up on you
When you think everything's okay and everything's going right
And life has a funny way of helping you out
When you think everything's gone wrong and everything blows up
In your face

A traffic jam when you're already late
A no-smoking sign on your cigarette break
It's like ten thousand spoons when all you need is a knife
It's meeting the man of my dreams
And then meeting his beautiful wife
And isn't it ironic, don't you think?
A little too ironic
And, yeah, I really do think

It's like rain on your wedding day
It's a free ride when you've already paid
It's the good advice that you just didn't take
And who would've thought, it figures

And, yeah, life has a funny way of sneaking up on you
Life has a funny, funny way of helping you out
Helping you out

Part II

Chapter 6

ON WHY 'FINANCES ARE LIKE OXYGEN'

How money is a necessity up to a point but why it contributes negligibly to incremental happiness beyond that point

"Money is much like Oxygen, excess of it does not make you necessarily happier or more alive, but without it, one would gasp to just stay alive."

–Author

"It is a kind of spiritual snobbery that makes people think that they can be happy without money."

–Albert Camus

Money is the 'Oxygen' of life. Without it, one would be gasping and struggling to survive. However, just like oxygen, one definitely needs a certain amount of it coming in at regular intervals for one's happiness. Any excess beyond a certain threshold contributes very little to incremental happiness; it is just an excess.

Interestingly, one could define how much money one would need. One could choose to build one's savings by limiting one's spending. As described in the chapter 'Living within your means', by clearly demarcating one's needs and spending accordingly, one could save oneself from a lot of trouble in the future.

In times of emergency, a 'Financial Cushion' would be extremely useful. It would prevent one from sliding down the slippery slope of financial ruin. This is the reason one needs to examine one's spending habits and not overspend. By saving enough for a 'Financial Cushion' and saving up enough for some 'Passive Income', one could overcome many of life's financial challenges and also have the bandwidth to think beyond one's immediate needs.

Just like the lack of oxygen would make us gasp in situations of emergencies and unforeseen circumstances, the lack of money in emergencies would pressurize us and make it difficult for us, to think and function normally. If we DO NOT have a 'financial cushion' and adequate resources set aside for emergencies, then the dearth of pre-planning would cause us to bleed financially and lead to poorer outcomes. When we are financially strained, we are pressurized and preoccupied with ways to earn money. Our preoccupation would make it almost impossible for us to think of anything else. We would be running and gasping on the treadmill of life. Hence, it is vital to have a constant flow of this 'Oxygen', whether it is through wages ('Active income') or returns from investments ('Passive income'). The constant supply of 'Oxygen' would allow us to not only stay alive but also be in a functional and thriving state. To this extent, money is critical and vital for one's well-being.

When Oxygen is in Excess

"You reach a point where you don't work for money."

– *Walt Disney*

"A wise man should have money in his head, but not in his heart."

–*Jonathan Swift*

When one hasn't been able to fulfill one's basic needs for living, one would only be preoccupied with those concerns and the methods of making money to fulfill those primary needs. However, once one does attain levels where those needs have been met, one needs to look at other sources of happiness to enrich our basket of life. Sometimes, people are still in the emergency mode of being preoccupied with money despite having attained a level of financial stability. They work harder and harder for more money, compromising their health and sacrificing time with their families. It is then that one needs to step back to reassess one's life.

People who have accumulated enough would do well to get off the treadmill of life and take care of their health and spend time with their families. Again, either way, money is like 'oxygen', and an excess of it has no linearly incremental benefits. Once one has enough of it, one should concentrate on the other aspects of one's life that contribute to one's happiness. Following one's passion, being kind to others, and engaging in some social work would increase one's happiness exponentially. Research has actually concluded that charity has a pivotal role in reducing one's blood pressure.

So from a philosophical angle, it is always necessary to remember that 'Money is like oxygen'. While one definitely needs some, more does not necessarily contribute greatly to one's incremental happiness.

It is also important to introspect on one's priorities. Let me explain; one can seek to help someone or be helped, whether in the form of a loan, charity, food, education, recommendation, etc. However, the one kind of wealth that we cannot beg, borrow, or steal for ourselves or from others is the 'wealth of good health'.

Once, the CEO of a well-renowned Indian company was making a presentation to investors. He laid out a long-term roadmap and described where he wanted to take his company. He had put forth his ambitious plans in that presentation. Though the CEO was middle-aged, he was in poor health and obese. He huffed and puffed as he gave his presentation and often stopped to catch his breath. Once he had completed his presentation, a foreign institutional investor got up with a question. He bluntly asked if the CEO would be around to take his company forward into the future that he had envisaged. He was point-blank and skeptical about whether the CEO, who could not even take care of his own health, could actually take care of the health of a large and growing company. The CEO's health did not exude the confidence that he would last the distance. Further, considering he was only middle-aged, it was also worrying that he was visibly breathless while presenting.

This was the cue that the CEO needed. He took up his health and fitness seriously. From then on, he set aside time to also work on his health. He became a marathoner, and in time, he was a regular at many marathon events around the globe. He found he enjoyed this workout, and it became a part of his lifestyle. This story goes on to illustrate that, firstly, one's life is to be looked at holistically and NOT just through the window of money and success. Secondly, where there is a will, there is a way. When we do assess our lives and choose to make that change, change is possible.

While there is no doubt that money is important and necessary, when in excess, one would do well to step off the treadmill and assess one's life honestly. Money beyond a certain point cannot buy us the intangibles that could enrich the other important dimensions of our lives. It is important for us to step back and fill our lives with those enriching and fulfilling aspects. This would require both independent thinking and truthful introspection. Beyond that, a will to make the change and persistence to stick with it would take us to the point where we could maximize our happiness and lead fulfilling and complete lives.

So love your money, but not so much that you forget other important things in life. As Sydney Madwed had rightly observed, "Poor is the man who does not know his own intrinsic worth and tends to measure everything by relative value. A man of financial wealth who values himself by his financial net worth is poorer than a poor man who values himself by his intrinsic self-worth.".

Time for some FUN

Here is a song originally written by **John Holt** in 1967. The **British** girl band **Atomic Kitten** released their version of the song as **'The Tide is High'** as the second song from their second studio album **'Feels So Good' (2002)**. Enjoy!!

'The Tide is High'

Atomic Kitten, [Album **'Feels So Good' (2002)**]

SCAN above to see **YOUTUBE** ***Video of the Song***

Lyrics

[The Tide is High]

Never give up
Yeah
Never give up

The tide is high, but I'm holding on
I'm gonna be your number one

I'm not the kinda girl
Who gives up just like that
Oh no

It's not the things you do that tease and hurt me bad
But it's the way you do the things you do to me
I'm not the kinda girl who gives up just like that
Oh no

The tide is high, but I'm holding on
I'm gonna be your number one
The tide is high, but I'm holding on
I'm gonna be your number one

Number one (my number one)
Number one (number one)

Every girl wants you to be her man
But I'll wait right here 'til it's my turn
I'm not the kinda girl who gives up just like that
Oh no

The tide is high, but I'm holding on
I'm gonna be your number one (the tide is high)
The tide is high, but I'm holding on
I'm gonna be your number one

Number one (my number one)
Number one

Every time that I get the feeling
You give me something to believe in
Every time that I got you near me
I know the way that I want it to be

But you know I'm gonna take my chance now
I'm gonna make it happen somehow
And you know I can take the pressure
A moment's pain for a lifetime's pleasure

Every girl wants you to be her man
But I'll wait right here 'til it's my turn
I'm not the kinda girl who gives up just like that
Oh no (not gonna let go)

The tide is high, but I'm holding on
I'm gonna be your number one
The tide is high, but I'm holding on
I'm gonna be your number one

Every time that I get the feeling
You give me something to believe in
Every time that I got you near me
I know the way that I want it to be

But you know I'm gonna take my chance now
I'm gonna make it happen somehow
And you know I can take the pressure
A moment's pain for a lifetime's pleasure

The tide is high, but I'm holding on

<u>Part II</u>

Chapter 7

'ACTIVE INCOME' VS. 'PASSIVE INCOME'

The difference between 'Active income' and 'Passive income' and the road to 'Financial Freedom'

"It's not how much money you make, but how much money you keep, how hard it works for you, and how many generations you keep it for."

– Robert Kiyosaki

"Financial peace isn't the acquisition of stuff. It's learning to live on less than you make, so you can give money back and have money to invest. You can't win until you do this."

– Dave Ramsey

The most important goal of any financially savvy person should be 'Financial Freedom'. When one takes up a job and earns one's daily income from it, we call that income 'Active income'. 'Active Income' is income that comes in as long as one is working. Earning that 'Active income' earns a person his 'Financial Independence'.

In Priyanka Chopra's words, "Financial independence is paramount. My mom always says that when a woman is financially independent, she has the ability to live life on her own terms. I think that was the soundest advice that I ever got. No matter where you go in life or who you get married to, you have to be financially independent - whether you use it or not.".

Whether you are male or female, having 'Financial Independence' allows one to make one's own decisions. As Salma Hayek put it, "I work hard, I make my own living, and I love it. I like having financial independence".

'Active income' helps one to pay off the bills and one's debt. It is best to start with paying off one's costliest debt first. So paying off one's credit card should be a priority. Following which, one should work on paying off student loans, car loans, and mortgage loans. However, 'Financial Freedom' is different from 'Financial Independence'.

The problems begin the moment we stop working or, for example, if unfortunately, one gets laid off and that income we call 'Active income' stops. Hence everyone has to look at something more than just 'Active income'. Most people start with 'Savings'.

'Passive Income'

"Stay in your bed as long as you want. Your money just left for work."

– Manoj Arora

"Rich people have their money to work hard for them. Poor people work hard for their money."

– T. HarvEker

'Savings' help one to tide over difficult times. Interestingly, when invested, savings would bring in earnings like another earning member of the family. More than just that, savings would earn for one even while one is asleep. For this reason, the earnings derived from 'Savings' are called 'Passive income'. This 'Passive income' is derived from the capital or 'Savings' one puts in. This 'Passive income' has a wonderful characteristic. It could earn for one round the clock, even while one does nothing and even when one is asleep.

Now, most people keep their savings initially in 'checking' or 'savings' accounts. This barely earns them returns. So the next question is about 'Investing'.

'Investing' involves deploying one's savings in a manner to minimize risk and maximize returns. As and when one begins to earn more money, one should begin to think in terms of how much money one would need over the short term, how much of a 'Financial Cushion' we may need for emergencies, and how much money we could put away for our long-term needs and retirement.

In other words, there are:

- Money to be set aside to pay the bills.

- Money allocated for paying debts (credit card, student loan, car loan, and home loan).
- Money to be reserved for a 'Financial Cushion' and insurance purposes.
- Money for immediate needs should be kept in 'Checking' and 'Savings' accounts.
- Money for short-term needs should be kept in 'CDs' (certificates of deposits) or in 'Money Markets'.
- Money to be saved for retirement in 'Retirement accounts' and employer matching accounts.
- Money for a steady income stream should be invested in 'Bonds'.
- Money for the long term should be held in stocks and invested in real estate.

FOR WEALTHIER INVESTORS

- Optionally, for a well-off investor: Money can be invested in commodities (only for sophisticated investors who understand the market very well and can make knowledgeable bets).
- For wealthy investors with excess cash, money should be invested in 'Hedge Funds' and 'PE' (private equity).
- For wealthier investors, money should be invested in 'VC' (Venture Capital) and/or deployed in 'Angel investing'.

In other words, 'Passive income' can be derived from a number of sources. Each source is suitable to one based on one's level of risk appetite. Wealthier people would begin to invest lower down the list because they have bigger risk appetites, and hence they can afford to seek higher returns WITHOUT compromising their financial stability.

The genius of passive income is that it is like an employee who earns and gives us his salary with minimum maintenance on our part. This frees us up to do other activities or follow our passions.

For most common folks, investing in bonds, stocks, and real estate are some of the best ways to derive 'Passive income'. As Suze Orman put it, "Cash - in savings accounts, short-term CDs, or money market deposits - is great for an emergency fund(s). But to fulfill a long-term investment goal like funding your retirement, consider buying stocks. The more distant your financial target, the longer inflation will gnaw at the purchasing power of your money".

Bonds give one a set coupon that is pre-set at the time the bond is issued. It is a stable and fixed return. It hence falls into the category of 'Fixed income' investing. Investing in stocks is actually buying a piece of a running and listed business, and the reward for investing in stocks is 'dividends'. This is variable and can vary depending on how well the company one has invested in fares. Real estate gives one return in the form of rent, which could be revised once the lease expires. It is automatically inflation-adjusted. Again, this could be a steady return as long as there are no vacancies. There are also other sophisticated options within these classes of investment which have been explained in the first part of this book.

If one could derive our running and capital expenses from a steady stream such as bonds, rental income, or dividends from stocks, one would be able to live off one's 'Passive income'. This would free one, and one wouldn't be obliged to report to a dreary 9-to-5 job. It would allow one to explore one's dreams and possibly discover one's true potential. Hence, 'Passive income' helps one to get closer and closer to 'Financial Freedom'. This milestone could be achieved when one limits one's expenses to the point that one accumulates enough resources and investments, which would generate adequate earnings that would enable one to regularly pay one's bills.

There is a theory that says that one's expenses expand with expanding income. While this may be true, one needs to work against the grain of this theory and keep one's expenses in check with expanding income. This is the secret to achieving 'Financial Freedom' earlier rather than later.

We are born to be free. Hence, achieving 'Financial Freedom' should be the first and foremost goal of every human being. So, one should limit one's needs, save up, and invest wisely to build up one's 'Passive income'. This will allow one to attain 'Financial Freedom' quickly. By attaining 'Financial Freedom', one would be able to explore and achieve one's true potential and goals. This would upgrade one's 'Happiness Quotient' (HQ) into an unlimited account. One could then reach for the skies!!!!

Time for some FUN

Time for the song ***'Chammak Challo'*** starring **Shahrukh Khan** and **Kareena Kapoor** from the **Hindi** movie, ***'Ra One'*** **(2011).** Playback singers are **Akon** and **Hansika Iyer**. It was **Akon's** first **musical collaboration** with Indian artists.

The song was composed by **Akon, Giorgio Tuinfort** as well as music director duo **Vishal - Shekhar (Vishal Dadlani** & **Shekhar Ravjiani**) and by **Gobind Singh**. The Movie was directed by **Anubhav Sinha** and Produced by **Shahrukh Khan** and **Gauri Khan.** Enjoy!!

SONG

'Chammak Challo'

('Glitter Girl')

MOVIE

'Ra One' **(2011)**

SCAN above to see **YOUTUBE** ***Video of the Song***

Lyrics **['Chammak Challo']**	***Translation*** **['Glitter Girl']**
Girl you're my chammak challo Where you go girl I'm gonna follow What you want girl just let me know You can be my chammak challo	Girl you're my chammak challo Where you go girl I'm gonna follow What you want girl just let me know You can be my chammak challo

Shawty I'm gonna getcha You know I'm gonna getcha You know I'll even letcha Letcha be my chammak challo	Shawty I'm gonna getcha You know I'm gonna getcha You know I'll even letcha Letcha be my chammak challo
Kaisa sharmaana aaja nachke dikha de Aa meri hole aaja parda gira de Aa meri akhiyon se akhiyaan mila de Aa tu na nakhre dikha	Don't be shy, show me your moves Get close to me, let down your guard Lock eyes with me C'mon, don't show me attitude
Wanna be my chammak challo? (x4) Tu meri chammak challo You're my chammak challo Teri picture ka main hero	Wanna be my chammak challo? (x4) Tu meri chammak challo You're my chammak challo I'm your movie's hero
Give it to me girl mujhko dedo You can be my chammak challo	Give it to me girl mujhko dedo You can be my chammak challo
Shawty I'm gonna getcha (i.e. get you) You know I'm gonna getcha Maybe I'll even letcha Be my chamak chamak chalo	Shawty I'm gonna getcha (i.e. get you) You know I'm gonna getcha Maybe I'll even letcha Be my chamak chamak chalo
Kaisa sharmaana aaja nachke dikha de Aa meri hole aaja parda gira de Aa meri akhiyon se akhiyaan mila de Aa tu na nakhre dikha	Don't be shy, show me your moves Get close to me, let yourself go Lock eyes with me C'mon, don't show me attitude
Wanna be my chammak challo? (x4)	Wanna be my chammak challo? (x4)

Unnai totta penn ullattai uruka maataya Ennai pola pennai paarthu mayanga maataya Kannil kannai poti vitaal sirika maataya Ennil unnai sooti vitaal ottika maataya	How can you not melt the woman who touched your heart How can you help falling for a girl like me If I lock eyes with you wouldn't that make you smile? If I bind you to me won't you get glued to me?
Kaisa sharmaana tujhe nachke dikha doon Mera ho jaaye jo main parda gira doon Aa tujhe akhiyon mein apne basa loon Aa tu na nakhre dikha	Let my dance show you how shy I am If I let my guard down, you'll be mine Let me hold you in my gaze C'mon now, don't show me attitude
Wanna be my Chammak Challo (x4)	Wanna be my Chammak Challo (x4)

<u>Part II</u>

Chapter 8

LIBERATION THROUGH 'FINANCIAL FREEDOM'

How and why 'Financial Freedom' is complete liberation and freedom

"Everyone chases a bit of what they say life is about: money, desire... But when you stop chasing, you realise life is a rhythm and it's very peaceful, very quiet. You see, it's quite a miracle."

– *Nick Nolte*

"Don't stay at the job for safe salary increases over time. That will never get you where you want - freedom from financial worry. Only free time, imagination, creativity, and an ability to disappear will help you deliver value that nobody ever delivered before in the history of mankind."

– *James Altucher*

As stated in the chapter on 'Active' and 'Passive' income, it is necessary for one to accumulate enough 'Passive income' to truly and safely liberate oneself from financial stress. 'Passive income' is the road to 'Financial Freedom'. 'Financial Freedom' brings with it the ability for one to follow one's passion and reach one's true potential.

Often following one's passion is a luxury, but with adequate 'Passive income', one could dabble in it without worries and without any stress. Ellen DeGeneres talks about passion when she says, "I say always follow your passion, no matter what, because even if it's not the same financial success, it'll lead you to the money that'll make you the happiest.".

A

'Sanskrit Slokha'

On Happiness

अन्तोनास्तिपिपासायाःसन्तोषःपरमंसुखम्।
तस्मात्सन्तोषमेवेहपरंपश्यन्तिपण्डिताः॥ - Mahabharata Vanaparva

antō nāsti pipāsāyāḥ santōṣaḥ paramaṃ sukham ।
tasmātsantōṣamēvēha paraṃ paśyanti paṇḍitāḥ ॥

Meaning:

There is no limit for greed, and contentment is the ultimate happiness,
So a wise man is always happy with what he has.

There was a graduate from one of INDIA's top schools who worked in Hong Kong as an investment banker making good money. He lived modestly in a simple apartment and limited his expenses for years. Many visiting friends would advise him to take a more luxurious living pad commensurate with his large income. However, he stuck it out for a decade because he had a dream.

He generated enough savings and invested them wisely. Incidentally, he was fired from his job. Taking this as an opportunity rather than a tragedy, he came back to INDIA and worked on his writing career. Following his return to India, he was able to comfortably maintain himself with his 'Passive income' to pursue his dream. He had attained 'Financial Freedom'. As he had attained that milestone, it allowed him to pursue his passion.

His dream was to be an author. He worked hard, researched, and wrote books relevant to the pulse of modern INDIA. Soon, he developed a large and faithful readership base. He went on to become one of INDIA's leading authors. In the year 2008, The New York Times cited him as "the biggest selling English language novelist in India's history". He was also featured in Forbes India magazine as one of the top celebrities of India in 2016.

He was listed 40th out of the top 100. The person is none other than Mr. Chetan Bhagat. He realized his greater potential and unlocked his talents.

All this was possible as he had made the initial sacrifices and generated enough 'Passive income' to liberate himself. Even in the face of job loss and the loss of 'Active income', he had the financial backing and strength from 'Passive income' to set him free. This allowed him to play out his passion. Following his passion allowed Mr. Chetan Bhagat to achieve greater success, and he lived his dream. He became a popular author, both rich and famous.

Such is the power of 'Financial Freedom'. When one's expenses are sky-high, one would have to work all through one's life, and one would be straddled to a fixed pre-set role. To liberate oneself and attain one's dreams, one needs to first attain 'Financial Freedom'. It is not easy, and it takes time. Nevertheless, believe in it, start now, and liberate yourself!!

Time for some FUN

Time for **American** boy band **Backstreet Boys,**with their hit song, **'Larger than Life'** from their third studio album, **'Millennium' (1999)**. Enjoy!!

'Larger than Life'

Back Street Boys, [Album **'Millennium' (1999)**]

SCAN above to see **YOUTUBE** ***Video of the Song***

Lyrics

[Larger than Life]

I may run and hide when you're screamin' my name, alright
But let me tell you now
There are prices to fame, alright
All of our time's spent in flashes of light

All you people can't you see, can't you see
How your love's affecting our reality
Every time we're down, you can make it right
And that makes you larger than life

Alright, lookin' at the crowd
And I see your body sway, c'mon
Wishin' I could thank you in a different way, c'mon
'Cause all of your time spent keeps us alive

All you people can't you see, can't you see
How your love's affecting our reality
Every time we're down, you can make it right
And that makes you larger than life

Larger than life
Yeah, All of your time spent, keeps us alive...

Everytime we're down, you can make it right

All you people can't you see, can't you see
How your love's affecting our reality
Every time we're down, you can make it right
And that makes you larger than life

Yeah, every time we're down
Yeah, you can make it right
Yeah, that's what makes you larger than life, yeah, yeah
All you people can't you see, can't you see?
How your love's affecting our reality
Every time we're down, you can make it right
And that makes you larger, that makes you larger
That makes you larger than life.

Part II

Chapter 9

THE '2% RULE', THE RULE TO 'FINANCIAL FREEDOM'

A simple rule of thumb for people to estimate the annual amount they could expend interminably and sustainably from their portfolio of investments.

"The best thing money can buy is financial freedom."

– Rob Berger

"I live, eat, spend, travel, support a family, entertain.....but I do not go to work. There is something wrong. My nest egg just keeps growing."

– Manoj Arora

When one truly analyzes one's life, one would realize one doesn't need more and more money, but one actually needs 'Financial Freedom'. Somebody measured 'Financial Freedom' as the measure of the length of time one could go without 'Active income' (income earned through salary/working). When we do attain it, it would mean we could continue to maintain our standard of living, even if we stopped working today. In other words, the amount of time one could maintain their exact same lifestyle WITHOUT any inflow of 'Active income' is a measure of their 'Financial Freedom'. 'Financial Freedom' liberates us such that we are not dependent on our monthly paycheck. It means living the same lifestyle and maintaining the same standard of living even when we stop our work and we don't receive our monthly paycheck i.e. our 'Active Income'. This would allow us to pick and choose how we would like to spend our time and live life on our own terms. It could be the freedom to choose our work and not to return to a distasteful job. Financial Freedom would mean more time or flexible timings. It could mean time and control in our own hands for us to do what is more meaningful to us, rather than doing only that which is more lucrative for us.

Essentially, 'Financial Freedom' allows one to work according to one's likes and passion. It is about not being forced to work because of the need for the paycheck. 'Financial Freedom' allows us to work on what we love rather than being FORCED to love our job.

Most people think they could only be happy if they were billionaires. Fortunately, this is not true. Not only that, if one goes on to believe that one would need to be a billionaire to be happy, one would actually be staking one's happiness on the improbable. A minuscule number of people go on to be that rich. The fact is one really does NOT need to be extremely wealthy to be happy. What one needs is actually just 'Financial Freedom'. 'Financial Freedom' is the state where one is not dependent on one's 'Active income' and one could just live off one's 'Passive income' for perpetuity.

So, one needs to have a 'Nest Egg' that earns while one goes about one's work or doing the things that one loves. With the 'Nest Egg' earning, one could choose to indulge in one's passions or work in occupations whose income one need not be dependent on. It could be any pursuit that would be of interest, a hobby, another degree, or one could follow one's dreams, or whatever one fancies. One could work shorter hours, have more time for family and friends, travel and explore, learn skills, and do the things one loves. The need for money would neither dictate one's life, nor would it occupy one's time, one's mental space, or one's physical energies.

How does one attain Financial Freedom?

"Too many people spend money they earned...to buy things they don't want...to impress people that they don't like."

– Will Rogers

"Wealth is not about having a lot of money; it's about having a lot of options."

– Chris Roc

How does one realize this 'Financial Freedom'? What would it take to create this, and could this really be achieved? It is possible, and as a first step, one needs to create 'Passive Income'. 'Passive income' is actually income earned from one's savings, which forms one's 'Savings Nest Egg'. Before one creates the 'Nest Egg', it is necessary for one to first define one's needs. This is very crucial and is pivotal to the entire plan. If one could sensibly limit one's needs, one could attain that 'Financial Freedom' faster, which would allow one to enjoy one's life and help one to live life on one's own terms. For defining needs, let us consider the hypothetical case of TWO people, Tom and Andy.

Tom is a senior partner in a consultancy firm and earns millions every year. Tom lives a BIG life. He has three big luxury vehicles, an eight-bedroom house with a swimming pool, a private theatre, a private library, designer bath, and kitchen. He has expensive club memberships and holiday homes in Florida and Naples, Italy. He changes his vehicles every year. He spends a lot on capital items, including big-screen televisions, costly furniture, crockery, and jewellery. He has a vast collection of designer clothes and footwear. He travels first class everywhere and stays only at seven-star hotels. Do you think he is happy? Well, Tom works really hard and travels weekdays. He actually has very little time to enjoy his possessions.

Andy is his colleague and is also a senior partner in the same consultancy firm and earns the same amount. He has a nice but modest three-bedroom house. He has two vehicles which he keeps for 5-7 years before selling. He travels economy and stays in places according to need. He doesn't buy things he does not need. He spends money on experiences rather than material things. He maintains his health, eats healthily, exercises, and tries to maintain balance in life. Like Tom, he too has a tough schedule and works very hard. While Tom's yearly expenses to maintain his lifestyle are in the millions of dollars every year, Andy's are a fraction of it.

Tom keeps working hard to keep the money coming so that he could continue to maintain the status quo. Since his savings are limited, he depends vastly on his 'Active income'.

Andy, on the other hand, has been living sensibly. Though he spends well to maintain a good life, he spends according to what he needs. He has been saving up half a million dollars every year for the past 10 years by keeping his expenses from spiraling. He plans to retire by the age of 40 and do the things he loves.

As one would guess, Andy is on the course to attain 'Financial Freedom'. The money that he saved has created a 'Nest Egg' with which he earns 'Passive income', allowing him to stop working for money. After his early retirement, Andy plans to pursue his passion for travel and writing. The great part is that his 'Nest Egg' would earn him enough 'Passive income' perpetually, so he could continue to maintain his current lifestyle indefinitely and leave the same for his children.

We can now see the prognosis: Tom would have to continue working indefinitely and then scale back his high-expense lifestyle during retirement as it may not be sustainable. Even after all those years of earning from a high-paying job, Tom, at retirement, would NOT be left with sufficient funds to retire with the same lifestyle. This is because any increase in his income has been matched by increased expenses.

These are very divergent and extreme examples meant to drive home an important point. As one achieves several financial milestones, one becomes potential 'customers' or 'clients' of each category of product/service. This is why one needs to be aware and observant about those products or services that one DOESN'T really 'need'. Whether it is to create or maintain an unsustainable standard or to please others or to impress our peer group, each one would feed off the other, and it could spiral out of control. If one maintains a standard of living that is always trying to fulfill a projected self-image to impress other people, one would be worse off, as that may push one down an insatiable chasm. Hence, the focus needs to be on one's expenses. One needs to know one's 'needs', 'wants', and 'luxuries'. One needs to cut out the fat and maintain a lean expense account. This is because how rich one is is NOT defined by how much we spend but by how much WE SAVE.

So, the first thing in attaining 'Financial Freedom' is to limit one's expenses to what one really needs to be happy. One needs to have an idea about one's annual expenditure that is required to maintain a happy lifestyle. It is then that one could work out how much one would need to create one's 'Nest Egg'. One's quantum of annual expenses and how one invests the remaining funds would determine the quantum of money required as capital in one's 'Nest Egg'.

The '2% Rule'

"The only way to permanently change the temperature in the room is to reset the thermostat. In the same way, the only way to change your level of financial success 'permanently' is to reset your financial thermostat. But it is your choice whether you choose to change."

– T. HarvEker

"You can be young without money, but you can't be old without it."

– Tennessee Williams

Once, I was talking to a very wealthy gentleman who I knew pretty well. He told me something interesting. He told me that he never knew how much was enough, and hence, he kept investing his time and energy towards earning money for decades. This set me thinking. Most folks do not really know HOW MUCH is enough. They keep working all their lives, compromising their happiness and health, to feel rich but miserable at the end of the day. For such folks, I have formulated a simple formula.

People should first ascertain their annual expenses. If they have invested their investable surplus in a diversified portfolio of stocks, bonds, and real estate, they are then entitled to spend a quantum of 2 percent of their capital invested every year towards their expenses. The surplus from their earnings beyond this 2 percent should be reinvested along with the capital. The rationale behind this is that a diversified portfolio of stocks and bonds, in most cases, should be able to beat inflation by 2 percent. In other words, after deduction for inflation, the real return for the portfolio would at least be 2 percent.

The capital and the surplus after the deduction of the 2 percent for expenses would continue to remain as the capital reserve. The underlying assumption here is that when the expenses are within the 2 percent margin, the investor would be able to comfortably finance his expenses with the return on the portfolio even after factoring in inflation and deductions towards expenses. Also, in most cases, the investors' return after this deduction would even surpass lifestyle inflation by a large margin.

So, for example, let us assume that inflation is at 5 percent, and an investor gets an average return of 12 percent on a diversified portfolio of stocks and bonds. After spending 2 percent of the return earned, the investor could reinvest the remaining 10 percent back into his/her invested capital reserve. With inflation at 5 percent, the amount reinvested would keep his/her reserve capital ahead of inflation while at the same time giving the investor a further cushion of 5 percent. Even if we assume that in a bad year, the investor gets poorer returns of only 7 percent from the diversified portfolio, he would still come out ahead.

Hence, an investor is entitled to spend a "guilt and carefree" 2% of the capital reserve every year without depleting the "Nest Egg". Further, the investor's "Nest Egg" would grow (inflation-adjusted) perpetually while accruing any excesses above inflation. This would keep the investor above the watermark of depletion, thus supplying him/her with the oxygen to perpetually fuel his/her dreams.

Hence, I went on to explain to the wealthy gentleman that as long as he maintained his expenses within 2 percent of his invested capital, he would be perpetually rich, and in most accounts, his wealth would grow significantly over the years. Of course, this was based on the simple yet powerful and effective assumption that his investable surplus would grow, at the very least, at a rate of 2 percent above inflation.

To flip the calculation, a person would need his/her "Nest Egg" to be fifty times his/her annual expenses for him/her to get to the threshold of "Financial Freedom". S/he could then spend 2 percent of it every year and do so perpetually.

In most cases, where people are starting out, they may not have such a large quantum of money. In such a scenario, people could spend 2 percent of their investable surplus and bridge the shortfall in expenses via "Active Income". In such cases, as the "Passive Income" grows, the quantum required from the "Active Income" to bridge the shortfall in meeting the expenses would shrink.

So, do use the "2% rule" to estimate how much you could spend annually to KEEP and GROW your "Financial Freedom". The rule will also help you to determine the size of the "Nest Egg" that would give you complete liberation.

Time for some FUN

Time for the song titled ***'Adada Mazhaida'*** from the **Tamil** movie ***'Paiyaa'*** **(2010)** starring **Karthi** and **Tamannah.** The Movie was directed and produced by **N.Linguswamy.**

Music was composed by **Yuvan Shankar Raja** (son of the illustrious music composer **Illayaraja**) and the songwriter was **Na MuthuKumar**. Enjoy!!

<table>
<tr><td colspan="2" align="center">SONG
'Adada Mazhaida'
MOVIE
'Paiyaa' (2010)

SCAN above to see YOUTUBE <u>Video of the Song</u></td></tr>
<tr><td align="center">Lyrics
['Adada Mazhaida']</td><td align="center">Translation
['Heavy down pour (of love)']</td></tr>
<tr><td align="center">(Tamil Music Beats)
Thantha Ne Thantha Nane, Thantha Nane Thana Ne,
Thantha Ne Thantha Nane, Thantha Nane Naa,

Adada Mazhaida Adai Mazhaida,
Azhaga Siricha Puyal Mazhaida,</td><td align="center">(Tamil Music Beats)
Thantha Ne Thantha Nane, Thantha Nane Thana Ne,
Thantha Ne Thantha Nane, Thantha Nane Naa,

There is a heavy down pour of rain (love)
If she smiles beautifully, it's a cyclone.</td></tr>
</table>

<table>
<tr>
<td>Mari Mari Mazhaiyadikka,
Manasukkulla
Kodaipidikka,
Kalgal Nalachu
Kaigal Ettachu,
Enna Achu Edhachu
Edhedho Ayachu,

Mayil Thogai Pola, Iva Mazhaiyil Adumbodhu,
Rayil Palam Pola,
En Manasum Adum Paru,
Enna Achu Edhachu
Edhedho Ayachu,

Adada Mazhaida Adai Mazhaida,
Azhaga Siricha Puyal Mazhaida,

(Tamil Music Beats)
Thana Nan Nan Nana, Thana Nan Nan Nana,
Thana Nan Nan Nana Na Na Na Na,
Thana Nan Nan Nana, Thana Nan Nan Nana,
Thana Nan Nan Nana Na Na Na Naa,

Pattu Pattu Padadha Pattu,
Mazhaithan Padudhu Ketkadhappattu,
Unnai Ennai Serthu Vacha,
Mazhaikkoru Salam Podu,
Ennai Konjam Kanalaye, Unakkulla Thedipparu,</td>
<td>It's (love) raining continuously and I'm holding umbrella
in my heart.
(as I dance) Legs have become four and hands have become eight
Don't know what's happening
Something has happened.

When she dances in rain like the peacock.
My heart shakes like a bridge trembling while a train is crossing it.
Don't know what's happening
Something has happened.

There is a heavy down pour of rain (love)
If she smiles beautifully, it's a cyclone.

(Tamil Music Beats)
Thana Nan Nan Nana, Thana Nan Nan Nana,
Thana Nan Nan Nana Na Na Na Na,
Thana Nan Nan Nana, Thana Nan Nan Nana,
Thana Nan Nan Nana Na Na Na Naa,

The song being sung has never been sung (before) The rain (love) is singing beautifully this original song.
My salutations to rain for uniting us.
I've lost my heart, search if it is with you.</td>
</tr>
</table>

Mandhiram Pola Irukku, Pudhu Thandhiram Pola Irukku, Bambaram Pola Enakku, Thalaimathiyil Suthudhu Kirukku, Dhevadhai Enge En Dhevadhai Enge, Adhu Santhoshamai Adudhu Inge,	It's like a mantra and new tantra. My head is feeling giddy (in love) I'm rotating like a top. Where is the angel? Where is my angel? Here is she dancing happily.
Onnappola Verarum Illa, Ennaivitta Veraru Solla, Chinna Chinna Kannu Rendu, Koduththenna Anuppivachan, Indha Kannum Podhalaiye, Edhukkivalai Padaichu Vachan,	No one is like you in this world. Nobody can say this other than me. These two eyes are not enough. Why did he (Creator) create only two eyes even as he sent her here?
Pattamboochi Ponnu, Nenjil Padapadakkum Ninnu, Poovum Ivalum Onnu, Ennai Konnupputta Konnu, Povadhu Enge Nan Povadhu Enge, Manam Thalladhudhe Boadhaiyil Inge,	My heart is fluttering like a butterfly. She's like a flower and has killed my heart. Where am I to go? Where am 1 to go? My heart is stuttering in this intoxication
Adada Mazhaida Adai Mazhaida, Azhaga Siricha Anal Mazhaida,	There is a heavy down pour of rain (love) If she smiles beautifully, it's a firestorm
Pinni Pinni Mazhai Adikka, Minnal Vanthu Kodai Pidikka, Vanam Rendu Achu Bhoomi Thundachu, En Moochu Kathala Mazhai Kooda Sudachu,	It's (love) pouring down heavily and it as though lightning is my umbrella Sky has broken into two and the earth is broken into pieces. Even rain has turned hot with my breath.

Kudaiyai Neeti Yarum, Intha Mazhaiyai Thadukka Venam, Anaiya Pottu Yarum, En Manasa Adakka Venam, Kondaduu Kondadu Koothadi Kondadu.	I don't need an umbrella (anymore) Don't try to stop this rain. Don't try to impound my heart with a dam. Have a blast and enjoy it (pouring of love) to the hilt.

Part II

Chapter 10

THE 'BIG SWAP'

How 'Time' and 'Money' are interchangeable and how to make that work for you and increase your HQ (Happiness Quotient)

"I have a fantastic relationship with money. I use it to buy my freedom."

– *Gianni Versace*

"It's better to waste money, than it is to waste time. You can always get more money."

– *Hal Sparks*

Beyond a point, having and earning more and more money does NOT necessarily lead to incremental happiness in one's life. A 2010 Princeton study by Daniel Kahneman and Angus Deaton found that at the national level in the United States, an increase in pay for people who made $75,000 per annum on average would NOT significantly improve their day-to-day happiness.

The study elaborates that our emotional well-being does NOT improve significantly once our household earning crosses $75,000. When our income crosses a certain threshold, further incremental increases in our income or wealth do NOT significantly cause any increase in the pleasure we derive from day-to-day activities and experiences. The study, however, said that "Life evaluation", which is how one feels about one's life and accomplishments, could continue to rise with higher income and education.

This is a significant conclusion. What it does tell us is that money is much like oxygen; one definitely needs a certain quantum for one's happiness, and one will be happier having more money, but only up to a certain threshold.

On the other hand, the lack or the dearth of money could cause significant distress, such that one would be completely preoccupied with ensuring one had enough of it. This is also a throwback to the chapter "Why a 'Financial Cushion' is Important", where one discusses why one should keep a financial cushion so that in an emergency, one is not left gasping and desperate. Such a situation would end up preoccupying one's thoughts and would force one to make suboptimal decisions, which could affect one's financial well-being and happiness.

Having said that, money is like oxygen, and while it is important, more of it beyond a certain point would actually NOT lead to more happiness. It is not a linear graph between money and happiness. As the Princeton study pointed out, emotional well-being does not improve significantly after a certain quantum. Hence, more oxygen does NOT mean more life happiness. It is just a surplus.

Examples are early-age high achievers who make significant amounts of money and then lose their balance in life. On their way up, they derive a lot of pleasure, but beyond a point, they feel something amiss, and the high is NOT there anymore. They end up doing things that are bad for their mental makeup and health, as they are constantly searching for the next high. They set themselves on the path of unhappiness and self-destruction, often being dissatisfied with their lives, with contentment and true happiness eluding them.

Materialism could make one happy up to a certain point, beyond which one needs other things to fill one's basket of life. If one approaches life with this wisdom, one would understand that there are other sources to realize true happiness, and one shouldn't be trying to just derive everything out of money. Beyond a certain threshold, materialism is NOT a recipe for happiness.

A classic example of this is the singer Michael Jackson, who attained fame and money at an early age. The initial high that money and fame brought did not last long. He was still unhappy with his life. He seemed to be dissatisfied with his identity and who he was. He went to great extents to correct his perceived imperfections through plastic surgery and skin bleaching, eventually singing "It does not matter if you're black or white". More "oxygen" does NOT necessarily lead to more happiness. Ironically, Michael Jackson is even rumored to have slept in an oxygen tent!

Nevertheless, if one does not have the requisite financial wherewithal, especially to sustain one's basic needs, one would feel like one is gasping for oxygen. Money is a necessity to live in this world, and one needs it to secure one's financial future and work towards achieving whatever benchmark or threshold that one has set for oneself. However, while one should work towards this benchmark, one should be aware and shouldn't build hope with the expectation that more money would solve all of one's problems. Beyond a point, "Money is not THE cure-all". It may actually make one more miserable. It is, therefore, important for one to work on how to allocate one's spending.

While the common phrase "Money can't buy happiness" is partly true, our awareness and observation in our journey should also look at "How we use money"; this could significantly alter or enhance our happiness. There is another study that talks about this. A study published in the Proceedings of the National Academy of Sciences talks about how money could be used to make us happier. Researchers led by Ashley Whillans, a professor at Harvard Business School, began with survey data from nearly 4,500 people from countries such as the United States, Canada, Denmark, and the Netherlands. The survey studies an unexplored and uncharted path to attaining and improving the Happiness Quotient. The survey takers were asked to pay other people to do "un-enjoyable daily tasks" and, in the process, free up time that they could use to pursue other activities. It was found that the survey takers who did engage help to increase their free time ended up increasing their Happiness Quotient. It was found that people who traded money for time were happier and more content than those who did not.

The survey was repeated among a study of 1,800 Americans, and the results were found to be the same. People who exchanged money for free time ended up being happier and more satisfied with their lives and reported less stress. This observation was found across the rich and poor and across the entire spectrum of the economic strata. It was demonstrated that we could make ourselves happy by paying other people to do our time-consuming and unenjoyable chores.

A more direct test was done by the Whillans team in Vancouver. Here, about 60 volunteers were given $40 to spend over two consecutive weekends. On one of the weekends, the volunteers were asked to spend the money on material things; on the other weekend, the volunteers were asked to spend the money on things that freed up their time. The researchers checked on the volunteers each weekend to see how they felt after they had spent the money. It was found that the volunteers reported more positive feelings such as joy and enthusiasm, and less time-related stress on the weekends where they spent their money on things that saved their time, as opposed to the weekends spent on shopping. They also experienced fewer negative feelings such as anger, fear, and nervousness in those weeks. In other words, they found a way to "buy" happiness.

World over, during the last hundred years, there have been significant increases in wealth among broad swathes of people, creating a large middle class and numerous wealthy people. However, there have been some unintended consequences. "Time" has become a casualty, with the rising sense of time scarcity parching people and vaporizing their HQs (Happiness Quotients). There is, however, strong evidence across the income spectrum that points to the fact that buying time could actually act as a buffer, thus containing this time famine and placing us firmly on the path to happiness. So, HOW one spends one's money is important.

The 'Time Factor'

"Waste your money and you're only out of money, but waste your time and you've lost a part of your life."

– Michael LeBoeuf

The pressures of "time-stress" could be linked to a lower sense of well-being. Lower levels of happiness and increased anxiety may even result in insomnia. People fail to eat healthy foods and exercise regularly under pressures of time. This is the underlying cause for the rise in obesity and unhappiness among people. Sometimes, spending that little extra to buy time—like getting our chores done, paying extra to reduce commute by living closer to work, or even taking up a job that may pay less but in turn gives us more free time—could actually make us richer as far as HQ (Happiness Quotient) is concerned. However, we have been conditioned to believe that everything we do should profit us materially, such that even those who are wealthy choose to spend on material acquisitions and swanky cars rather than buy more free time for themselves. Sometimes it's the intangibles that actually count.

It is important to underline that "Time" is a finite commodity and one is given only 24 hours each day. On the contrary, by being smart about earning, investing, and spending one's money, one could actually buy more time to be spent on oneself and thus reduce the negative effects of the "modern time famine". This would greatly increase one's HQ (Happiness Quotient).

Women over the last half a century have truly come ahead to claim their space, to access better education and opportunities. However, it is difficult to first achieve financial independence while building and managing their homes. In most cases, they have been achieving this without actual support from their partners. This has created a time famine and has decreased their life satisfaction. The increasing demands on time have led to decreasing satisfaction levels. For such busy women, spending money to save time may have particularly beneficial consequences. While we are discussing how swapping money for time may be beneficial, we are not discussing the larger issues pertaining to gender dynamics. As the gender that predominantly suffers from time famine, I have only said that women should work towards financial freedom to reward themselves with more time.

This is particularly useful information for employers. Employers who reward employees with vouchers for time-saving services would find that their employees then report being better equipped mentally and emotionally, and thus deliver better results. Employees rewarded in this way particularly benefit from better work-life balance and performance. The employers would also see increased retention rates and benefit immensely. In a small pilot initiative by Stanford University, there was concurrence with the above observations. Doctors who were given time-saving vouchers reported better work-life balance and had better retention rates. Employers would hence do well to make employees more "Time rich" and reduce the "Time famine".

'Time affluence' proved to be more rewarding than just 'money affluence'. This would also help the trickle-down effect in economies where the wealthy actually create more employment for people who would do their chores for them, rather than hoarding wealth, which will serve no one.

A significant barrier that people need to overcome is the guilt they feel when they outsource time-consuming tasks or chores. Rather than looking at the situation as providing the service provider an opportunity to earn money, wealthier people may feel guilty that they are burdening the less wealthy. This may lead to less participation in the sharing economy. The 'sharing economy' could actually lead to the sharing of wealth in a manner that would benefit society as a whole, provided fair wages and benefits are ensured.

At the individual level, spending money on buying time acts as a buffer against the effects of time stress, as it enhances our perceived control over our life. People who are always busy perceive a lack of control over their time. Spending money wisely would free up one's time and actually give one what one needs most: more time for ourselves to do things we actually like.

One caveat to this observation is that spending too much money on time-saving services, which use many people such as house helps, nannies, and cooks, would not actually take away from the time spent on 'managing' the help. Also, with so many service providers, it could bring on a sense of lack of control. Hence, the graph of benefits of buying time and life satisfaction may be curvilinear, and it is necessary to find the point that is optimum for oneself. This optimum may differ from person to person and probably depend on one's current circumstance and personality. So to conclude, we need to spend money to save time, but we also need to find the optimal balance to give ourselves control but not to give up control over our lives.

Time for some FUN

Here is **American** rock band **Smash Mouth** with their first major smash hit single **'Walkin' On The Sun'** from their first album **'Fush Yu Mang' (1997).** Enjoy!!

'Walkin' on the Sun'

Smash Mouth, [Album **'Fush Yu Mang' (1997)**]

SCAN above to see **YOUTUBE** ***Video of the Song***

Lyrics

[Walkin' On The Sun]

It ain't no joke, I'd like to buy the world a toke
And teach the world to sing in perfect harmony
And teach the world to snuff the fires and the liars
Hey, I know it's just a song, but it's spice for the recipe
This is a love attack, I know it went out, but it's back
It's just like any fad, it retracts before impact
And just like fashion it's a passion for the with-it and hip
If you got the goods, they'll come and buy it
Just to stay in the clique

So don't delay, act now, supplies are running out
Allow if you're still alive, six to eight years to arrive
And if you follow there may be a tomorrow
But if the offer's shunned
You might as well be walking on the Sun

Twenty-five years ago, they spoke out and they broke out
Of recession and oppression and together they toked
And they folked out with guitars around a bonfire
Just singin' and clappin', man, what the hell happened?
Then some were spellbound, some were hellbound
Some, they fell down and some got back up
And fought back against the meltdown
And their kids were hippie chicks, all hypocrites
Because fashion is smashing the true meaning of it

So don't delay, act now, supplies are running out
Allow if you're still alive, six to eight years to arrive
And if you follow, there may be a tomorrow
But if the offer's shunned
You might as well be walking on the sun

It ain't no joke when a mama's handkerchief is soaked
With her tears because her baby's life has been revoked
The bond is broke up, so choke up and focus on the close up
Mr. Wizard can't perform no god-like hocus-pocus
So don't sit back, kick back and watch the world get bushwhacked
News at ten, your neighborhood is under attack
Put away the crack before the crack puts you away
You need to be there when your baby's old enough to relate

So don't delay, act now, supplies are running out
Allow if you're still alive, six to eight years to arrive
And if you follow, there may be a tomorrow
But if the offer's shunned

You might as well be walking on the sun
You might as well be walking on the sun
You might as well be walking on the sun
You might as well be walking on the sun
You might as well be walking on the sun

<u>Part II</u>

Chapter 11

RECIPE FOR 'TIME AFFLUENCE'

Why regaining control of 'Time' in your life is a step towards achieving your goals and happiness in your life

"My favourite things in life don't cost any money. It's really clear that the most precious resource we all have is time."

– *Steve Jobs*

"Time flies. It's up to you to be the navigator."

– *Robert Orben*

Previously, we explored how one could build one's HQ (Happiness Quotient) by spending money to save time. However, one also needs to reflect on HOW one could optimally utilize the time one has. Like stated earlier, all of us have finite days filled with the same fixed twenty-four hours. How one uses it would take one to the next level. The internet/mobile era today provides one with many conveniences. It is a boon, and yet it brings with it several shackles that are baneful. This tool provides one with many options but is truly like a double-edged sword. While on one hand, one has more options on how to spend one's time, on the other hand, the demands on one's time have increased. With the advent of the smartphone era, the demand on OUR time has increased exponentially. So, one has fallen victim to time deprivation even while having control of what is ours. Ironically, this has caused a widespread 'Time Famine'. Wherever we go, we are people who are always busy and short on time. The very tools that were meant to make one's lives richer and lighter have contributed to greater stress and, in many cases, unhappiness and psychological disorders.

Companies in the mobile era are furiously working toward having larger slices of our time, demanding our attention and hooking us onto our smartphones and computers in unprecedented ways. The more they are able to engage us, the more money they make. While some tools have saved us time, many others do not actually contribute to our happiness and could sometimes make us more miserable. We have a plethora of choices today, but most will not lead us to a consistently balanced and happy state. It is important for us to step back and evaluate the situation. We need to take control of our lives rather than let these electronic devices control us. These tools are meant to serve us, to be used to our advantage, and are to be at our disposal. Yet sometimes, we are not smarter than the devices that we use and are often addicted to those artificial highs that make us dance to their tune. As the saying goes, "Some things are good slaves but bad masters".

FOMO

"Time passes irrevocably."

– *Virgil*

"When you fear missing out, you are missing the moment."

– *Anonymous*

We all understand, believe, and speak out against the ills of different screens and online platforms, yet we are also driven due to FOMO (Fear of Missing Out). FOMO is the fear of NOT wanting to miss out on things that our friends and neighbors may be indulging in. FOMO has made us constantly come back to our tools, to keep scrolling, to kindle our curiosity to just see what's next, until we look up and realize we have been at it for the last hour! The FOMO thinking has led us to make choices which cause imbalances in our lives. We have to decide to choose and make choices we can control. Tools that are addictive and consume disproportionate time in our lives are to be shunned. In other words, it is best to DETOX.

It is human tendency to not want to be left behind, and sometimes one is comfortable only when following the herd. However, it is necessary for one to really step back, control the primal instincts, and think for ourselves. One should always be in a position to choose. The choices one makes in a calm and balanced state are the best, and they need to be set in our minds. These pre-decided options should be the ones we stick with. This is done so that one is not swayed by the moment or by the herd. Once one begins to overcome FOMO (Fear of Missing Out), one will find one's bearings and stand by what one wants rather than letting the herd decide for one. It is important that one does not worry about what other people do or say. One only needs to engage in those activities that contribute to one's well-being and shun the rest. Doing a re-evaluation and DETOX from electronic gadgets and setting rules for oneself and our loved ones will help us reclaim our most valuable asset: 'Time'.

As Rick Smolan says, "Every time there's a new tool, whether it's the Internet or cell phones or anything else, all these things can be used for good or evil. Technology is neutral; it depends on how it's used.".

Social Networking applications, Online Games, Virtual Games, etc., are both time-fillers and time-hoarders; they have voracious appetites for one's time. While they are fun if one can control the way we use them as tools of recreation, when they begin to control one's choices and one's time, they could be very detrimental to one's happiness and well-being. We can't just blame these companies who go about manipulating us in ways that one gets addicted to their products. That is their job. They find reasons to give us doses of dopamine highs. Studies have shown that the highs we get from 'likes' and game rewards all release small doses of dopamine in our brain. That's the reason we get addicted and desire more. This high is similar to what sugars in processed food and drinks have done, and continue to do.

The ICMR, Indian Council for Medical Research, recently concluded a year-long study on close to 3,000 subjects in the age group of 18-40 years in select urban communities across India. The study found alarming levels of technology dependence. India's premier mental health hospital, The National Institute of Mental Health and Neurosciences, has seen a steady stream of parents seeking treatment for their teenagers' obsession with social networking, instant chatting, texting, and mobile gaming. The issues arriving at their doorstep are wide-ranging, but predominantly, technology addiction (or internet addiction) has now been recognized by mental health professionals as similar to addiction disorders related to the consumption of drugs or alcohol. Excessive engagement in activities involving screen devices, the internet, and social networking sites has been found to be detrimental to our health, social life, and/or mental state. Teenagers are particularly prone to the addiction, which manifests itself in acts like constantly checking instant messaging apps, frequently changing status messages and profile photos on social networks, and uploading selfies daily. In many cases, the addiction leads to insomnia, depression, and social withdrawal.

When one steps back and honestly evaluates their effects on one's happiness, one would see that the happiness generated by electronic gadgets is very brittle and fleeting. So, while one may choose to play a video game or network socially, one should do so within time limits. The limits should be such that one does NOT compromise other important activities that contribute to one's happiness and well-being.

As Ales Ohanian said, "It takes discipline NOT to let social media steal your time". If we are unable to engage and disengage at will, it is better to shun and disengage completely.

It is unfortunate that children have become pawns in the hands of companies that make these electronic devices and applications. They have never had a chance to evaluate what is better for them. They are bombarded by choices that are designed to attract and retain them WITHOUT concern for their well-being. Nowadays, children all over the world are addicted to their mobile devices and tablets. They would RATHER play a video game THAN find joy in playing outdoors in the sun.

It is just a throwback to a few decades earlier when children would RATHER have a sugar-filled soft drink THAN drink plain water. Children would RATHER have packaged fruit juice THAN eat a fruit. Similarly, today's children would RATHER play tennis as a video game than actually hit a ball on the grass court. These choices NOT ONLY affect the health of children BUT also their emotional development. Children have to deal with problems of obesity and insomnia. Even mental health has become a casualty. The rise in prescriptions written for children and increases in aggressive behavior are evidence of the problems at hand.

The Way Out

"Time is more valuable than money. You can get more money, but you cannot get more time."

–Jim Rohn

"While money can't buy happiness, it certainly lets you choose your own form of misery."

– Groucho

It is important for adults and children alike to "Step back" and "Detox". Spending time as a family is critical to our emotional well-being. It is important to focus and practice choosing outdoor activities and spending time in an unhurried atmosphere. World over, people have taken to meditation and physical activities such as *yoga* and *Tai-chi* to find mind and body balance. While this chapter is not meant to be a lecture on how to live, it is important that one makes proper choices that could enhance rather than degrade one's quality of life.

In the words of John C. Maxwell, "Time management is an oxymoron. Time is beyond our control, and the clock keeps ticking regardless of how we lead our lives. Priority management is the answer to maximizing the time we have.".

So, prioritize and make wise choices with YOUR time.

I would conclude by saying that while earning money and investing wisely are important, it is as important to use that money to buy "Time Affluence". On the other hand, we need to reclaim OUR time by detoxing ourselves from our electronic and virtual worlds and prioritizing rightly. This would make the right recipe that could bring balance and happiness in our lives. So, make your choices and make them wisely.

If I were to take the words of Lilian Russell, "It is time to open up a new chapter in life and to explore a larger center."

Time for some FUN

Time for the song ***'Kal Ho Na Ho'*** starring **Shahrukh Khan, Saif Ali Khan,** and **Priety Zinta** from the **Hindi** movie *KHNH,* a.k.a. ***'Kal Ho Na Ho'* (2003).** The Movie was directed by **Nikhil Advani** and produced by **Karan Johar** and **Yash Johar.**

The music is composed by the trio **Shankar-Ehsaan-Loy,** and the playback singer is **Sonu Nigam.** Enjoy!!

SONG

'Kal Ho Na Ho'

('This Story, may not be there Tomorrow')

MOVIE

***'Kal Ho Na Ho'* (2003)**

SCAN above to see **YOUTUBE** ***Video of the Song***

Lyrics **['Kal Ho Na Ho']**	***Translation*** **['This story, may not be there tomorrow']**
Har ghadi badal rahi hai roop zindagi Chaav hai kabhi kabhi hai dhoop zindagi Har pal yahan jee bhar jiyo Jo hai sama, kal ho na ho	Life is changing form every moment Sometime there's shade, at times there is sun Live every moment to the fullest This very moment may not be there tomorrow

Har ghadi badal rahi hai roop zindagi Chaav hai kabhi kabhi hai dhoop zindagi Har pal yahan jee bhar jiyo Jo hai sama, kal ho na ho	Life is changing form every moment Sometime there's shade, at times there is sun Live every moment to the fullest This very moment may not be there tomorrow
Chaahe jo tumhe poore dil se Milta hai woh mushkil se Aisa jo koi kahin hai Bas vohi sabse hasin hai	It is very difficult to come by the one who loves you with all her heart If there is someone like that somewhere She is the one who is the most beautiful
Us haath ko tum thaam lo Woh meherbaan kal ho na ho Har pal yahan jee bhar jiyo Jo hai sama kal ho na ho	Take her hand in yours NOW because Time may not be so kind as to wait Live every moment to the fullest This very moment may not be there tomorrow
Palko ke leke saaye Paas koi jo aaye Lakh sambhalo paagal dil ko Dil dhadke hi jaaye	When someone comes as close to your heart as the shadow of your eyes lashes is to your eyes The heart starts beating harder Even when you try to manage it really hard
Par sochlo is pal hai jo Woh dastan kal ho na ho	Do understand and don't take that moment for granted, It may or may not be there tomorrow

Har ghadi badal rahi hai roop zindagi Chaav hai Kabhi Kabhi hai dhoop Zindagi Har pal yahan jee bhar jiyo Jo hai sama kal ho na ho Har pal yahan jee bhar jiyo Jo hai sama kal ho na ho	Life is changing form every moment Sometime there's shade, at times there is sun Live every moment to the fullest This very moment may not be there tomorrow Live every moment to the fullest This very moment may not be there tomorrow

Part II

Chapter 12

INVEST IN EXPERIENCES AND PEOPLE AND NOT IN MATERIAL ACQUISITIONS

How experiences and investing in people trumps material acquisitions and how investing in them increases your happiness manifold

"Materialism is the only form of distraction from true bliss."

– Douglas Horton

"Acquisition means life to miserable mortals."

– Hesiod

For most people, money is a limited resource, and the question that crops up is how to best allocate it so that one can maximize one's happiness. Should we spend it on material acquisitions or on experiences? Material possessions last longer; a holiday would last a week or, at best, ten days, hence most people tend to prefer material possessions. How long do holidays actually last? Could one say material acquisitions are better because they last longer?

When I was dating, one of the questions I would ask my date would be, "Given a bounty of $100,000, how would you spend it? Would you rather buy a new BMW, or would you prefer to go on seven holidays over a seven-year period?" The answer to this question gave me an insight into whether I would like to go out with that person.

If the person said she would rather spend time with me on a holiday than in a BMW, I would go on to think we have matching thought processes. Personally, I value a holiday MORE than a BMW in the garage.

A holiday with one's loved ones would leave one with memories and shared experiences, which would be talking points for decades to come. It could have wonderful or adventurous memories, shared escapades, and all these create bonds that would last one a lifetime. Reliving those wonderful moments and talking about them would also create points of conversation and special bonds, which would make one happier and more complete. Decades later, it's more likely that holiday experiences with photos, videos of the experience could be relived with animated discussions on the experience. Decades later, the memory of a BMW or any other luxury car in the garage would be less exciting. I rest my case.

I believe spending money on experiences contributes to happiness far more than spending on material things. I knew a couple in their 40s who were bickering and on the verge of splitting up. Nevertheless, they decided to go on a holiday together. Two weeks later, they came back arm in arm, unable to get enough of each other. Their closeness and bonding grew with their shared experience. A holiday is something a Mastercard could buy, but the bonding is certainly priceless.

A

'Sanskrit Slokha'

Describing attributes and sources of Happiness

सन्तोषःपरमोलाभःसत्सङ्गःपरमागतिः।
विचारःपरमंज्ञानंशमोहिपरमंसुखम्॥

santōṣaḥ paramō lābhaḥ satsaṅgaḥ paramā gatiḥ ।
vicāraḥ paramaṃ jñānaṃ śamō hi paramaṃ sukham ॥

Meaning:

Contentment is the highest gain, Good Company the highest course,
Enquiry the highest wisdom, and Peace the highest enjoyment.

While I may prefer and independently advise people to spend more on experiences and holidays, I have also found that research points in the same direction. Most people, when given a choice, choose material acquisitions such as jewellery or expensive cars over experiences. This is because most people believe material acquisitions last longer than a one-off experience. This is a very logical conclusion, indeed, yet the assumption on which the conclusion is based is actually flawed. Research suggests that spending on trips, concerts, activities, and dine-outs provides one with greater joy and satisfaction, which lasts longer.

One of the elements of human nature to consider is one's ability to get accustomed and to adapt. While new things make one happy, they do so only for a while. They are exciting at first, but then, one adapts to them and gets used to them quickly. This diminishes the happiness that one's new acquisitions provided in the beginning. Therefore, most psychologists suggest that it is better to spend our money on experiences. One could go outdoors, visit a beach, go trekking, try hand gliding, do bungee jumping, go fine dining, travel, learn a new language or skill, or visit art exhibits. One has endless options. Indulging in the next big impulsive purchase, like buying the next-generation phone or a luxury sports car, would NOT, however, lead to lasting happiness.

Research has also found that when one makes either a material purchase or buys an experience, the initial excitement is the same. However, over time, people's satisfaction with material things fades and fizzles out. On the contrary, people's satisfaction with experiences goes up. Even though this is counterintuitive—as the material object would remain with one and is in one's possession—it is somewhat like the economic term 'Diminishing Marginal Utility'. This means that the utility derived from the consumption of every additional unit of the same product diminishes; likewise, there is no incremental happiness derived from material objects after a certain point. The 'high' gained from objects is short-lived, and thus, with time, the utility derived begins to decline or diminish. It seldom contributes to one's long-term happiness. Ironically, the constant presence of the material possession makes it easier to adapt to and makes it less exciting.

On the other hand, when one makes a sojourn to a tropical island or enjoys a weekend hike, it gets etched in one's memory and becomes a bigger part of one's identity, while material possessions actually remain outside of us, just taking up space that one gets accustomed to. Ultimately, one is really the SUM TOTAL of one's experiences and NOT one's possessions.

Experiences are also invaluable as they form bonds and could also become reasons for animated discussions. They kindle associations and fire relationships with people around us. One is more likely to connect with someone because one took a vacation together to Greece than to connect with someone because one bought them an expensive phone or watch. People bond over experiences that they discuss. A discussion on the trek up the Himalayas is far more interesting as a topic of conversation than, say, the new 'curvy television' that one had bought.

Moreover, the phenomenon of "keeping up with the Joneses" causes negative comparative benchmarks. When we compare material things, one realizes that they DO NOT contribute to our overall happiness in any way.

Research done and published by Gilovich and Amit Kumar in the academic journal of 'Experimental Social Psychology' confirms these observations. It would hence be smart to allocate one's limited resources towards experiencing new things rather than material possessions.

That's why one needs to take that vacation and go out and spend time experiencing new things, rather than getting stuck with one's PlayStations playing mindless games. One should maximize one's happiness and do so smartly.

Investing in people

The other important thing is investing in people. There was once a picture I saw in a publication. One side of the picture depicted hell and the other half portrayed heaven. Actually, there was virtually no difference BETWEEN the two. Both sides had people dining at a table and being served with bowls of soup. Both halves of the picture had diners who were given soup spoons with really long stems.

The DIFFERENCE, however, was that in the half portraying hell, the diners were busy trying to consume their soup using their long spoons, and it was hell. It was painfully difficult and downright impossible to feed oneself. The long stems of the spoon made scooping the soup and eating it a nightmare, and thus the people in hell were miserable and hungry. In the picture of heaven, everything was the same, EXCEPT that the diners, INSTEAD of feeding themselves, fed the person opposite to them, and it was all harmony and sweet.

A

'Sanskrit Slokha'

Describing Generosity

गौरवंप्राप्यतेदानात्नतुवित्तस्यसञ्चयात्।
स्थितिरुच्चैःपयोदानांपयोधीनामधःस्थितिः॥

gauravaṃ prāpyatē dānāt na tu vittasya sañcayāt ।
sthitiruccaiḥ payōdānāṃ payōdhīnāmadhaḥ sthitiḥ ॥

Meaning:

Respectability comes NOT from collecting BUT from giving
Hence Clouds (attain) a higher position and the Oceans, a lower one.

The allegory of the long spoons is a parable, a folklore that has become part of many cultures: Jewish, Hindu, Buddhist, Christian, and is narrated with variations. It speaks of people and our interdependence. When one is selfish and thinks only of self-gratification without acknowledging or recognizing the other, one would only hurt oneself and build misery and pain. It is here on earth that one could make one's heaven when one empathizes, learns to be considerate, and thinks of our fellow beings.

To stand alone, as an island, one would slowly perish without nourishment for one's inner self. However, when one builds ties and real relationships, which are beyond mere courtesy, one would then build a sense of community that nurtures one another. Having a serving mentality and valuing your neighbor does have its paybacks to one as an individual and to society as a whole.

Time for some FUN

Time for the song **'Wonderful World'** by **American** R&B singer-songwriter **Sam Cooke** from his album **'The Wonderful World of Sam Cooke' (1960).** Enjoy!!

'(What A) Wonderful World'

Sam Cooke, [Album **'The Wonderful World of Sam Cooke' (1960)]**

SCAN above to see **YOUTUBE** ***Video of the Song***

Lyrics

[(What A) Wonderful World]

Don't know much about history
Don't know much biology
Don't know much about a science book
Don't know much about the French I took
But I do know that I love you
And I know that if you love me, too
What a wonderful world this would be

Don't know much about geography
Don't know much trigonometry
Don't know much about algebra
Don't know what a slide rule is for
But I do know that one and one is two
And if this one could be with you
What a wonderful world this would be.

I don't claim to be an 'A' student
But I'm tryin' to be
For maybe by being an 'A'-student, baby
I can win your love for me

Don't know much about history
Don't know much biology
Don't know much about a science book
Don't know much about the French I took
But I do know that I love you
And I know that if you love me, too
What a wonderful world this would be (La, ta, ta, tata, ta, ta)

History (Hmmmm)
Biology (Woah, la, ta, ta, tata, ta, ta)
Science book (Hmmmm)
French I took (Yeah)
But I do know that I love you,
And I know that if you love me, too
What a wonderful world this would be

Part II

Chapter 13

LESS GREED, MORE PASSION

Choose 'Financial Freedom' and NOT 'Financial Freedom'

Why you should set aside greed and live life according to your passions

"O gentlemen, the time of life is short!
To spend that shortness basely were too long,
If life did ride upon a dial's point,
Still ending at the arrival of an hour."

– ***Shakespeare*** *(Henry IV, Act 5, Scene 2)*

"Your time is limited, so don't waste it living someone else's life. Don't be trapped by dogma – which is living with the results of other people's thinking. Don't let the noise of others' opinions drown out your own inner voice. And most important, have the courage to follow your heart and intuition."

– Steve Jobs

"...not doing what we love in the name of greed is very poor management of our lives."

– Warren Buffett

No billionaire in the world is going to carry his/her bank balance or assets with him/her when his/her time is up. Everyone is EQUAL in death. It always makes one wonder at the pointless scorekeeping, when one's life is much richer when looked at holistically.

The Result of 'Financial Freedom'

The famous work by Russian author Leo Tolstoy, 'How Much Land Does a Man Require?' is apt for today's time. In that story, a group of rich landlords, landowners known as Bashkirs, tell a peasant named Pahom that for a thousand roubles he could have as much land as he wants. There was a catch, though: Pahom had to circle the land he wanted and return to the starting point by sunset. He would only accrue the land that he could walk around from sunrise to sunset.

Pahom starts out at dawn and covers vast swathes of land, running all through the day. He arrived at the starting point at dusk only to drop dead. He was then buried in a grave six feet in length, WHICH ironically answered the question posed by the title of the short story by Leo Tolstoy. As simple as the story is, it carries the powerful message that GREED burns and destroys one's valuable and intangible possessions. In turn, it finally comes back to destroy us.

While money is a definite need, as laid out in the chapter 'Why Finances Are Like Oxygen', too much greed for it could slowly kill off one's intangible wealth: like our health, family relationships, friendships, one's passions, and ultimately our happiness. It is therefore important for one to take a step back and understand how much one really needs and why one would need that much. This could provide one with a better perspective and would stop one's blind pursuit of material possessions. The mindless pursuit of mere monetary wealth would not only limit one's happiness, it could also harm one back.

Following one's Passion

"A runner must run with dreams in his heart, not money in his pocket."

– Emil Zatopek

"I learned from a very young age that if I pursued the things that truly excited me that they would reward in more important ways, like happiness."

– Brandon Boyd

To feel complete, one definitely needs to find a calling. We are most happy in one's purposeful journey that we set for ourselves. It is the most important thing we could do for ourselves to sustain our drive and happiness. Very often, following one's passion may involve making some initial sacrifices. Yet the rewards reaped give one a sense of achievement. The exhilaration gained from having accomplished something, in terms of happiness and contentment, would make the journey well worth it.

To quote Ellen DeGeneres, "I say always follow your passion, no matter what, because even if it's not the same financial success, it'll lead you to the money that'll make you the happiest".

Once, I was at a famous outlet dealing with electronic goods. The owner, who was a hefty and relatively obese gentleman, was seated near the cashier's desk, monitoring all the cash transactions that were being made. He had been doing this for decades, reporting to work right from his younger days until today. He made tons of money in the process, working long hours with very few days off. He was still at it, accumulating wealth at an increasing pace. However, his health was deteriorating at an equally rapid rate. He heaved and panted as he stood up to have a closer look at some of the transactions. He lost his temper at employees, who cowered in fright and helplessness. It made one wonder: why was he so clued into making money when what he should be doing is taking care of his health? Well, the answer was greed. It would have been best if he had considered other aspects of his life that would have made him holistically richer than just the accumulation of wealth.

Money can take one up to a certain point in life; beyond that, the baton is to be handed over to better sense and passion to guide us through our lives.

To quote Pablo Picasso, "Never permit a dichotomy to rule your life, a dichotomy in which you hate what you do so you can have pleasure in your spare time. Look for a situation in which your work will give you as much happiness as your spare time.".

Blessed are those who understand that and those who have the wherewithal to follow up on it. The rest of us will just trudge along, dragging our lives through a desert, searching for that elusive oasis and hoping it isn't a mirage that has been drawing us in endlessly.

Most people are in a rat race, running on the treadmill of life, too scared to get off. One needs to ask honest questions to oneself, and by introspecting, one could truly understand what one would really like to do. Of course, it is easier when one attains the threshold of 'Financial Freedom', and the first half of the book could help one accomplish that. One can and should dream. Following one's passion is one's rightful path to happiness. One's responsibilities and one's work have always made up for one's time. Many who have attained financial freedom still fear making the change. It is important for one to introspect and to understand what is holding one back. This inner inquiry should be guided by one's heart, while the chatter around us should be ignored. We need to listen to our inner voice, as it would have something to say about our aspirations and our intrinsic self-worth.

Conclusion

"Success is not the key to happiness. Happiness is the key to success. If you love what you are doing, you will be successful. "

– Albert Schweitzer

"I always was a rich person because money's not related to happiness."

– Paulo Coelho

One is rich NOT because one has a billion dollars, but because one has a billion dreams. Live your dreams when you can, and do it now! Drop greed and embrace your passions. One day, when you do look back, you will feel complete and bask in the warm glow reflected from the rich, interesting, and happy life lived. So, fill your life with things you want to do. The time is NOW!

Time for some FUN

Time for a song written by **Savan Kotecha** and producer **Rami Yacoub,** titled **'What Makes You Beautiful'.**

The song is performed by the **English-Irish** boy band **One Direction.** The song is their debut single and their lead single from their debut studio album, **'Up All Night' (2011).** Enjoy!!

'What Makes You Beautiful'

One Direction, [Album **'Up All Night' (2011)**]

SCAN above to see **YOUTUBE** ***Video of the Song***

Lyrics

[What Makes You Beautiful]

You're insecure, don't know what for
You are turning heads when you walk through the door
Don't need makeup to cover up
Being the way that you are is enough

Everyone else in the room can see it
Everyone else, but you, ooh

Baby, you light up my world like nobody else
The way that you flip your hair gets me overwhelmed
But when you smile at the ground, it ain't hard to tell
You don't know, oh-oh
You don't know you're beautiful

If only you saw what I can see
You'll understand why I want you so desperately
Right now I'm lookin' at you, and I can't believe

You don't know, oh-oh
You don't know you're beautiful, oh, oh-oh
That's what makes you beautiful

So c-come on, you got it wrong
To prove I'm right, I put it in a song
I don't know why you're being shy
And turn away when I look into your eyes

Everyone else in the room can see it
Everyone else, but you, ooh

Baby, you light up my world like nobody else
The way that you flip your hair gets me overwhelmed
But when you smile at the ground, it ain't hard to tell
You don't know, oh-oh
You don't know you're beautiful

If only you saw what I can see
You'll understand why I want you so desperately
Right now I'm lookin' at you, and I can't believe

You don't know, oh-oh
You don't know you're beautiful, oh, oh-oh
That's what makes you beautiful

Na-na-na, na-na-na, na, na, na
Na-na-na, na-na-na
Na-na-na, na-na-na, na, na, na
Na-na-na, na-na-na

Baby, you light up my world like nobody else
The way that you flip your hair gets me overwhelmed
But when you smile at the ground, it ain't hard to tell
(You don't know, oh-oh)
You don't know you're beautiful

Baby, you light up my world like nobody else
The way that you flip your hair gets me overwhelmed
But when you smile at the ground, it ain't hard to tell
You don't know, oh-oh
You don't know you're beautiful

If only you saw what I can see
You'll understand why I want you so desperately
Right now I'm lookin' at you, and I can't believe

You don't know, oh-oh
You don't know you're beautiful, oh, oh-oh
You don't know you're beautiful, oh, oh-oh
That's what makes you beautiful

Part II

Chapter 14

HQ (HAPPINESS QUOTIENT)

How to prioritize and balance the various facets of one's life to derive and maximize one's happiness

"It's good to have money and the things that money can buy, but it's good, too, to check up once in a while and make sure that you haven't lost the things that money can't buy."

– George Lorimer

"You aren't wealthy until you have something money can't buy."

– Garth Brooks

Earlier chapters in this book discussed 'Time Affluence' and why it has to be prioritized over 'Money Affluence', and thus, how it could increase our happiness. Further, the chapter 'The Big Swap' talks about how money and time can be interchanged to achieve our objectives.

Changes in time and outlook are reflected in what we say nowadays: "The Father in his time spent 30 minutes to save $30, but the Son now spends $30 to save 30 minutes". Our priorities should change according to our circumstances. As people are pressured by time constraints, they should find help and swap 'money' for 'time'. Some may also be in a position to swap 'time' for 'money'.

In the chapter 'Recipe for Time Affluence', the discussion veered towards why, in the modern world, we should pick and choose what we wish to spend time on. This could mean fewer electronic gadgets, less of what big corporations want us to do, and more of what we want to do. It also includes a good 'DETOX' from electronic gadgets and more time spent in the real world.

As Napoleon Bonaparte said years ago, "There is one kind of robber whom the law does not strike at, and who steals what is most precious to men: time". So, DO NOT let the big corporations steal your time.

Going back a full circle to the first chapter, we said the essentials for happiness were:

- Health
- Family and Friends
- Financial Freedom

Above all these, our happiness lies in our attitude, the way we handle stress, the way we handle failure, and the way we treat our friends, peers, the less advantaged, or less privileged.

Our attitude, our outlook, also influences the way we are motivated, the way we are driven. It is our attitude and determination that nudge us out of our beds every morning to put on those sneakers and head out for a morning run. We cannot beg, borrow, or steal good health. Our health is made and needs to be maintained by us, and we need to recognize that responsibility and consistently work on maintaining our health. Adequate exercise is a casualty of modern living. Children prefer the indoors to outdoors, virtual games to actual sports, junk food to healthy options. This is a modern phenomenon that is destroying our health and the health of our children.

As John Wanamaker wisely put it, "People who cannot find time for recreation are obliged sooner or later to find time for illness.".

A fine balance of good sleep, wholesome nutritious food, and exercise has to become a consistent part of our lives.

Warren Buffett has said about taking care of oneself, "Imagine that you had a car and that was the only car you'd have for your entire lifetime. Of course, you'd care for it well, changing the oil more frequently than necessary, driving carefully, etc. Now, consider that you only have one mind and one body. Prepare them for life, care for them. You can enhance your mind over time. A person's main asset is themselves, so preserve and enhance yourself".

This is important because it adds up to our financial and our mental well-being. Having good health is the greatest wealth. Even a billion in the bank is no substitute for good health. In fact, such a situation would actually make one feel more miserable.

Family is what you Have

"Peace is the beauty of life. It is sunshine. It is the smile of a child, the love of a mother, the joy of a father, the togetherness of a family. It is the advancement of man, the victory of a just cause, the triumph of truth."

– Menachem Begin

"Family is not an important thing. It's everything."

– Michael J. Fox

Everyone in their lifetime will go through difficult periods. Our ability to navigate those hard times, our mental and emotional stability during those periods, vastly depend on the support that our family provides us with. Even if it weren't a habit, it's never too late to make a habit of spending time with our parents; to listen better and understand the needs of our near and dear, to travel, dine out, visit the beach, or make a meal. These are small memories that we build together. These are the moments that our children will recall when they are old enough to reminisce and experience nostalgia.

As Irina Shayk said, "Nothing is better than going home to family and eating good food and relaxing.".

Those bonds that sustain through time, kindle the sense of warmth and emotional connection, are the intangibles that money cannot buy. Spending money on holidays, in my opinion, is more valuable than a depreciating luxury in the garage. Money spent on our loved ones is money well spent. Yet, most of this requires intent and mind-space more than just money.

Voltaire once said, "Don't think money does everything, or you are going to end up doing everything for money.".

Money is not central to happiness; it only helps in laying out options for you. It is up to you to pick the good options. So, paying attention to family is the second most important thing after good health. What is the use of money if we do not have people whom we want to spend it on? We are rich when we have health and family checked in our favor. We need to nurture them both; they matter.

'Financial Freedom': Your ticket to living your Life on Your terms

"Only the guy who isn't rowing has time to rock the boat."

– *Jean-Paul Sartre*

"Working because you want to, not because you have to is financial freedom."

– *Tony Robbins*

The chapters in this book have widely discussed 'Financial Freedom'. Put another way, 'Financial Freedom' comes from having adequate 'Passive Income'. 'Passive Income' is nothing but 'Residual Income'.

In the words of Steve Fisher, "Residual income is passive income that comes in every month whether you show up or not. It's when you no longer get paid on your personal efforts alone, but you get paid on the efforts of hundreds or even thousands of others and on the efforts of your money! It's one of the keys to financial freedom and time freedom.".

When this 'Residual Income' is adequate to support our living, we will have attained the 'Financial Freedom' to move on and pursue our dreams and passions. Pursuing our passion could unlock our potential, often leading to greater financial security and wealth. Since people are happy doing things they like the best, I would say 'Financial Freedom' is one of the important pillars of contentment and lasting happiness.

Harvard Study on People Living Longer and Happier lives

A Harvard study led by Mr. George Vaillant, which studied a large group of people from youth until old age, tried to figure out what made people live longer and happier lives. While coping ability and ability to deal with others made a significant difference, SIX key factors were found to impact longevity and happiness.

The six factors were

1. **Avoid smoking and alcohol**

   Broadly, it was found that indulging in smoking and alcohol was the No. 1 predictor of bad health. People who smoked heavily were ten times more likely not to be included among the "happy-well". Drinking, on the other hand, not only destroyed health but, over longer periods of time, led to relationships that were poor and less happy. Alcohol abuse was a cause of increased stress, depression, and downward social mobility, often damaging future social supports.

2. **Positive impact of years of education**

   The study found that pursuing more education often led to more self-care, self-awareness, and perseverance. The higher the education, the more likely people were to stop smoking, use alcohol in moderation, eat sensibly, and exercise.

3. **A happy childhood and a good marriage at 50**

   It was found that what goes well and right in childhood predicted the future better than what went wrong. How much someone was loved as a child made a huge difference. It also stated that if one found a loving spouse and a trusted friend in adulthood, even a troubled childhood could heal completely.

4. **Relationships are everything**

   Successful relationships built on the foundation of the right attitude and gratitude were found to be the key. People who aged well gave to others joyously while receiving from others gratefully. People's ability to deal with others and their coping skills were good predictors of longevity and happiness. People's social aptitude and their emotional intelligence played key roles in their ability to build and nurture relationships. Continuing to learn new things and making new friends at age 50 was just as important to good psychosocial aging as emotional maturity.

5. **Coping Skills**

   Having "Mature Defenses" with the ability to respond to painful thoughts and feelings when faced with them had far-reaching and long-term consequences. People who aged best had coped well with something very horrific in their past and handled really stressful situations with grace. The four coping strategies associated with maturity were doing good to others (altruism), the ability to creatively resolve conflict and spin straw into gold, or make lemonade out of life's lemons (sublimation), having patience and seeing the brighter side (suppression), and the ability to NOT take oneself so seriously (humor).

6. **'Generativity'**

   People who focused on building a good life and then on giving back and helping other people with their lives often improved their own happiness and longevity. Ability and willingness to give back and participate in community building were seen in happy people. Acting as a guide, mentor, or coach to younger adults helped to serve society.

   The good thing about the study is that most of these factors are in our control and not in our horoscopes or genes. All these are actionable.

Being Less Cynical

"Cynicism masquerades as wisdom, but it is the farthest thing from it because cynics don't learn anything. Because cynicism is a self-imposed blindness, a rejection of the world because we are afraid it will hurt us or disappoint us."

– Stephen Colbert

"I think the reason I was successful is that I was never cynical."

– Carol Burnett

An old woman who lived by the sea was walking by the shore; the tide had receded and several fish were stranded, gasping and tossing in the sands that were too hot. Few managed to reach the waters, while many were dying, suffocating slowly. The old woman, who was pained by the sight, kept picking up the fish she could reach and threw them back into the waters that had betrayed them. A man who was watching all this unfold walked up to her and spoke, "Dear Lady, why are you doing this?" he asked. "The shore is full of these fish, and you won't be able to save all. How many are you going to pick? This is such a futile exercise; it's not going to make any difference", he said. The woman looked at the man and smiled. She then bent down and picked up another struggling fish, and as she tossed it back into the cool waters, she said, "But it has made a difference to this life, at least."

We may have passions and dreams, yet we may shy away from pursuing them, as we are held back because of our cynicism. We tend to believe we can't change the world, and it is not in our hands.

Whether it is our effort to reach out a helping hand to one person who is needy, sponsoring the education of someone who is underprivileged, planting one tree, one direct action enabling another life toward helping themselves will make a difference to that one life that we have touched. By understanding the interdependence of life, we should at least strive to make a difference to the lives around us. Like the old woman said, it would certainly make a difference to that one being that we reached out to.

The Power of a Smile

"Nothing you wear is more important than your smile."

– Connie Stevens

"Smile, it is the key that fits the lock of everybody's heart."

–Anthony J. D'Angelo

There is an airline in INDIA that I often fly in. The CEO of that airline is a champion campaigner who often reiterates to his employees and air hostesses to smile often and serve with a smile. In contrast, there is a competing airline that provides better service, but the air hostesses are grumpy. Guess which airline I fly in?

There is a name for people who carry the weight of the world on their shoulders and have expressions that are grim and burdened. I call them "Atlas".

Atlas Telamon, or "enduring Atlas" in Greek mythology, is condemned to bear the weight of the sky on his shoulders. So do not think you are bearing the burden of the entire universe on your shoulders. Refuse to be an "Atlas" and smile.

When we smile, we communicate a positive energy that is infectious and spreads the joy around. It changes the mood of both the beholder and the beholden and sends positive vibrations through our little universe. So lastly, do smile, as it's God's gift to humanity. It is good for our health, mood, and pocket, and it also changes the atmosphere around us in our favor.

As Tom Wilson said

"A smile is happiness you'll find right under your nose."

Time for some FUN

A fun song to set the mood as we end the chapter, from the title track of the **Tamil** movie ***'Alaipayuthey'*** (2000), starring actor **R. Madhavan.**

The movie is directed by **Mani Ratnam,** while the music is composed by **A. R. Rahman** (with a hint of 'The Backstreet Boys'). Enjoy!!

SONG

'Enendrum Punnaigai'

(Always a Smile)

MOVIE

'Alaipayuthey' **(2000)**

SCAN above to see **YOUTUBE** ***Video of the Song***

Lyrics **['Enendrum Punnaigai']**	***English Translation*** **[Always a Smile]**
Enrendrum punnagai Mudivilla punnagai Indru naan meendum meendum Piranden oru thuli paarvaiyilae [x2]	Always Smiling A Smile (in joy) that is everlasting Now, I was born again and again To catch that ONE small glimpse (of you) [x2]

Ohhhhhhhh.. Enuyirae	Ohhhhhhhh....(equivalent to) My life
Ohhhhhhhh.. Enuyirae	Ohhhhhhhh....(equivalent to) My life
Ohhhhhhhh.. Enuyirae	Ohhhhhhhh....(equivalent to) My life
Oh..ohhhhhhhh.. Enuyirae	Oh..ohhhhhhhh....(equivalent to) My life
Dheem dheem thanana	(Humming)..Dheem dheem thanana
Dheem thananana	Dheem thananana
Ohooo vaanamae Ellaiyo	Ohooo..is the sky the Limit?
Dheem dheem thanana	(Humming)..Dheem dheem thanana
Dheem thananana	...Dheem thananana
Ohooo kaadhalae Ellaiyo [x2]	Ohooo ...has love got any Limits?? [x2]
(Rap) Hey.. here we go	**(Rap) Hey.. here we go**
I revved up on the marches	**I revved up on the marches**
Singing with the hip-the-hop	**Singing with the hip-the-hop**
Once again in effect	**Once again in effect**
Feel the constant	**Feel the constant**
Slamming of the bassline	**Slamming of the bassline**
Never mess around	**Never mess around**
With the funk	**With the funk**
Because I'm sticking	**Because I'm sticking**
Kicking always finger lickin	**Kicking always finger lickin**
I don't need halloween	**I don't need halloween**
Just to be trick or trippin	**Just to be trick or trippin**
Cause I'm always on top	**Cause I'm always on top**
(Humming)...Ki wiggudu waggudu	**(Humming)...Ki wiggudu waggudu**
Jiggudu joganna	**Jiggudu joganna**
Hey wassup..	**Hey wassup..**
Enrendrum punnagai	Always Smiling
Mudivilla punnagai	A Smile (in joy) that is everlasting
Indru naan meendum meendum	Now, I was born again and again
Piranden oru thuli paarvaiyilae	To catch that ONE small glimpse (of you)

Ohhhhhhhh.. Enuyirae Ohhhhhhhh.. Enuyirae Ohhhhhhhh.. Enuyirae Oh..ohhhhhhhh.. Enuyirae	Ohhhhhhhh....(equivalent to) My life Ohhhhhhhh....(equivalent to) My life Ohhhhhhhh....(equivalent to) My life Oh..ohhhhhhhh....(equivalent to) My life
Dheem dheem thanana Dheem thanananа Ohooo vaanamae Ellaiyo Dheem dheem thanana Dheem thanananа Ohooo kaadhalae Ellaiyo [x2]	(Humming)..Dheem dheem thanana Dheem thanananа Ohooo..is the sky the Limit? Dheem dheem thanana (Humming) ...Dheem thanananа Ohooo ...has love got any Limits?? [x2]

The remake of ***'Enendrum Punnaigai'*** (from the Tamil movie ***'Alaipayuthey'*** **(2000)**) is ***'Humdum Suniyo re'*** (in Hindi from the movie ***'Saathiya'*** **(2002)**). The song is the title track of the movie and stars **Vivek Oberoi.** The music is by **A R Rahman.** Enjoy!!

Hindi Remake of Movie and Song as below
SONG ***'Humdum Suniyo re'*** **(Listen my Love)** MOVIE ***'Saathiya'*** **(2000)**  **SCAN** above to see **YOUTUBE** ***Video of the Song***

Part III

The THREE Pillars of SOCIETY

KNOWLEDGE, WEALTH & POWER

Part III

Chapter 1

THE THREE PILLARS OF THE SOCIETAL CONSTRUCT

The way the THREE Pillars of the societal construct are established often determines the fate of that society

"The poor and the rich quarrel with one another, and whichever side gets the better, instead of establishing a just or popular government, regard political supremacy as the prize of victory."

– Aristotle

"Some men see things as they are and say why. I dream things that never were and say why not."

– Bobby Kennedy

THREE Pillars of Society

There are 3 major pillars or engines of society namely:

i. Knowledge
ii. Wealth
iii. Power

If one takes any civilization, from any part of the world, and at any point in time, one would find these three pillars were structured in a certain way to presumably do the best for society. However, the fate of that society often hinged on how these three pillars were structured and how they withstood the ravages of time.

To quote Ray Dalio (from his book 'The Changing World Order'):

"The biggest thing affecting most people in most countries through time is the struggle to make, take, and distribute wealth and power, though they also have struggled over other things too, most importantly ideology and religion."

Typically, throughout history, people who owned the means of production were the wealthy ones. They in turn, needed to work with the people who had the political power to keep order. This symbiotic relationship is common across countries and civilizations in time. In early times, agricultural land and livestock were the basis for the means of production, and therefore, the wealth.

In early Europe, the wealth was a monopoly of the 'Nobles', who owned the (agricultural) land, while the 'Monarchs' maintained political power. The 'Clergy', on the other hand, helped in lending legitimacy to the monarchs, while presumably keeping order and harmony in society.

It is to be noted, though, that the monopoly of wealth and power was confined to a very small percentage of the population. This small minority controlled exceptionally large percentages of wealth and power. This left out large swathes of the population, who did not have a say in this setup.

In times when this privilege was taken for granted and got overextended, it led to rebellion and serious conflict. Often, society plunged into unrest, revolutions, and/or civil wars. This has played out across civilizations and across time.

In India, the societal system that came into being was similar to what happened in Europe. 'Birth' ended up being the criteria that decided one's position, privilege, wealth, and status in society. Similar to the feudal system comprising Nobles and Vassals, with the Clergy and the Monarchs completing the socio-economic stratification, as in Europe, the 'caste system' took root in India. Whether this was incidental or intentional is irrelevant. What is relevant, however, is whether these systems did a great disservice to that society and humanity as a whole?

Often, a system that decides one's position and role in society based on birth would fail to maximise its societal and human potential. When power, wealth and knowledge is privileged based on birth it ends up being a double whammy. A double whammy when one considers that with time such a system leads to mistrust, disenchantment, turmoil and even conflict. This sadly wasted the societal potential TWICE over.

The 'Caste System' Experiment in INDIA and Why did it fail?

While the original objective of the caste system in India was to encourage specializations and prevent a SINGLE group from enjoying all privileges of society, namely 'Power', 'Knowledge', and 'Wealth', it led to major problems.

While one group was to enjoy 'Power', the second group was to enjoy 'Knowledge', and the third group was to enjoy 'Wealth', NO assigned group was to enjoy all three and have a monopoly over society.

While on the face of it, it seemed to be a system where ALL the societal advantages were NOT held by only ONE group of people, the system also led to the formation of groups that enjoyed NEITHER 'Power', 'Knowledge', nor 'Wealth' and were bereft as victims of oppression. Moreover, it failed to allow a person to choose his or her profession based on natural proclivity and talents. This innately was a huge disservice to society. In the long run, such a system did not allow for the society to harness the strengths of its inhabitants to the fullest extent.

For instance, the knowledge of metallurgy was confined to a closed group of blacksmiths and transmitted orally to the long line of blacksmiths in the family. There were THREE key problems that this created.

The FIRST is that the knowledge was easily lost over the centuries; the SECOND was that, without the ability to disseminate the knowledge, it was not built on or furthered with the collective knowledge or wisdom of the larger population; the THIRD was that, if the knowledge was to be kept confined within a group, mass production of goods was not possible.

All these factors led to the demise of an amazing golden period in the history of the world, where, while several inventions and innovations were created, many of them perished due to the limitations brought on by the social hierarchies.

> While there are many evils in the caste system, this aspect alone is highlighted to show how society limited progress and hurt itself. When the ability to transmit knowledge to the masses is hindered, it precludes the abilities of the larger populace and its capacity to evolve and develop a larger knowledge base for the advancement of humankind. Education, by nature, has to be disseminated to a larger group who could gain and later contribute to it.
>
> This is why the innovation of the 'Printing Press', which came much later, was the ground-breaking innovation that first broke through this challenge for the dissemination of knowledge.

These feudal systems or caste-based systems FOCUSED on maintaining privileges. These feudal or caste-based system often failed to recognise the potential of EVERY human being based on their individual strengths and motivations. These societal constructs failed to recognise them as individual entities, who had natural interests, inclinations, and talents to contribute to society and mankind.

To cut to the chase, the basic problem with these societal systems that took hold was that they not only did great injustice by preventing a large portion of the population from attaining their inherent potentials, but also, the fact that the reward systems inherent in these societal constructs were a recipe for turmoil. This often, led to great conflict and consequently great distress.

The THREE pillars of the societal construct, however, have their roles. Knowledge was meant to bring out human ingenuity and is the magic seed that grows into the tree of prosperity. Wealth was meant to be an enabler and act as a force multiplier. Power was meant to act as a stabilizer to keep order and harmony for the smooth functioning of society. If managed well, everyone in society would benefit, and society would see harmony and prosperity.

However, if knowledge becomes a privilege, while wealth becomes a barometer for exclusivity, and power is used as a tool of oppression, it would only end badly for that society.

Society is always in flux, and in this context, 'change is the only constant'. Hence, society needs to constantly allow for adaptations with time while simultaneously maintaining a balance.

A fair, meritorious, and inclusive societal construct with the 3-engines firing in order and acting in harmony, is the recipe for peace, wealth, and prosperity. Often, adapting the systems along the way would allow one to stay the course.

"An **evolution in time** is **less painful** than **a revolution** in **the end."**

Time for some FUN

Time for the song **'Stayin Alive',** from the motion picture soundtrack, **'Saturday Night Fever' (1977).** The song is performed by the **Australian** music group **'Bee Gees',** comprised of the brothers **Barry, Robin,** and **Maurice Gibb**. Enjoy!!

'Stayin Alive'

Bee Gees, [Motion Picture Soundtrack **'Saturday Night Fever' (1977)]**

SCAN above to see **YOUTUBE** ***Video of the Song***

Lyrics

[Stayin Alive]

Well, you can tell by the way I use my walk
I'm a woman's man, no time to talk
Music loud and women warm
I've been kicked around since I was born

And now it's all right, that's okay
You may look the other way
We can try to understand
The New York Times' effect on man

Whether you're a brother or whether you're a mother
You're stayin' alive, stayin' alive
Feel the city breakin' and everybody shakin'
And you're stayin' alive, stayin' alive
Ah, ah, ah, ah, stayin' alive, stayin' alive
Ah, ah, ah, ah, stayin' alive
Oh, when you walk

Well, now I get low and I get high
And when I can't get either, I really try
Got the wings of heaven on my shoes
I'm a dancin' man and I just can't lose

You know, it's all right, it's okay
I'll live to see another day
We can try to understand
The New York Times' effect on man

Whether you're a brother or whether you're a mother
You're stayin' alive, stayin' alive
Feel the city breakin' and everybody shakin'
And you're stayin' alive, stayin' alive
Ah, ah, ah, ah, stayin' alive, stayin' alive
Ah, ah, ah, ah, stayin' alive

Life goin' nowhere, somebody help me
Somebody help me, yeah
Life goin' nowhere
Somebody help me, yeah
Stayin' alive
Well, you can tell by the way I use my walk
I'm a woman's man, no time to talk
Music loud and women warm
I've been kicked around since I was born

And now it's all right, it's okay
You may look the other way
We can try to understand
The New York Times' effect on man

Whether you're a brother or whether you're a mother
You're stayin' alive, stayin' alive
Feel the city breakin' and everybody shakin'
And you're stayin' alive, stayin' alive
Ah, ah, ah, ah, stayin' alive, stayin' alive
Ah, ah, ah, ah, stayin' alive

Life goin' nowhere, somebody help me
Somebody help me, yeah
Life goin' nowhere
Somebody help me, yeah
I'm stayin' alive [x4]

Part III

Chapter 2

KNOWLEDGE: 'IT'S A KIND OF MAGIC'

[The First Pillar of Society and Magic Seed]

The Infinite Power of Human Ingenuity

"Where the mind is without fear and the head is held high
Where knowledge is free
Where the world has not been broken up into fragments
By narrow domestic walls
Where words come out from the depth of truth
Where tireless striving stretches its arms towards perfection
Where the clear stream of reason has not lost its way
Into the dreary desert sand of dead habit
Where the mind is led forward by thee
Into ever-widening thought and action
Into that heaven of freedom, my Father, let my country awake."

– *Rabindranath Tagore*

"Technology has the ability to democratize knowledge, to spark explosive growth and bring about progress, by tapping into the potential of every human mind across the world."

– *Author*

"For a knowledge system to be a success, it needs to address 3 major factors namely; relevance, cost, and delivery."

– *Author*

KNOWLEDGE

In early times, 'wealth' (based on agricultural land and livestock) and 'power' were the powerful constructs of society.

With time, as humans began to capitalize on their brain power, knowledge became a significant factor that not only increased wealth, but also projected power.

While knowledge, by itself was powerful, the dissemination of knowledge and exchange of information were even more potent. As time went by, there were breakthroughs that led to greater access and dissemination of knowledge for the masses. Soon, the true power of human ingenuity and knowledge began to be unlocked as barriers began to be broken.

There was a time when knowledge gained or developed was difficult to disseminate. The first attempts to transfer knowledge across society and generations included efforts in the Egyptian Civilization through Hieroglyphs.

Cursive hieroglyphs were used for religious literature and were written on papyrus and wood. While these had their limitations in terms of dissemination, they were, however, the first real organized attempts at preserving and disseminating knowledge over generations.

Egyptian Hieroglyphs

Ancient Egypt developed a formal writing system called 'Egyptian Hieroglyphs'. These had over 1,000 distinct characters combining logographic, syllabic, and alphabetic elements.

The Egyptian hieroglyphic scripts were pre-cursors to the majority of scripts in modern use, most prominently the Latin and Cyrillic scripts (through Greek) and the Arabic script. Hieroglyphics survived well into the Roman period, extending into the 4th century A.D.

With the final closing of pagan temples in the 5th century, knowledge of hieroglyphic writing was lost. Many attempts were made to decipher the hieroglyphics throughout the Middle Ages and the early modern period.

Finally, in the 1820s, Jean-François Champollion, with the help of the Rosetta stone, managed to decipher the hieroglyphic writings.

It is estimated that the known number of words contained in all ancient Egyptian hieroglyphic and hieratic texts numbered approximately over 5 million. If one were to account for duplicates (such as the 'Book of the Dead' and the 'Coffin Texts'), then the approximation would be close to 10 million.

While the earliest written texts were inscribed on birch bark or palm leaves, later ones were on parchment. The *Vedic* texts from India are considered the oldest of the texts, dating back to over two millennia B.C. These books of knowledge were vast compilations and reached their peak in periods spanning the mid-2nd to mid-1st millennium B.C. during the Iron and Bronze Ages.

The Vedic Texts

The transmission of the Vedic texts was oral by tradition, with precision and accuracy maintained through elaborate mnemonic and chanting techniques. These texts were mostly in Sanskrit, often considered the mother of languages, alongside Tamil, which is regarded as the oldest living language in the world. Bearing in mind how vast this body of knowledge was and how consistently it had been transmitted over millennia, it is widely believed that the texts were conveyed in both oral and written forms.

Again, the problem with the oral tradition and limitations of handwritten texts was that they could NOT be WIDELY disseminated. Since knowledge was shared orally, one had to attend a 'Gurukula', a school run by a 'Guru', to partake in the knowledge dissemination. This meant that knowledge did NOT spread easily and remained confined to a smaller privileged group. This led to the 'caste system' in India, where knowledge was passed on from one generation to the next, eventually becoming an inheritance or birth-based system. While attempts were made to reach a larger audience through the establishment of universities in that era, they did NOT have the mass effect desired.

The oldest of these universities were established at *Nalanda, Vikramshila,* and *Taxila* as early as the sixth century B.C. However, these did NOT succeed in breaking the monopoly over knowledge held by a few privileged individuals.

Much later, the groundbreaking innovation of the 'Printing Press' allowed, for the first time in human history, reliable written records in the form of books to be created and disseminated. This mass production enabled the quick and cost-effective production of books.

The 'Printing Press' was as significant an invention in human history as the wheel or the discovery of fire. It shattered a major limitation that had hindered the sharing of knowledge and laid the groundwork for further human progress. To paraphrase the famous quote by the first man on the moon, Neil Armstrong, this was a small step for man but a giant leap for humankind.

The Revolution called the 'Printing-Press'

One of the most powerful and revolutionary inventions in the second millennium was the 'Printing-Press'. The invention of the 'Printing-Press' allowed for knowledge to be widely disseminated and laid the base for great strides to be made for the progress of humanity.

The early technologies to print were prevalent since the *Tang dynasty.* During the early part of the millennium, movable type printing had been invented during the *Song Dynasty* in China and later used during the *Goryeo Dynasty* in Korea, where metal movable type printing was used as early as the 13th century. Woodblock printing based on screw presses was widely used in Europe during the 14th century. Until then, the metal movable type printing technology had been unknown in Europe.

A goldsmith by the name Johannes Gutenberg adapted existing technologies, innovated, and perfected his innovation to mechanize the printing press. It was developed around the year 1440 A.D., and this revolutionized the spread of knowledge and information. Within several decades of the invention, it spread to hundreds of cities in Europe. Its reach went further, and the output from printing presses soon touched hundreds of millions of copies.

As printing presses became popular, sufficient paper needed to be made available. Paper manufacturing processes needed improvement, and new innovations mechanized the manufacturing methods. The introduction of water-powered paper mills replaced handcrafted techniques used by Chinese papermakers. The mechanization of paper making and improvements in printing technology stoked the 'print revolution'.

The Foundation for the 'Education Revolution'

It won't be far-fetched to say that the Renaissance in Europe had been fueled by the arrival of the printing press. A new medium of expression and mass communication called 'The Press' had come into being. This altered the very structure and fabric of society in Europe. It threatened the established wealthy (Nobles), political (Monarchs), and religious (Clergy) order and set the stage for mass reformation.

Literacy spread and broke the stranglehold of the literate elite who until then had dominated over the masses. Furthermore, the 19th century ushered in the era of the steam-powered rotary press, which allowed for mass industrial-scale printing, thus fueling the spread of knowledge and information. This accelerated the progress made in science, technology, and literature, which caused the 'education revolution' over the next two centuries.

The power of education and its dissemination began to take root across the Atlantic in the United States of America, which was then a young nation trying to get its feet wet. A number of 'Land Grant' Universities were set up in the United States, and a large number of public libraries were set up across the United States. While some were state-funded, others were set up by wealthy philanthropists who understood the power of education of the masses.

In the United Kingdom, the state began to fund education in the 19th century. While early education became more democratized, college education was still elusive for most.

However, barriers related to cost and access were still hurdles. Books were mass-printed but remained expensive; libraries had memberships but were sometimes exclusive. The knowledge available was in books, but its dissemination, the cost of training, and the cost of education were still significant barriers, especially in the so-called third world.

The Rise of Electronics and its Impact on Knowledge, Productivity and Empowerment

In the past and for centuries, in the southern state of Tamil Nadu, in South India, the mathematics required for the accounting of agricultural produce was done by a person called the *'Kanukku pillai'* or the 'Village accountant'.

Ledgers were maintained, and calculations were manual. While there were tables and formulas in existence that were put to use as required, the fact remained that calculations were tedious and laborious.

The invention of the 'Slide ruler' made calculations less tedious. It was a boon for engineers and scientists. Other tools, such as 'Logarithmic tables', helped reduce the time of computation. I remember using 'Logarithmic tables' extensively in the late 1980s and 1990s in both school and college. (Schools and colleges did not allow calculators in class in India then.)

Slide rulers and conversion slide rulers were used to convert between measurement systems. Thanks to my Dad being a civil engineer (who had passed out of college in the 1950s), I happened to have access to them.

The Human Computers

'Hidden Figures'

[How Black Women Did the Math That Put Men on the Moon]

Author Margot Lee Shetterly (a native of Hampton in the state of Virginia, USA), in her book released in 2016, tells the story of the black women who worked tirelessly as human computers and behind the scenes to help the United States win the Space Race against the Soviets in the 1950s and 1960s.

Ms. Margot, who was the daughter of a former Langley scientist, narrates the story in her book 'Hidden Figures: The American Dream and the Untold Story of the Black Women Who Helped Win the Space Race'. The book follows the lives of three black women mathematicians, namely Katherine Johnson, Dorothy Vaughan, and Mary Jackson, who worked as computers (then a job description) at *NACA* and *NASA* during the space race.

These enterprising women played the role of human computers, writing the extensive equations that kept the craft in orbit. One of these black women, Katherine Johnson, played a pivotal role in the calculations that took Senator and Astronaut John Glenn's craft to orbit. This turned out to be a pivotal moment in the space race between the United States and the Soviet Union.

This was also the time when electronic computers were taking over much of the task of calculating the necessary numbers involved in the increasingly complex space missions.

However, even in that moment of transition from the 'human computers' to the 'electronic computers', there was an iconic handoff moment when Senator and Astronaut John Glenn actually asked for "the girls" to double check the computations of the electronic computer manually. John Glenn trusted 'the girls' (human computers) rather than the program on the electronic computer in its early days. Such was the role that these women played in making sure all key parts of the mission were in order and in its success.

On February 20, 1962, astronaut and Senator Mr. John H. Glenn became the first American to orbit the Earth during the three-orbit Mercury-Atlas 6 mission aboard the spacecraft he named Friendship 7.

Ms. Margot's non-fiction book was adapted into the film 'Hidden Figures', starring Taraji P. Henson (as the mathematician Katherine Johnson), Octavia Spencer (as Dorothy Vaughan, who was an African-American mathematician who worked for NASA in 1949), and Janelle Monáe (as Mary Jackson, the first female African-American engineer to work for NASA).

Texas Instruments was the first to invent the handheld electronic calculator in 1967 and subsequently improved it in the early 1970s. It may surprise most people to realize that, barely 50 years ago, even a handheld electronic calculator was considered a novelty.

As the World Turns

On his visits to China in the mid-1980s, Mr.Ray Dalio (Co-Chief Investment Officer and Co-Chairman of the famous hedge fund *'Bridgewater Associates'*) stated that he took hand-held calculators costing $10 each as gifts for the high-ranking people in power whom he was scheduled to meet.

> The people receiving the gift of the $10 hand-held calculator were astonished, grateful, and delighted by the simple and (now) humble calculator. But this was then, and now when you think of where China is in terms of going from being a beginner in electronics to being a leader in 'AI' (artificial intelligence), it would simply astonish most observers.
>
> It will be good to keep in mind that the world does spin on its axis every 24 hours!

While handheld calculators were considered a novelty in the early 1970s, it didn't take much longer for scientific calculators, graphic calculators, and even financial calculators (I only encountered a financial calculator in 2003) to gain popularity.

'Mainframe Computers', courtesy of *IBM,* and 'Desktop Computers', thanks to *Apple,* made swift entries into the scene. *Microsoft* revolutionized the 'Desktop operating system' with *Windows,* and the 'Internet browser', with *Netscape,* quickly began capturing the public's imagination.

'The Information Super Highway'

As the internet created a storm, telecom companies rushed to lay infrastructure for the backbone of the internet; the force was unstoppable. Companies like *Google* and *Amazon* surfed the power that was the internet, and the rest, as they say, is history.

I would often say that the coming of the internet was a 'new dawn'. The Information superhighway built on the back of the internet boom allowed for information to be disseminated over the *World Wide Web* and across the globe to reach people in far-off regions who were otherwise disconnected. Most of the world was now armed with the tools for connectivity and had access to information which until then they had been excluded from. Well YES, in terms of access to this knowledge, the world had truly begun to shrunk.

Vast bodies of information were now available to anyone who had a web connection to search and find. The establishment of search engines such as *Google* truly allowed for information on the web to be indexed so that they could be searched for and found. It had truly revolutionized and opened doors to what was impossible.

It is to be noted that the world has moved into another era. We are well into the internet and mobile revolution. Any information on any subject can be obtained in a jiffy, and there is no value in storing all the data and information in one's head. Rather than memorizing without comprehension, efforts can be better channeled towards training people to find information, collate, analyze, and draw deductions from the informational data.

The Mobile Phone Revolution

At the turn of the century, a new and quite revolutionary era driven by the 'mobile phone' with *Nokia, Blackberry,* and *Motorola* was beginning to open a world of new possibilities. The computing device called the mobile was beginning to fit in the palm of the hand of the consumer, and at a price point that was within reach for the then-excluded many.

At the peak of the feature phone revolution, a technologist-cum-entrepreneur asked me who I thought was the 'largest computer company' in the world (at that point in time). As I hesitated for a moment, lost in thought, he said, *Nokia*, as he sat back with a satisfied smug. He was right; the biggest computing company in the world at that point was *Nokia*, indeed.

Not for long though, as within less than a decade, (at the height of the internet and feature phone revolution), a new power in the form of the smart phone had been unleashed. *Apple* with its *'iPhone'* ignited a new fire that consumed the competition and gave impetus to the 'smartphone revolution'.

The *Android* (*Google*-owned) and *iOS* (*Apple*-owned) operating systems rode the wave of the power of the smartphone, unleashing a tsunami of 'Apps' and dreams. A number of 'smartphone makers' fought for market share as they drove down the prices of these phones, even as their features and offerings exploded.

Now, why is this story important? The story simply tells one a story of the empowerment of mankind. How the continuous waves of innovation and enterprise, when put to scale, unleashed new opportunities. It forever changed how information and data moved around our planet.

When we now connect the dots, we begin to see the emergence of a NEW World. The democratization of access to knowledge and information has led to the empowerment of billions of people around the world.

The AI (Artificial Intelligence) Revolution

As I write this piece, the AI (Artificial Intelligence) revolution is exploding and beginning to challenge everything we have known. The 'leap of productivity' and the 'intensity and volume' of information that will be accessed, analyzed, and presented to us in distilled form will add a layer of 'computation and intelligence' that will simply take humanity to another level (provided, of course, it doesn't spiral out of control).

The first time I heard of a real-world application of Artificial Intelligence was when my professor (during my Masters in Engg.) at ISU handed out to all students in class a newspaper article about a company that made a billion-dollar IPO in the 1990s. The company made supply chains of companies more efficient by using intelligent software powered by AI. This saved millions of dollars for the companies involved, making this company worth billions of dollars on listing.

The company that made the IPO was *i2 Technologies*. That was close to three decades ago. If that was possible then, just imagine what is possible now. Everything you touch, see, or hear will use AI in the coming future at a level of computation and presentation that will boost human productivity, liberate humans from drudgery, and elevate them to levels that cannot be easily fathomed at the moment.

A

'Sanskrit Slokha'

<u>Describing the Importance of 'Knowledge and Skill'</u>

धान्यानामुत्तमंदाक्ष्यंधनानामुत्तमंश्रुतम्।
लाभानांश्रेयआरोग्यंसुखानांतुष्टिरुत्तमा॥ - Source - Mahabharat vanparva

dhānyānāmuttamaṃ dākṣyaṃ dhanānāmuttamaṃ śrutam ।
lābhānāṃ śrēya ārōgyaṃ sukhānāṃ tuṣṭiruttamā ॥

Meaning:

Skill is superior to Material things. Knowledge is superior to Wealth. Health is superior to Profits and Contentment is the best form of Happiness.

Conclusion

"I want to break free."

– Freddie Mercury of Queen
[lyrics by bassist John Deacon], The Works (1984)

"It's a Kind of Magic."

– Freddie Mercury of Queen
[original lyrics by Roger Taylor], A Kind of Magic (1986)

'Humanity progresses only at the rate at which information is exchanged'. The exchange of information allows for knowledge to be built upon and compounded as it criss-crosses the globe.

Technology acts as a catalyst and accelerates growth. It increases the 'pace at which information' is exchanged. Technology, whether it is the computer, internet, mobile, or finally artificial intelligence, has led to the greater intensity of exchange and processing of knowledge, ideas, and information. It can be said that with the dissemination of knowledge, learning, and the exchange of ideas, one would see huge benefits and a quantum leap in the prosperity of humankind.

With AI distilling the information and saving humans time and effort, we are going to see even more acceleration of the processing and exchange of information and consequent learning. This will accelerate and lay the foundation for the explosive growth of humankind, leading to prosperity for all!

When people interact, exchange ideas, trade goods, transfer money, and open themselves to other cultures and possibilities, well, magic happens!!

Time for some FUN

Like **Freddie Mercury** of the **British** band **Queen** sang in the **1980s**, **'A Kind of Magic'** from their album **'A Kind of Magic'.** Scan below for your listening pleasure. Enjoy!!

'A Kind of Magic'

Queen, [Album **'A Kind of Magic' (1986)**]

SCAN above to see **YOUTUBE** ***Video of the Song***

Lyrics

[A Kind of Magic]

It's a kind of magic
It's a kind of magic
A kind of magic (No way)

One dream, one soul
One prize, one goal
One golden glance of what should be
It's a kind of magic

One shaft of light that shows the way
No mortal man can win this day
It's a kind of magic

The bell that rings inside your mind
Is challenging the doors of time
It's a kind of magic

The waiting seems eternity
The day will dawn of sanity (Ooh ooh ooh ooh)
Is this a kind of magic?
It's a kind of magic

There can be only one
This rage that lasts a thousand years
Will soon be done
This flame that burns inside of me
I'm hearing secret harmonies
It's a kind of magic

The bell that rings inside your mind
Is challenging the doors of time
It's a kind of magic
It's a kind of magic

This rage that lasts a thousand years
Will soon be, will soon be, will soon be done
This is (this is) a kind (a kind) of magic (yeah)
There can be only one (one, one, one)
This rage that lasts a thousand years
Will soon be done (done)

Magic (it's a kind of magic)
It's a kind of magic
Magic magic magic (magic)
(Magic) Aa ha ha haa, it's magic (Magic)
It's a kind of magic

Part III

Chapter 3

WEALTH: 'THE ENABLER'

[The Second Pillar of Society and Force Multiplier]

Wealth earned brings along with it the Inherent responsibility of Optimal Allocation of it for the Best of Society.

"Wealth is the ability to fully experience life."

– Henry David Thoreau

"Empty pockets never held anyone back. Only empty heads and empty hearts can do that."

– Norman Vincent Peale

Early Wealth

In early times, the wealth of humans, who were 'hunters and gatherers', was related to the environment in which they functioned. As they began to rear cattle, horses, hens, goats, and sheep, wealth began to be measured by the number of cattle they owned. The early humans were nomadic and wandered from pasture to pasture, feeding and taking care of their domesticated stock.

Wealth in those times came to be measured by the count of domesticated stock in one's possession. It is interesting to note that even today, in many parts of the world, cattle wealth is taken as a serious barometer of personal wealth and status.

In parts of Africa and India, a person is introduced as an owner of such and such number of domesticated cattle. In fact, in this day and age, the practice of gifting a set number of cattle as dowry in marriage still prevails in quite a few places.

The advent of agriculture spurred human settlements, and land soon became a resource. Land was fenced, and ownership of land and homes became possible and necessary. Wealth began to be measured in terms of acres of land held, along with the count of domesticated livestock.

Land even today holds great importance, and many people, including the likes of the richest men in the world today, Jeff Bezos, all hold large tracts of land. In fact, Mr. Bezos is rumored to have one of the largest land holdings in the US to his name.

Real estate in the form of land or (timber land, commercial property, housing properties) has and will always be a kind of wealth that humans value because it is a piece of this limited Earth. However, its value relative to other forms of wealth has and will continue to undergo sea changes, moving it up and often down the pecking order in comparison to newer forms of wealth.

Gold and the beginning of 'Modern Banking'

Gold has been a wealth barometer for some centuries now, and it simultaneously took root as a currency across many different civilizations, as gold began to be used in barter and trade.

As a currency, it is highly valued for its consistent appearance, aesthetic qualities, rarity, durability, and malleability. Gold is also one of the Noble metals. Noble metals are metals that don't corrode or undergo oxidation when exposed to moist air.

Gold treasures belonging to ancient *Thracians* dating back to as far as the 5th millennium B.C. have been found in *Varna Necropolis* in Bulgaria. In 3100 B.C., the Egyptian ruler Menes laid the foundation for incorporating gold into the Egyptian economy and decreed that "one part of gold in value was equal to 2.5 parts of silver." Gold was also an integral part of the 'Indus Valley Civilization' in India and was used in jewellery and as barter.

The first official declaration of gold as money came in 600 B.C. when King Alyattes of Lydia oversaw the first recorded mint. Coins, which were an alloy of gold and silver called electrum, were stamped with denominations.

Darius I of Persia introduced a 95.83% pure 8.4g gold coin minted from his treasury, which was deemed equivalent to 20 silver coins.

Roman Society, which had been using coins for exchange, also introduced gold coins in 300 B.C., and this was continued by the *Byzantine Empire* until the Middle Ages. The *Italian Florin* became the most dominant gold coin, along with the *German Augustalis* introduced under Frederick II. By the 14th century, England had also moved towards using gold as a currency by minting its coins known as Noble.

Unsurprisingly, most treasures in the world involve gold. One famous surviving treasure vault was discovered at the famed *Shree Padmanabhaswamy* Temple in Thiruvananthapuram, Kerala, India. The vaults of the temple are rumored to hold an estimated Rs. 1 Trillion (US $20 Billion) of wealth in gold and other precious commodities in just ONE of its many vaults. When the Vault-B of the temple was opened and audited under the aegis of the Supreme Court of India, unimaginable wealth in the form of gold coins and necklaces were discovered inside.

Apart from being a part of treasures around the world, gold also helped kickstart the first banking system. The fractional banking system first took hold in England, where the goldsmiths started to re-lend gold that was deposited with them for storage. The gold was lent in lieu of receipts in the early gold markets. The confiscation of large amounts of gold as a forced loan by King Charles-I, led many merchants to store gold with the goldsmiths. This was the genesis of the 'fractional banking system'. As a convenience and for the safety of the gold traded, the system would circulate the titles of ownership of gold rather than the gold itself.

In the year 1816, the UK officially defined the pound sterling relative to gold. With the entry of the United States of America, the 'Classic Gold Standard' was adopted in 1879 and was further solidified in 1900.

The *Bretton-Woods* agreement signed in 1944 laid the foundation for 'convertible currencies', where countries settled their international balances in dollars, and the US dollar became fully convertible to gold. The exchange rate applied at that time was $35/ounce, which was the responsibility of the United States. While the major powers constantly undermined the gold standard, it was not until 1971 that the Federal government in the United States jettisoned the 'gold standard' once and for all.

From then on, it was the dollar trade that became the central theme of global trade, and the 'US dollar' became established as the standard and preferred currency for trade.

Wealth Redefined

"If money is your hope for independence you will never have it. The only real security that a man will have in this world is a reserve of knowledge, experience, and ability."

– Henry Ford

While 'CATTLE', 'LAND', and 'GOLD' were initial bedrocks of wealth, the 'Industrial Revolution' created new forms of wealth. Industrialization brought on rapid growth, mass production of goods, large-scale factories with a significant workforce. These not only created jobs but also generated multi-millionaires and billionaires who amassed unimaginable wealth.

A factory may only require small acreages, but it had the capacity to churn out goods that got traded far and wide, making its owners unimaginably rich and powerful. The first few factories produced products including agricultural items, textiles, and machine parts. The invention of the 'ASSEMBLY LINE', famously pioneered by Henry Ford, manufactured and assembled goods with much-improved efficiency. For those days, the output production rates were phenomenal. Vast amounts of wealth were created in the process, and wealth began to be redefined. One became wealthy by NOT just owning vast tracks of land and gold, but by ownership of companies. Companies that managed factories and supply chains. These assets opened new avenues for the creation of wealth.

In his time, Andrew Carnegie was the richest man in the world. He amassed his vast fortune from the production and sale of factory goods. He amassed his wealth, namely from his 'vertically integrated' businesses. He owned the entire supply chain upstream, which included mines, railroads, and factories. This allowed him to have complete control over the pricing of the end product, making him supremely rich.

Unlocking of Wealth and 'Paper Money'

The 'East India Company' became the first publicly traded company in the world. Trading across the globe was very risky, as ships could get lost or destroyed in storms, or have their cargo plundered by pirates, and many times they suffered mutinies.

These risks were too numerous for ONE investor to withstand, and it was but natural that the *'East India Company'* was formed to spread the risk and rewards of its endeavors. Thus, it became the first limited liability company. It was formed in the year 1600 A.D. and was called the 'Governor and Company of Merchants of London trading with the East Indies'.

This helped to diversify and mitigate risk, by spreading the investment and consequent risks over a number of voyages. This reduced the risk and the chance of catastrophic failure if investments in a particular voyage drew a blank. In the year 1602 A.D., the first shares of the 'East India Company' were released on the *Amsterdam Stock Exchange.*

While the *New York Stock Exchange (NYSE)* was formed in 1817 A.D., the *NASDAQ* was created in the year 1971 A.D. Since then, a number of stock exchanges have been established in various countries around the world.

Large amounts of wealth today reside in these stock exchanges as paper money. Many entrepreneurs have listed their businesses on the stock markets of the world, and they dominate the Forbes list of the richest people in the world.

The Oil Economy

The initial demand for oil was satisfied by hunting whales and extracting oil from their blubber by flensing. This became a major occupation across Europe, the United States, and many countries in East Asia. The whaling industry reached its peak during the latter half of the 18th century. In fact, whale hunting was a significant part of the GDP of many countries during that time.

The discovery and production of oil from drilling and the ability to extract kerosene from coal caused the whaling industry to wane. However, until the signing of 'The International Convention for the Regulation of Whaling', whale hunting continued. The convention not only brought international action to prohibit and discourage the hunting of whales but also emphasized the conservation of whale stock.

Ever since the 'Industrial Revolution', the demand for coal and oil has grown exponentially, and businesses involved in the extraction of coal/oil have, and continue to, mint a lot of money. Initially, the 'Carbon Economy' was defined by coal mining. Since then, the demand for kerosene and gasoline has been growing ever since the automobile revolution.

In the 20th century and right into the 21st century, spanning from the 'Industrial Revolution' to the 'Information Revolution', the 'Carbon Economy', as it is called, defined wealth. The proliferation of personal transport and global trade through automobiles and gasoline/diesel-powered vehicles led to successive peaks in the oil economy. Wealth remained deeply rooted in the 'Carbon Economy' over the years. In the 19th century, businessman J.D. Rockefeller Sr. controlled 90% of the oil economy in the United States, at one point making him the richest American until he was surpassed by Andrew Carnegie.

The 'Carbon Economy' and industrial reliance on fuel spurred the rise and growth of several countries, especially those in the Middle East. These nations were blessed with vast reserves of natural wealth in the form of oil and gas. Due to the insatiable demands of the 'Carbon Economy', their resources held significant value and were in high demand. Oil has consistently defined wealth and continues to do so.

However, headwinds have begun to appear as there is talk that the 'Carbon Economy' would give way to the 'Renewable Energy Economy'. A new era with the advent of Electric Vehicles and Solar power has been initiated. Just as IC engines and thermal power plants defined the 20th Century, these new technologies that use renewable energy are expected to define the 21st century.

The Computer and Chip revolution

Talking about sources of wealth, the 20th Century saw the rise of computers and faster chips. Sources of *'Intangible wealth'* beyond just tangible product or traded commodities, began to become significant. This caused a paradigm shift in the genesis and creation of wealth. The dimensions of wealth was no more confined to just something tangible like land, cattle, gold or factories but also included the intangibles like tools that jumped productivity and maximised the 'factors of production' and moved the bar with higher efficiencies and innovation. Software codes were written to power the hardware, and its usefulness has led to its rise as a source of intangible wealth.

In the 1980s, *Microsoft*, a company that envisioned an 'Operating System' (OS) on every 'desktop PC', foresaw the future. It became one of the world's most sought-after stocks in the late 20th century. Computer chip companies such as *Intel* grew in tandem, producing faster and faster microprocessors to power the ever-increasing demand for the next version of software and software upgrades.

Wealth in the late 20th century and even today lies in these intangibles. These wealth-creating teeny-weenie chips are certainly far removed from wealth constituted by land, cattle, and gold of yesteryears.

The Information Superhighway

The coming of the 'Internet' or the 'Information superhighway' simply began a revolution that SPAWNED a hundred others.

The internet and the flow of information provided the basis for smart entrepreneurs to reach out to markets, offer services, control supply chains, outsource manufacturing, market directly to consumers, and take in e-payments in a manner never seen before.

A staggering number of businesses riding on the back of the internet were born, and many continue to flourish even as new businesses with newer business models come into vogue. The 'Information Superhighway' provided the basis for 'Creative Destruction' at its best. Giants (like *Amazon* and *Google*) were born and have created new kinds of wealth.

These companies have provided customers with tools to find exactly what they want and give them access to ways to fulfill their needs. There has been a tectonic shift as the flow of information has increased the efficiency of supply chains, opened new markets, increased convenience to customers, enabled targeted marketing, and has even changed the way that people lived their lives. This new wealth redefined the way money was seen since the late 20th Century and early 21st Century.

The Mobile Revolution

The 'Smartphone revolution', however, was the real game changer. Taking off from the feature phone, the smartphone is a powerful computing device in a customer's hand, constantly relaying information to and fro to company servers via a variety of applications called *'Apps'*.

This has not only created new avenues to serve the customer but has also made the computing device omnipresent and omnipotent. Customers can now hail a cab, look up restaurants, order food delivery, shop, play games, pay, and chat all through ONE device in their pocket.

There is a paradigm shift where customization and in-depth customer information allowed one to cater more specifically and effectively to the customer's needs. New models for the delivery of services and new models to reach out to each individual consumer, to get their attention, time, and money, are effected by these technologies. These are new ways of reaching out and fulfilling business opportunities. This is the new reality where wealth has been created by taking a number of businesses and their offerings right into a device and right into the hands of the consumer.

Social Media Revolution

It would be pertinent to mention the 'Social Media Revolution' in this context. The 'Social Media' companies allow consumers to use their services for free, and in exchange, they obtain personal data. These companies also own all data posted on their servers. They comb and analyze the data to understand the profile of consumers and use that to help third parties target customers with products and services.

A better understanding of customers means better targeting of advertisements. Such services are invaluable to advertisers, product, and service providers around the world. Rather than the 'spray and pray' advertising of the past, targeting occurs at a micro level, and each customer can be individually and effectively marketed to.

Any manufacturer or service provider could define their target market, and these social media channels would be invaluable channel partners to reach out to customers with their marketing messages. These manufacturing and service companies are willing to pay big dollars to anyone who helps them sell more.

This is how 'Social Media' giants rake in the moolah, sometimes 'cents at a time' for 'every target' they connect with. Like little drops make an ocean, when we consider the extent of their global networks and the number of users, these 'cents per click' translate into billions of dollars in revenue.

Data the 'New Oil'

Consequently, data has now become the 'new oil'. It has become the resource that companies seek to harness to better understand and serve their customers.

Companies appear intent on gathering this data and deep mining it for insights to sell better to their customers. Companies on social media platforms like *Facebook, Linkedin, WhatsApp, Instagram, Twitter,* etc., sit on a treasure trove of data that can be mined for various new applications and services.

With 'IoT' (Internet of Things) and 'AI' (Artificial Intelligence) taking center stage in the 21st century, we are at the helm of an age where large quantities of data will be available and exploited. In this regard, the 'raw material' is DATA.

Companies are in a race to gather as much of this gold as possible. It matters significantly who owns the data and who has access to it. The entire wealth of the new age companies resides on 'server farms' in the form of this data.

AI requires huge amounts of data to feed its engine to enable machine learning. This aids machine response to new situations as and when they arise. The *Google* car, for instance, has recorded over 1.5 million miles of testing, providing invaluable insights that could help train the self-driving software to respond to the varied situations it may confront in the future. The learning is such that it may be able to respond to situations it may not have confronted in the past.

These kinds of insights that help in training an AI system, however, need vast amounts of data. Another example is healthcare. As 'wearables' become a rage, and as more and more data is collected from the devices that people wear, greater insights can be obtained to make these devices more accurate and also to break new ground in the fitness and health segment. Hence, it does not come as a surprise that bits of data on servers are the new wealth or, as some call it, the 'New Oil'.

As a civilization that measured wealth by literally counting sheep and livestock, we have certainly come a long way. Today, bits and bytes of information are a major source of wealth.

However, going forward, as the world becomes wealthier, it can be hoped that people may move towards a more holistic definition of wealth focused on at an individual and at a societal level.

One can call this new wealth, the 'True Wealth'.

A

'Sanskrit Slokha'

Greed as an endless Chasm and Contentment as source of Ultimate Happiness

अन्तोनास्तिपिपासायाःसन्तोषःपरमंसुखम्।
तस्मात्सन्तोषमेवेहपरंपश्यन्तिपण्डिताः॥ - Mahabharata Vanaparva

antō nāsti pipāsāyāḥ santōṣaḥ paramaṃ sukham ।
tasmātsantōṣamēvēha paraṃ paśyanti paṇḍitāḥ ॥

Meaning:

There is no limit for greed, and contentment is the ultimate happiness, So a wise man is always happy with what he has.

'True Wealth'

Philosophically speaking, real wealth is more than just money. In the simplest terms, 'True Wealth' is the ability to live life on one's own terms to the fullest extent of one's potential and happiness. It's freedom to have and exercise choices.

Individually speaking, there are different kinds of wealth.

You can be wealthy in....

- Money & Possessions (Financial Wealth)
- Fame & Fortune
- Health & Happiness (Health Wealth)
- Purpose & Direction in Life
- Family & Friends (Relationship Wealth)
- Love & Laughter
- Freedom & Time (Time Wealth)
- Talent & Wisdom (Wealth of Wisdom)
- Peace of Mind & Spirituality (Spiritual Wealth)

As people move up the economic ladder, wealth, as defined by money, has diminishing rates of return, and smart people look beyond it. People in many developed nations are valuing fewer working hours and more family time. More and more people are beginning to believe that blind consumption, with disregard for the environment, would only hurt the planet and come back to bite us as a race.

Movements to work and care for the environment are growing. People have begun to believe that environmental health is the 'True Wealth' we could leave for future generations. There is also greater awareness among the new generation to stay healthy. The shift towards vegetarianism and veganism is an example of how people are making better choices to not only safeguard the environment but also to take care of their health. Healthy environment and healthy living are maxims that people are swearing by today. They choose organic food and prefer sustainable agriculture. More and more people are taking their health and fitness seriously. This only goes to show that wealth has many dimensions. 'Health is Wealth' goes an old adage, and the new generation has made an early start. The world is moving towards holistic living where they value physical fitness and living a stress-free life. In this context, it would be pertinent to mention how popular *Yoga* has become.

Individual wealth, seen through the prism of 'True Wealth', is a function of our environment, the food we consume, the water we drink, and the air we breathe. These need to be healthy just like our immediate living environment. This is part of our 'True Wealth'.

This 'True Wealth' will be affected by our lifestyle and the choices we make. How we consume and how we discard what we don't need, all make up our carbon footprint and could build or break our future. As inheritors of the planet, future generations are more attuned to the need to save the environment. We have come a long way, and we are on a path where our views and perceptions about wealth will change to include that which makes holistic and sustainable living possible.

As the world becomes wealthier, wealth will begin to be seen beyond just GDP and per capita income. 'True Wealth' will be measured by the physical, mental, and spiritual health of the population. These will be seen as the measure of true wealth.

GDH, or Gross Domestic Happiness, as a central measure, will take hold once the world has gone through this 'mindless and soul-less' materialism cycle. This will happen gradually with greater realization.

'True Wealth', which is wealth seen holistically, has begun to see the dawn. With greater realization in this century, there is going to be a fundamental shift in what basically contributes to and constitutes wealth. The traditional definitions of wealth are going to undergo a major overhaul once again!

Time for some FUN

Here is **British** rock band **'Dire Straits'** with one of their biggest hits, **'Money for Nothing'** from the album **'Brothers in Arms' (1985).** Enjoy!!

'Money for Nothing'

Dire Straits, [Album **'Brothers in Arms' (1985)]**

SCAN above to see **YOUTUBE** ***Video of the Song***

Lyrics

[Money for Nothing]

I want my
I want my, I want my MTV
I want my, I want my MTV
I want my, I want my MTV

Now look at them yo-yos, that's the way you do it
You play the guitar on the MTV
That ain't workin', that's the way you do it
Money for nothin' and your chicks for free

Now that ain't workin', that's the way you do it
Lemme tell ya, them guys ain't dumb
Maybe get a blister on your little finger
Baby, get a blister on your thumb

We gotta install microwave ovens
Custom kitchen deliveries
We've got to move these refrigerators
We've got to move these colour TVs

See the little faggot with the earring and the makeup
Yeah buddy, that's his own real hair
The little faggot got his own jet airplane
The little faggot, he's a millionaire

We gotta install microwave ovens
Custom kitchen deliveries
We've got to move these refrigerators
We've got to move these colour TVs

Got to install microwave ovens
Custom kitchen deliveries
We've got to move these refrigerators
We've got to move these colour TVs (look at him)

I shoulda learned to play the guitar
I shoulda learned to play them drums
Look at that mama, she come in stickin' in the camera
Man, we could have some fun

And he's up there, what's that? Hawaiian noises?
He's bangin' on the bongos like a chimpanzee
That ain't workin', that's the way you do it
Get your money for nothin', get your chicks for free

We gotta install microwave ovens
Custom kitchen deliveries
We've got to move these refrigerators
We've got to move these colour TVs, lord

Listen here
Now, that ain't workin', that's the way you do it
You play the guitar on the MTV
That ain't workin', that's the way you do it
Money for nothin' and your chicks for free

Money for nothin'
Chicks for free
Get your money for nothin'
And your chicks for free
Oozin' money for nothin'
And your chicks for free
Get your money for nothin'
Chicks for free

Money for nothin' (all that money for nothing)
Chicks for free
Get your money for nothin'
Get your chicks for free

Get your money for nothin'
And your chicks for free
Get your money for nothin' (what's that?)
And your chicks for free (look at that, look at that)

Get your money for nothin' (I want my, I want my)
And your chicks for free (I want my MTV)
Money for nothin' (I want my, I want my)
Chicks for free (I want my MTV)

Get your money for nothin' (I want my, I want my)
And your chicks for free (I want my MTV)
Get your money for nothin' (I want my, I want my)
And your chicks for free (I want my MTV)

Easy, easy money (for nothing)
Easy, easy chicks (for free)
Easy, easy money (for nothing)
Chicks for free (I want my MTV)
That ain't workin'

Money for nothing
Chicks for free
Money for nothing
Chicks for free

Part III

Chapter 4

POWER: 'THE STABILIZER'

The Third Pillar of Society and Stabilizer
Power when Entrusted brings along the Inherent Duty to Stabilize and Serve Society

"Power has in it the inherent ability to stabilize and serve Society. When entrusted, that ability transcends to a duty towards society."

–Author

"Believe in the power of your own voice. The more noise you make, the more accountability you demand from your leaders, the more our world will change for the better."

***–Al Gore,** Former US Vice President*

While the saying goes, "Power corrupts; absolute power corrupts absolutely", it does highlight the fact that as a person's power increases, their moral sense tends to diminish. However, it does NOT have to be this way.

A 'great leader' would look at leadership as an opportunity to serve and NOT as some kind of affirmation of his/her greatness. Being a leader is NOT about one's ego being stroked, but it is about recognizing that one has been entrusted with a responsibility. Leadership is about responsibility towards one's countrymen, employees, or followers, as in the case of nations, corporate settings, or organizations, respectively.

The biggest danger of any performing leader is in them getting ahead of themselves because of their ego. It is very easy for a leader to get drunk on power and start believing in their own greatness and consequently, invincibility. Also, there is a risk that a leader's leadership starts becoming all about the leader, rather than focusing on the challenges ahead. At that point, that leader would have reached the highest point of his/her competence, and it just goes downhill from there on. No matter how much they are praised (often by sycophants and rent-seekers), a great leader would maintain focus on the unfinished business and ignore the weave of adoration around them.

An **effective leader** could be **defined** by **10 important qualities.**

They are as follows:

i. *Integrity*
ii. *Competence*
iii. *Energy*
iv. *Humility*
v. *Empathy*
vi. *Wisdom*
vii. *Inspirational Vision*
viii. *Tolerance for Ambiguity*
ix. *Decisiveness and ability to take Tough Decisions*
x. *Equanimity Under Pressure*

Why Integrity is the Most Important of the Traits

Competence and Energy while being excellent traits would backfire if the leader has susceptible integrity. To quote the legendary investor Warren Buffett -

"Somebody once said that in looking for people to hire, you look for three qualities: integrity, intelligence, and energy. And if you don't have the first, the other two will kill you. You think about it; it's true. If you hire somebody without [integrity], you really want them to be dumb and lazy."

There is a French proverb, "The fish rots from the head". A leader who is corrupt will end up creating a system that is institutionally corrupt. It would be like a virus that, when introduced at the top, percolates into the entire organization while weakening and ultimately destroying it.

A leader sets an example, and their cue is followed by the rest. Founders of a company or any organization set the DNA of the organization, which replicates itself. So the seed needs to be right to set the tone for a constructive and meritorious entity.

While competence and energy are obviously good and useful traits for a leader to rise in stature and move to higher levels, qualities such as humility and empathy play a pivotal role in maximizing the leader's capacities.

While leaders in popular imagination are tough, no-nonsense people, these qualities can only take a leader up to a certain point. By its very definition, a leader is someone who people should identify with and look up to. He or she has to be a person who leads by inspiring every level in the organization rather than using fear. While inspiring leadership acts as an enabler, leadership based on fear only paralyzes the organization from top to bottom.

The reason humility is an 'essential and effective' trait is that it makes room for a leader to grow in the role and do so 'constantly and consistently'. This elevates their capability and ability to make an impact. Constant learning and growth can only be achieved if a person is humble enough to know that any ONE person alone can't be the fountainhead of all knowledge, wisdom, or ability.

A

'Sanskrit Slokha'

Conveying the importance of 'Humility'

ज्ञानंयस्यसमीपेस्यात्मदस्तस्मिन्नविद्यते।
यस्यपार्श्वेभवेत्गर्वःज्ञानंतस्यकुतोभवेत्॥

jñānaṃ yasya samīpē syāt madastasminna vidyatē ।
yasya pārśvē bhavēt garva:jñānaṃ tasya kutō bhavēt ॥

Meaning:

Who has knowledge then, he cannot have arrogance.

One who has ego then, he doesn't have the knowledge.

Humility is a trait that allows the leader to grow by being open to learning from others, no matter their hierarchy, while at the same time recognizing and correcting one's own mistakes. Humility helps a leader to recognize his/her mistakes and introspect. This paves the way forward by leading to corrective action. Humility also happens to make a leader smarter by allowing him to learn from mistakes made by others. A focus on the problem rather than the individual allows learning by focusing on what needs to be learned, rather than sitting in judgment of others.

Empathy is another great trait of a great leader. The ability to empathize raises the stature of a leader in the eyes of the people he wishes to enable and empower. Empathy allows a leader to look at the human resources of the organization in a manner that empowers, enables, and maximizes their potential synergistically.

There is a quote that says, "If you judge a fish by its ability to climb a tree, it will live its whole life believing that it is stupid." Empathy is a trait that allows a leader to look at the talent in a way that their strengths are captured and enhanced.

An empathic leader creates a climate of empowerment in the organization, where people are unafraid to make decisions because they know their honest mistakes would NOT be held against them. This allows organizations to move forward without being paralyzed by fear. It also eliminates a toxic and blaming work culture, replacing it with an enabling environment. An empathetic climate allows individuals to enable each other. Such an atmosphere creates a conducive environment for teamwork and collaboration.

An empathetic leader will find that his troops place their faith in him/her as much as the leader had placed faith in them. He would earn the respect and loyalty by being an enabler, in contrast to leaders who rule by fear.

Decisions that a leader of a country, organization, or company must make are never easy. No decision is black or white. The ability of a leader to navigate the lack of clarity or fog involved in the process would often define the leader's ability to emerge successfully.

There is never full information to make the "RIGHT" decision. The leader has to be comfortable enough to hold the contradictions and ambiguity involved in his head and yet not be swayed by his/her biases and still come out on top.

A good leader needs to be decisive and not let time slip away. Often, even a 'less than perfect decision taken' is better than 'no decision taken'. This is because "complete" information is often never available; hence, no decision that has to be taken is perfect.

Therefore, weighing the situation and acting quickly enough can work out much better than being paralyzed and letting things drift. This is especially true when decisions made (even with imperfect data) can be course-corrected (as fresh data emerges) along the way. In most cases, this would work out better than letting the situation drift. The worst situation is to have a leader in a constant state of analysis-paralysis. Such organizations will end up being dead on arrival.

There is a Sanskrit Slokha (Sanskrit verse) that talks about the qualities of a great king. It states that a king has to be as 'soft as a petal and yet tough as a thunderbolt'. The ability to have humility, empathy, and compassion while at the same time being tough enough to make difficult decisions are just necessary traits. It is just that tough decisions are to be tempered by wisdom.

A

'Sanskrit Slokha'

Describing the Qualities of the Extra-ordinary

वज्रादपिकठोराणिमृदूनिकुसुमादपि।
लोकोत्तराणांचेतांसिकोहिविज्ञातुम्अर्हति॥

vajrādapi kaṭhōrāṇi mṛdūni kusumādapi ।
lōkōttarāṇāṃ cētāṃsi kō hi vijñātum arhati ॥

Meaning:

Who can easily understand the minds of the extra ordinary, which are firmer than diamonds and as tender as flowers!

Incisive intelligence alone will not cut it. This is because intelligence can only cut like a knife and maybe do it really well. However, even a very sharp knife needs a good guiding hand for it to lead to the correct outcomes. Wisdom and equanimity, allow the intelligence to be directed towards decisions and actions that lead to desirable and better outcomes.

A knife does not know what it is cutting. It needs a guiding hand for it to be able to discriminate. Wisdom is that 'guiding hand' which allows the leader to exercise his power for good and well-meaning outcomes. A knife in the hand of a madman only leads to bad outcomes. Often, in such cases, the bigger the knife, the worse the outcome. This is the reason the bigger the knife, the more one needs to be careful about who one hands it to.

Also, a great leader maintains poise and equanimity in high-pressure situations. Equanimity allows the leader to apply his intelligence and wisdom without being crushed by the massive pressures, that accompany difficult and critical situations.

Equanimity allows for the leader to absorb the information and process it calmly, without being consumed by the chaos of the moment. Combined with humility and listening skills, a leader in balance will have the mental space to absorb and process the information to arrive at balanced decisions.

A

'Sanskrit Slokha'

On why 'equanimity' and 'being in balance' is important

क्रोधःप्रीतिंप्रणाशयतिमानोविनयनाशनः।
मायामित्त्राणिनाशयतिलोभःसर्वविनाशनः॥

krōdhaḥ prītiṃ praṇāśayati mānō vinayanāśanaḥ ।
māyā mittrāṇi nāśayati lōbhaḥ sarvavināśanaḥ ॥

Meaning:

Anger destroys love, Pride destroys modesty,

Hypocrisy destroys friendship, while Avarice destroys everything.

Finally great leaders know when to step up when the time comes, and know when to step down when the time comes. They clearly understand that power is a responsibility and that the position entrusted in an organisation is bigger than any individual, no matter how great the individual.

Power and Society

"When societal leaders fail to 'lead and evolve' with the needs of the society, it is only a matter of time before the 'lack of evolution' necessitates a 'revolution'."

–*Author*

"Only a power structure that gives voice to subjects can maintain harmony and act as a societal stabiliser."

–*Author*

While having a great leader at the helm is invaluable, the power structure of society needs to be fair to all comprising the society. Decisions made by leaders in political arenas need to be done after due consultation and reflection.

The larger the country, the greater the power, and the greater is the impact of the decisions taken. Hence, decisions need to be made with wisdom and an understanding that they can massively impact the lives of many.

Around the world and across time, the lack of representation of the concerns and voices of the subjects ultimately led to unrest, sometimes ending in destabilizing and violent ends. The French Revolution is just one case in point. Sometimes, the disconnect between the masses and the people in power can be such that the people in power have no idea of the tsunami on the way. The last queen of France, Marie Antoinette, is alleged to have commented, *"Qu'ils mangent de la brioche!"* ("Let them have cake"), when told that her subjects did not have bread to eat. Her final destination ended up at the guillotine.

Revolutions have happened across societies and countries when the level of discontent among the subjects reached a breaking point. These often have been violent transitions sparked when the 'disconnect between the rulers and the subjects' went past the breaking point. Such transitions have happened in countries including China, Japan, the United States, France, and Russia. These transitions were not exactly smooth.

When people in power refuse to 'evolve' and make necessary changes along the way, a 'revolution' comes knocking. When societal leaders fail to 'lead and evolve' with the needs of the society, it is only a matter of time before the 'lack of evolution' necessitates a 'revolution'.

In England, the struggle for greater representation of the 'Nobles' led to the Treaty of *'Magna Carta'*. These developments gradually led to the transfer of power from the 'Monarchy' to the 'Nobles'. Though the 'Magna Carta' was about the transfer of certain powers to the 'Nobles', it became a symbol of liberty.

It was the starting point and the foundation of the constitution as a sacred document. It was the foundation of the right to freedom of the individual and insurance against an authoritative despot. It finally paved the way for the establishment of the Constitution and the modern-day elected parliament.

A

'Sanskrit Slokha'

<u>On why the 'Seed' is important</u>

उप्तंसुकृतबीजंहिसुक्षेत्रेषुमहाफलम्। -कथासरित्सागर

uptaṃ sukṛtabījaṃ hi sukṣētrēṣu mahāphalam ।

Meaning:

The seed of good works, sown in the right place gives great results.

The advantage of a democratic system is that the pressure for change that builds, is released at the ballot box. This helps preclude the necessity for a painful and violent revolution. Though imperfect, a democratic system still gives the common man a voice and a sense of control over their collective destinies. Democracies are by nature for the people, of the people, and by the people. As long as democracies maintain the required separations between its constituent power structures, and the checks and balances, they can help keep society in harmony and humming along.

Only a power structure that gives a voice to its subjects can maintain harmony and act as a societal stabilizer. May the power always be in the hands of those it seeks to serve.

Time for some FUN

Ok time for a song. The song is **'That Don't Impress Me Much'** by **Canadian** singer **Shania Twain** from her album **'Come on Over' (1998).** The song was co-written by **Robert John "Mutt" Lange** and **Twain**. Enjoy!!

'That Don't Impress Me Much'

Shania Twain [Album **'Come on Over' (1998)**]

SCAN above to see **YOUTUB*E*** ***Video of the Song***

Lyrics

[That Don't Impress Me Much]

ow

(Han han, uh-uh) uh-huh, yeah, yeah

(Han han, uh-uh) uh-huh

I've known a few guys who thought they were pretty smart

But you've got being right down to an art

You think you're a genius, you drive me up the wall

You're a regular original, a know-it-all

Oh-oh, you think you're special
Oh-oh, you think you're something else
Okay, so you're a rocket scientist

That don't impress me much (han han, uh-uh)
So you got the brains, but have you got the touch?
Now, don't get me wrong, yeah, I think you're alright
But that won't keep me warm in the middle of the night
That don't impress me much
(Han han, uh-uh) uh-huh, yeah, yeah
(Han han, uh-uh)

I never knew a guy who carried a mirror in his pocket
And a comb up his sleeve, just in case
And all that extra hold gel in your hair ought a lock it
'Cause heaven forbid it should fall outta place

Oh-oh, you think you're special
Oh-oh, you think you're something else
Okay, so you're Brad Pitt

That don't impress me much (han han, uh-uh)
So you got the looks, but have you got the touch?
Now, don't get me wrong, yeah, I think you're alright
But that won't keep me warm in the middle of the night
That don't impress me much
Han aho
Yeah

You're one of those guys who likes to shine his machine
You make me take off my shoes before you let me get in
I can't believe you kiss your car good night
Now come on, baby, tell me, you must be joking, right?

Oh-oh, you think you're something special
Oh-oh, you think you're something else
Okay, so you've got a car

That don't impress me much (han han, uh-uh)
So you got the moves, but have you got the touch?
Now, don't get me wrong, yeah, I think you're alright
But that won't keep me warm in the middle of the night
That don't impress me much (don't impress me)
Oh-oh no, you think you're cool, but have you got the touch?
Now, now, don't get me wrong, yeah, I think you're alright
But that won't keep me warm on the long, cold, lonely night
That don't impress me much
(Han han, uh-uh) uh-huh, yeah, yeah
(Han han, uh-uh)

Okay, so what do you think, you're Elvis or something? (Han han, uh-uh)
(Han han, uh-uh) that don't impress me much
(Han han, uh-uh)
Ho no (han han, uh-uh)
(Han han, uh-uh) that don't impress me
(Han han, uh-uh) ho no
(Han han, uh-uh) han aho
(Han han, uh-uh) yeah
(Han han, uh-uh) woo (woo, woo)
(Han han, uh-uh)

Part III

Chapter 5

DIMENSIONS OF KNOWLEDGE, WEALTH AND POWER

Knowledge, Wealth and Power have many more dimensions that become apparent at different moments in our life and in time

"It is unwise to be too sure of one's own wisdom. It is healthy to be reminded that the strongest might weaken and the wisest might err."

– *Mahatma Gandhi*

"Minds are like parachutes – they only function when open."

– *Thomas Dewar*

As humans, we often take for granted what we have and what we've been given. It's just human nature. When handed wealth without work, we are more likely to squander it. This is because while we know the price of things in the material world, we may not have realized their true value. There's a saying in the Tamil language that briefly comments on the fate of such wealth: *"Andhu Pannum Ottaddu"*. In other words, "such wealth does NOT stick".

The Chinese have a proverb that translates to, "Slipper to Slipper in Three Generations." It succinctly captures how even as wealth is made by one generation that worked hard for it, the next might squander it, ultimately coming full circle back to where the first generation began.

The important thing to realize is that the greatest wealth we can give our children is NOT necessarily just material wealth, but a great work ethic, independent thinking, worldly wisdom, good habits, and an understanding of the value of things, not just their price.

A dose of wisdom and spirituality will allow them to attain happiness and focus on the right aspects of living. Spiritual wealth will ensure our children do NOT take themselves or the material world too seriously.

An attached-detachment will allow them to achieve maximum happiness and face any failure or suffering with equanimity. Challenges and losses are simply a part of existence and should be taken in a balanced manner, just as one needs to remain sober and grounded when successful.

'Maintaining Balance' is the key. While wisdom will allow our children to navigate this world, a more philosophical and spiritual approach will keep them happy and healthy.

A

'Sanskrit Slokha'

Describing why giving our children wings (skills & wisdom) rather than a branch (wealth) to rest on, is superior

वृक्षेसीदन्पक्षीशाखाखंडनान्नबिभेति।
यतःसःशाखायांनस्वपक्षायोस्तुविश्वसिति॥

vṛkṣē sīdanpakṣī śākhākhaṃḍanānna bibhēti ।
yataḥ saḥ śākhāyāṃ na svapakṣāyōstu viśvasiti ॥

Meaning:

A bird sitting on a tree is never afraid of the branch breaking because her trust is NOT on the branch but on her OWN wings.

There are things that money can't buy. Well, even *MasterCard* can't ☺. Money CANNOT buy happiness. Assuming you have the 'oxygen-money' in your life covered, then money alone CAN'T bring much more happiness. If you are miserable, you'll only become MORE miserable with a million dollars and EVEN MORE miserable with a billion.

It's like building a house on a poor foundation. One might feel it's NOT enough, add another floor, still feel discontented, and continue adding floors. A weak foundation will only worsen results as you add more floors, leading to a likely impending collapse.

The foundation of life is grounded in the basics of philosophy, wisdom, and spirituality. Someone with a strong foundation can build ANY number of floors, limited only by that foundation. The stronger the foundation, the better one can handle the money, power, and fame that come with success. The trappings of success WON'T consume or destroy such a person. That's why it's crucial to instill children with proper grounding. This will guide them later when they are inevitably exposed to the material world.

One can certainly understand unhappiness in people who DON'T have their basic needs met. Practically speaking, money is like oxygen; you do need it, but only up to a point. Excess of it is NOT going to significantly enhance your happiness.

If, however, one remains miserable even after their basic needs ('oxygen-money') are covered, then it's time to look INWARD and REFLECT.

Simply having more money won't help. As mentioned earlier, it's like adding another floor to a building with a shaky foundation. In real-world terms, it's like handing a teenager a million dollars in cash and perhaps a gun. Unless he's grounded, the outcome is likely to be troubling. While this example may seem overtly clear, it underscores that most times, situations are more complex. The simple example was just to highlight a blatant fact.

When one mentions wealth, the immediate thoughts are cash, cars, mansions, boats, and private jets. But let's not soar too high and lose focus because wealth HAS many dimensions. The facets of wealth include health, happiness, time, family, friends, integrity, honesty, wisdom, spirituality, children, and even grain.

Now, what's with the 'grain'? Where did that come from?

Time for the joke!

An American teenage girl was at a breakfast table, putting cereal into a bowl. Her dad was seeing the news on TV about mad cow disease and said, "This mad cow disease is killing cows; either they are dying or are going to be culled". As the teenage daughter was pouring milk into the bowl, she remarked, "Who needs cows when there is *Krogers?*"

* Krogers is an American Grocery Chain

** Ok American Girls don't hate me for this, It is JUST a joke 😂

So how come grain is wealth? This is actually obvious, but for those who are still at a loss, let me put this in a different context. Let us take another example and look at this differently.

A

'Sanskrit Slokha'

Highlighting the many dimensions of Wealth

सुवर्णरौप्यमाणिक्यवसनैरपिपुरिता ।
तथापिप्रार्थयन्त्येवकृषकान्भक्ततृष्णया ॥

suvarṇaraupya māṇikyavasanairapi puritā ।
tathāpi prārthayantyēva kṛṣakān bhakta tṛṣṇa yā ॥

Meaning:

Even after being full of gold, silver, rubies and clothes, humans have to depend on the farmer for food.

Let us assume you have a huge 20-room mansion by the lake, about 10 miles from the nearest habitation. You also have a 7-series *BMW* and a *Mercedes GLS* SUV, among other cars in your 10-car garage. Let's assume you have a nicely manicured lawn in front of your home. You also have a backyard an acre in size at your mansion, which is great for your dog to run around. Cool, right? Let's also assume you have an old bicycle lying in your garage, which, of course, you ignore because your gleaming cars do the trick for you now.

I'm going to keep this really simple. Let's say an event occurs that suddenly constricts the oil supply around the world. As the situation nosedives due to global cascading events that follow, gas stations run out of gas. It also seems like things aren't going to normalize soon. Now, you need to get to the grocery store 10 miles away. You also need to do this before there's a panic run on the grocery store.

If things globally become very uncertain and you need cash at some point, your two cool cars, along with the rest in your garage, will be worth junk. Neither can you quickly cash in on your 20-room mansion (which guzzles heating oil to keep warm) if you wished to sell. Well, heating oil is running out, and so is your time.

That dusty, 'humble' bicycle lying in your garage, though, would be worth more at that point than your two luxury cars combined. If you had to make a decision about dusting off and polishing the bicycle and selling it, you might want to weigh that decision against the long walk to the grocery store and back. I really hope you practiced 'The Farmer's Walk' properly in your gym sessions! You'll need that on your way back, carrying whatever you manage to get at the store.

At this point, seeds that you can plant for food will become more valuable than gold. Your backyard will transform into your farm, and while the dog might have to be barred from running around, the dog's poop — and yours — will become invaluable for fertilizing your veggies. As for your Harvard Law degree, it won't be of much use unless you took some electives related to agriculture.

It has been a while since I saw a really funny advertisement in a magazine. In the advertisement, there was a man in an expensive suit hanging from the wing of a plane that was in flight. There was a caption that said something to the effect: "Your Harvard Law degree is not as useful when you are hanging from a plane, is it?"

The idea behind these examples is just to highlight that wealth has many dimensions. Wealth in a holistic sense is not just money.

For Instance, isn't 'Love', a kind of wealth too?

The point that was being made earlier was that wealth has many dimensions. Just ask Steve Jobs as he lay on his deathbed, unfortunately suffering from pancreatic cancer. All the wealth, fame, and success were useless at that point, even as he pondered that he could get someone to mow his lawn but not someone who could take his place in the hospital bed. Incidentally, just after he passed away, Steve Job's $500 million yacht was ready to sail.

The truth is, "We came with NOTHING and will leave with NOTHING".

My Father, who was a Civil Engineer, spent about 20 years in the Oil Industry in INDIA with *O.N.G.C.* (Oil and Natural Gas Commission), a public sector undertaking. He spent the next decade of his life in the U.A.E. He went to Abu Dhabi in the mid-1970s when it was essentially a desert. My Dad had vast experience building infrastructure for the Oil Industry. By then, he had built everything from bridges to townships, and from highways to large oil storage facilities. He was an expert civil engineer who, at that time, had about 20 years of experience in building oil infrastructure and townships.

He was called for an interview for a senior position at *ADNOC* (Abu Dhabi National Oil Company). He was provided a flight ticket to attend the interview. My Dad's mother was strongly opposed to her son going to what was, to her, an unknown land.

Her perceptions were clouded by fear, as she 'imagined' people having their hands cut off and enduring corporal punishment by being whipped in the middle of a mosque at noon. These are, of course, stereotypes people form based on limited knowledge or hearsay.

My Maternal Grandmother was an equally enterprising lady, and she encouraged my Dad to go. She made her calculations and advised him to take a calculated risk and proceed. So, my dad left his job, potential pension, and other benefits, and decided to give it a shot.

Story of my Dad becoming a Civil Engineer

My Paternal Grandfather had lost his father very young, around 1910. He pretty much had to fend for himself. He managed to pass the metric after a lot of financial struggle. In fact, he did not have money to pay the metric exam fees and loaded sacks of grain, carrying them on his back and to trucks, to get the money needed to appear for his high school exam. When life became unbearably hard, he left his village in Thanjavur and caught a train to Bombay (Mumbai).

He managed to get a job as an accountant in the railways, making and tallying account entries. He was an extremely calm person; he rarely spoke unless necessary. He had the personality of a *Sadhu*—calm and self-contained. However, the lady he married was a daring woman. She dared to dream big. Nothing was going to stop her.

At some point, my Paternal Granddad retired from the railways after almost 30 years of service. I said 'almost', because he was 6 months short (at 29 years and 6 months) and therefore was NOT eligible for a pension. Through those years of work in the accounts department, my Granddad kept turning down promotions. Promotions always came with a transfer to another location. He sacrificed his promotions so that his two children could get an uninterrupted education.

When my Paternal Grandfather retired, money was tight, and my father had just completed schooling. My Granddad asked my dad to apply for a job as a ticket collector in the railways. However, my Grandma would have none of it. She said that even if her son became a cook, he would be the head of the kitchen or own a restaurant. She had bigger plans for her son.

She was only a 3rd or 5th grade pass, but she was an ambitious and daring woman. She had heard of engineering being a good field and asked her son to apply to college. When my Dad pointed out that there was basically no money in the house, she told my Dad to focus on studying. Paying college fees was not his concern. My Paternal Granddad was a very calm person. He was a man of peace and contentment. He was a wise man and consequently never challenged his wife! What a wise man he was!

My Dad first got admission to an engineering college in Pune (a smaller city south of Mumbai). He consulted his Mother on what stream to take. My Grandma, of course, had no idea what engineering meant in the first place, let alone the streams of engineering. But she had her logic. It went as follows:

Grandma's deduction:

1. Electrical Engineering, well, 'dismiss', because one could 'get a shock'.
2. Mechanical Engineering, well, 'dismiss', because one could 'lose one's limbs'.
3. Civil Engineering, well, sounds ok and reasonable, pass that!

That is HOW my dad took to the 'Civil Engineering stream'!

So my Dad lands up in a hostel and in an engineering college in *Pune.* My Paternal Grandmother had pawned all her jewelry to pay the fees and boarding. However, with my Paternal Granddad retired, there was money for only one semester.

My Father had a roommate in the hostel. My Father was of the upper *Brahmin* caste, and his roommate was of a much lower caste. It did not matter to my Dad anyway. They bonded completely. When they spoke about their lives, they realized they were both in identical situations. Both had no roadmap past the first semester.

Both were very worried. One afternoon, they decided to go to the famous *Goddess Parvathi* temple, which was on a hill. They went by foot, climbed to the top, and prayed with all their hearts. On the way back, they chatted about how dire their state was, even as they walked back to the hostel. It was late evening and dark as the night fell.

When they reached the hostel, a big surprise awaited them. Much to their delight, BOTH had received a telegram that cryptically told them to return home immediately as they got admitted to respective colleges in their home cities. They were overjoyed. Now, without having to pay for boarding, they could manage two semesters. At least some progress had been made.

The next day, they met with the dean of their Pune engineering college and requested a transfer and refund. Though initially reluctant, the head ultimately, after some persuasion, agreed to let them go. My dad and his roommate made it back to their respective homes. My Father joined *V.J.T.I.* in Mumbai in the 1950s.

However, with my Paternal Granddad retired and without a pension, there was no way to pay the fees past the first two semesters. My Paternal Granddad asked my Father to apply for a scholarship being offered to children of railway employees. As luck would have it, my dad applied and got the scholarship.

My Paternal Granddad later said that, even though he was deprived of a pension after having served 29 and a half years, he was grateful his son had gotten a railway scholarship (the scholarship even paid for the instrument box imported from Germany whose price was Rs 60 in those days, a time when a salary of Rs 100 was a princely sum). The scholarship allowed my Dad to complete his engineering education.

My Dad graduated in the late 1950s as a Civil Engineer.

*In railways a ticket collector checks for tickets.

I get reminded of Mahendra Singh Dhoni, a.k.a. MSD, every time I think about my dad and my granddad. MSD started out as a ticket collector but ditched it to reach for his dream of playing cricket for India. (We all know what happened next.)

In his career, MSD went on to lead India as captain to the *T20 World Cup* victory (in 2007), the *50-over World Cup* Victory (in 2011), and the *World Test Championship* Trophy (2013), becoming the only captain (until then) to have achieved the pinnacle in all three formats.

MSD is also considered one of the most charismatic and successful captains in the *IPL [Indian Premier League]*, leading his team *CSK (Chennai Super Kings)* to innumerable IPL titles.

MSD has recently retired from international cricket. Wish him luck on his next!

Returning to the story, with two decades of extensive experience, my Dad decided to fly to Abu Dhabi. When the plane landed and as it taxied to its parking spot, a peculiar thing occurred. The plane's doors weren't opened immediately. Passengers were instructed to remain in their seats for half an hour. That was to let the dust settle!

In those days, few were attracted to the U.A.E. It was mostly vast stretches of sand and desert. However, with the discovery of oil, a boom was imminent. There was a demand for skilled personnel to drive this transformation. Now, 50 years later, we all recognize the U.A.E.'s status, with Dubai, Abu Dhabi, and Sharjah standing as exemplary cities.

The Sheikh's Vision

My Father would tell me many wonderful stories of his time in the Gulf. He was in charge of executing very large projects.

In one instance, my Dad and some consultants were at the site when the then-Sheikh of U.A.E. came with his entourage. They were caught by surprise. My Dad was working with many consultants, British, American, and so on. There was a diagram and an outlay spread before them as the consultants were in discussion.

The Sheikh came and took one look at the outlay and dismissed it. He pointed with his stick at the vast, endless miles of sand across the horizon. He asked them to change the plan to occupy the vast expanses of endless desert before just raising extremely tall buildings. My Dad later said that though the Sheikh was no town planner, he had a bigger vision and was right in his infinite wisdom.

The Sheikh and his Conference room

A huge conference room was made for the Sheikh. The size of the room and the number of people it would accommodate, when taken along with the heat outside, meant that the air conditioning had to be powerful. Having understood the huge task, the consultants had put together a plan. The plan was then executed, and the conference room was completed.

On the first day the conference room was used, the Sheikh simply found the noise made by the air blowing in from the air-conditioned ducts annoying. He asked the engineers to do something about it. Even the best 'central air-conditioning' technology of its time had limitations. While the massive cooling units were isolated elsewhere, the cool air was powered through ducts. The size of the room meant that the cool air had to be blasted through the vents.

With the limited technology of those days, the ability to cool such a massive conference hall against the sweltering heat outside was a challenge. One simply had to blast cold air through vents to keep the room cool. In theory, this was great, but it made a humming noise, which annoyed the Sheikh. Now, the plan had to be reworked.

Since the calculation meant that a certain quantum of cool air had to be powered to cool such a huge room, The only solution the engineers could think of was to increase the size of vents or to re-distribute the air through a larger number of vents.

The layout of the room was such they picked the former. The vents increased in size. My Father said that feeding vents (suitably camouflaged) were so big in size that one could drive a car through them!

One intriguing story my dad would recount was about the 'Shah of Iran'. I'm uncertain about the story's accuracy, but it centered around the immensely powerful Shah, who seemed to have the world at his fingertips. He wielded unimaginable wealth and power for that era. However, fortunes shifted, and adversity befell him. After a cascade of events, he found himself fleeing for his life. Situations deteriorated to such an extent that, upon the Shah's death – a man who once ruled over the vast expanses of Iran – his closest aides struggled to find a 6ft. x 4ft. plot to bury him. As mentioned before, wealth can be elusive and sometimes ephemeral, unless one truly grasps its nature.

Another tale revolves around a notorious drug lord from the 1980s. He wouldn't hesitate to eliminate rivals and potential threats, seemingly wielding boundless power and possessing vast caches of hidden money. On one occasion, he was at a bar surrounded by his bodyguards when adversaries recognized him. A gunfight broke out. The drug lord narrowly escaped amidst the chaos, even as his bodyguards exchanged gunfire with the assailants. With enemies in hot pursuit, he found himself fleeing on foot.

The don desperately sought a place to hide and to make a call for backup. He spotted a telephone booth and quickly ducked inside. With his pocket brimming with wads of cash, what he crucially needed was just a coin to make that call. As he frantically rummaged for that SINGLE coin, the stark realization hit him: despite the millions stashed away and the numerous armed men at his disposal, none of it was of any use at that critical moment. Lacking that ONE essential coin, his fate hung in the balance. Eventually, his pursuers located him in the phone booth and riddled it with bullets.

A

'Sanskrit Slokha'

Describing Dharma

सत्येनोत्पद्यतेधर्मोदयादानैर्विवर्धते।
क्षमयास्थाप्यतेधर्मःक्रोधलोभैर्विनश्यति॥ - महासुभाषितसंग्रह

satyēnōtpadyatē dharmō dayādānairvivardhatē ।
kṣamayā sthāpyatē dharmaḥ krōdhalōbhairvinaśyati ॥

Meaning:

Dharma arises from Truth. Through compassion and offerings it grows.

Through forbearance, it endures (remains in existence).

Through anger and greed it disappears.

Wealth, Health & Character

There is an **English proverb**

"When **'Wealth'** is lost, **nothing** is lost.

When **'Health'** is lost, **something** is lost.

When **'Character'** is lost, **everything** is lost."

Most young people will initially scoff at this, dismissing it as old school, but as they age, the health aspect will begin to resonate. As they navigate their careers and lives, the latter point will also become clear.

While health is far more important than wealth, character holds even greater value. Integrity, likened to wealth, has many dimensions. It can indirectly provide health, peace, and happiness. The right kind of people will be drawn to you, and it will keep you above the line (w.r.t. Integrity) regarding money matters and relationships.

A

'Sanskrit Slokha'

Describing 'Truth' as Supreme

सत्यमेवेश्वरोलोकेसत्यंपद्माश्रितासदा।
सत्यमूलानिसर्वाणिसत्यान्नास्तिपरंपदम्।।

satyamēvēśvarō lōkē satyaṃ padmāśritā sadā।
satyamūlāni sarvāṇi satyānnāsti paraṃ padam ॥

Meaning:

Truth is God. The goddess of wealth always takes refuge in truth.

Truth is the root of everything. It is supreme and there is nothing above it.

That's why it's critical to maintain your stance regarding integrity. Many people have lost everything when they couldn't uphold their integrity.

A

'Sanskrit Slokha'

Describing why 'Good Conduct' is central

आचाराल्लभतेधर्मम्आचाराल्लभतेधनम्।
आचाराच्छ्रियमाप्नोतिआचारोहन्त्यलक्षणम्॥ - Mahasubhashitsangrah

ācārāllabhatē dharmam ācārāllabhatē dhanam ।
ācārācchriyamāpnōti ācārō hantyalakṣaṇam ॥

Meaning:

Through good conduct one attains Dharma; through good conduct one attains wealth;

Through good conduct one attains a High position; good conduct scares bad luck away.

Even health can be managed. While it's a limiting and debilitating factor, one can still get by. However, it's much harder if you compromise your integrity. As idealistic as this might sound, it's timeless wisdom.

To quote Warren Buffett, "It takes 20 years to build a reputation and five minutes to ruin it. If you think about that, you'll do things differently".

That's surely worth contemplating and embracing.

Time for some FUN

Time for a song by **Canadian** songwriter and singer **Bryan Adams** titled **'Here I am'** from the album **"Spirit: Stallion of the Cimarron" (2002)**. The song was co-written by **Bryan Adams, Hans Zimmer**, and **Gretchen Peters**. Enjoy!!

'Here I Am'

Bryan Adams [Album, **'Spirit: Stallion of the Cimarron' (2002)**]

SCAN above to see **YOUTUBE** ***Video of the Song***

Lyrics

[Here I Am]

Here I am, this is me
There's nowhere else on earth I'd rather be
Here I am, it's just me and you
Tonight we make our dreams come true

It's a new world, it's a new start
It's alive with the beating of young hearts
It's a new day, it's a new plan
I've been waiting for you
Here I am
Yeah, yeah, here I am

Here we are, we've just begun
And after all this time, our time has come
Yeah, here we are, still goin' strong
Right here in the place where we belong, oh

It's a new world, it's a new start
It's alive with the beating of young hearts
It's a new day, it's a new plan
I've been waiting for you
Oh, here I am
Yeah, here I am
Oh, here I am, yeah-yeah
C'mon

Here I am, this is me
There's nowhere else on earth I'd rather be
Here I am, it's just me and you
Tonight we make our dreams come true

Oh, it's a new world, it's a new start
It's alive with the beating of young hearts
It's a new day, it's a new plan
I've been waiting for you (waiting, waiting, waiting)

Oh, it's a new world, it's a new start
It's alive with the beating of young hearts (young hearts)
It's a new day, it's a new plan
I've been waiting for you (waiting waiting waiting)
Oh, here I am
Here I am, oh
Right next to you (right next to you, here I am)
And suddenly, the world is all brand new

Here I am (here I am) oh
Here I am (here I am) oh
Where I'm gonna stay (I'm gonna stay) oh
There's nothing standing in our way
Oh, here I am (here I am) oh
Here I am
This is me

PART IV

Finding SUCCESS & HAPPINESS in Life
Philosophies in a Nutshell

Part IV

Chapter 1

WHY THE EARTH IS OUR WINDOW TO THE CREATOR

Just like a Child's Window to the World are his Parents, the Earth is Our Window to Our Creator

"Sooner or later, we will have to recognise that the Earth has rights, too, to live without pollution. What mankind must know is that human beings cannot live without Mother Earth, but the planet can live without humans."

– Evo Morales

"Earth provides enough to satisfy every man's needs, but not every man's greed."

– Mahatma Gandhi

Introduction

In *Sanatana Dharma's* philosophies, Lord *Shiva* and his consort, Goddess *Parvathi,* had two sons: *Ganesha,* the elder, and *Karthikeya,* the younger. While both brothers were fond of each other, they did exhibit the usual sibling rivalries. In particular, Karthikeya often felt the need to compete, win, and prove his worth to his parents.

Ganesha was the calm and wise one with a hint of wit, while Karthikeya was impulsive and had a short temper.

The Story of Baby Ganesha

One day, *Narada Muni,* a sage who loved to create conflicts between divine beings to test them and keep them rooted, approached Lord Shiva on

Mount Kailash and presented a beautiful and shiny fruit. He claimed this fruit was given by Lord *Brahma* and the one who ate it would be blessed with infinite knowledge and wisdom.

Lord Shiva held the beautiful shiny fruit and looked at his consort, seemingly asking whom among their two sons he should offer it to. His consort believed the best way to decide was to hold a contest and challenge their two sons to win it. The reward for the contest would be the 'fruit of wisdom' given by Brahma.

So, Lord Shiva and his consort Parvathi summoned their two sons and informed them of the challenge. Goddess Parvathi highlighted that the winner would receive the 'fruit of wisdom' as a reward.

The contest was that one would have to circle the world three times. The one who did it first would receive the 'fruit of wisdom' as a prize.

The moment the younger of the two sons, Karthikeya, heard of the challenge, he impulsively took off on his peacock, which was his *vahan* (vehicle) as depicted in Hindu philosophy.

Ganesha, being the calm one, paused and took one look at his *vahan* (vehicle) – a big, fat mouse – and decided on a different approach. With reverence and folded hands, Ganesha calmly circled his parents three times. Lord Shiva and his consort Parvathi were initially perplexed.

As little Ganesha completed his third circle, he stood before his parents and, taking their blessing, stated with a twinkle in his eye,

"For a child, the parents are his window to the world. Both of you mean the world to me, and hence, as far as I am concerned, I have completed your challenge!"

Pleased with Ganesha's wit and overwhelmed by the young one's wisdom, Lord Shiva and his consort Parvathi had no choice but to declare him the winner and award him the 'fruit of wisdom'.

The story goes that young Karthikeya, after completing three rounds around the world and returning, learns of his parent's verdict. He becomes upset and angry. In a huff, he takes off on his *vahan* and heads south, settling on a hillock to meditate. This hillock is popular in South India as the abode of Karthikeya and is called the Palani hills.

Something to Think About

"To look out at this kind of creation out here and not believe in God is to me impossible."

*–**John Glenn** (On his second space flight on space shuttle Discovery in 1998)*

"Our planet's alarm is going off, and it is time to wake up and take action!"

– Leonardo DiCaprio

In 1998, as the Space Shuttle Discovery orbited the Earth, astronaut and senator John Glenn looked out of the window of his orbiting spacecraft. As he gazed at Earth from space, he couldn't help but marvel at its creator. In his words, "To look out at this kind of creation out here and not believe in God is, to me, impossible." Implicit in this was his awe and recognition that the Earth was his window to the Creator, God Himself.

Much like the young child Ganesha had said, "For a child, his parents are the window to the world". And just as he exhibited profound wisdom beyond his years, we need to recognize that the Earth, our precious home, is our window to God, the Creator, Himself.

Closing Thoughts

"What is the use of a house if you haven't got a tolerable planet to put it on?"

– Henry David Thoreau

"Environment is no one's property to destroy; it's everyone's responsibility to protect."

– Mohith Agadi

We need to recognize that Earth is much like our 'Parent'. Just as young Ganesha exhibited wisdom in recognizing his parents as "his window to the world", we need to understand that the "Earth is our window to God", our creator and the architect of this universe. We must respect the Earth and protect it from our own shortsightedness and greed.

Much like astronaut and Senator John Glenn realized when looking out of his window while orbiting the Earth, we need to acknowledge and respect the fact that the "Earth is a precious gift" to us and humanity, from God.

We bear a responsibility to the next generation and our children to pass on this divine gift in as pristine a condition as possible.

Time for some FUN

We end the chapter with a melody-love song to set the mood. This is from the movie soundtrack of the romantic **Tamil** movie ***'Minnale'* (2001)**. The movie stars actors **R.Madhavan** and **Reema Sen** and is directed by **Gautam Vasudev Menon**.

The song ***'Vaseegara'*** or **'Magical Charmer'** is penned by **Thamarai** and sung by **Bombay Jayashri**, with music composed by **Harris Jayaraj.** Enjoy!!

SONG

'Vaseegara'

(Magical Charmer)

MOVIE

***'Minnale'*(2001)**

(Lightning)

SCAN above to see **YOUTUBE** ***Video of the Song***

Lyrics **['Vaseegara']**	*Translation* **['Magical Charmer']**
Vaseegara En Nenjinikka Un Pon Madiyil Thoonginal Poathum, Athae Kanam En Kannuranga Mun Jenmangalin Aekkangal Theerum [x2]	Hey Magical Charmer, let me just lay on your lap to my heart's contentment And in that moment even if my eyes sleep forever then all my yearnings from my previous births and rebirths will be satiated! [x2]
Nan Nesipathum Suvasipathum Un Thayaval Thane, Aengugiren Aengugiren Un Ninaival Nane Nan,	I Love & Breathe in the benevolent shadow of your love I wish to yearn and re-live that love because of your memories.
Adai Mazhai Varum Athil Nanaivome, Kulir Kaychalodu Sneham Oru Poarvaikkul Iru Thookkam,	When we get drenched in the pouring rain and end up with love fever. We shall sleep together as one in a single blanket even though two
Kulu Kulu Poigal Solli Enai Velvaaye, Athu Therinthum Kooda Anbe, Manam Athaiyethan Ethirparkkum,	Even as you win me over with your sweet lies Even when knowing that, my dear. My heart yearns and wants more
Engeum Poagamal Thinam Veetilee Nee Vendum, Sila Samayam Vilaiyataye, Un Aadaikkule Nan Vendum,	I do not want you to go away from me I feel a need for you to be always around me at home all the time Sometimes and just for fun I wish to wear and feel your clothes on me

Vaseegara En Nenjinikka, Un Pon Madiyil Thoonginal Pothum, Athe Kanam En Kannuranga, Mun Jenmangalin Aekkangal Theerum,	Hey Handsome, I would like to sleep in your lap to my heart's contentment and in that moment even if my eyes sleep forever then all my yearnings from my previous births and rebirths will be satiated!
Thinamume Kulithathum Ennai Thedi, En Selai Nuniyal Unthan, Thalai Thudaipaye Athu Kavithai,	After your bath, when you come searching for me and when you wipe your wet hair with my Saree! Those moments feel like Poetry!
Thirudan Pol Pathungiye Thideer Enru, Pinnalirunthu Enai Nee Anaipaye Athu Kavithai,	When you silently enter through the back door and suddenly hug me from behind! Those moments feel like Poetry!
Yarenum Mani Ketal, Athai Solla Kooda Theriyathe, Kathalenum Mudiviliyil, Gadigara Neram Kidaiyathe,	If anyone asks me what the time is I really don't know what to say as when in love one just loses track of time
Vaseegara En Nenjinikka Un Pon Madiyil Thoonginal Poathum, Athae Kanam En Kannuranga Mun Jenmangalin Aekkangal Theerum [x2]	Hey Magical Charmer, let me just lay on your lap! to my heart's contentment And in that moment even if my eyes sleep forever then all my yearnings from my previous births and rebirths will be satiated! [x2]
Nan Nesipathum Suvasipathum Un Thayaval Thane, Aengugiren Aengugiren Un Ninaival Nane Nan,	I Love & Breathe in the benevolent shadow of your love I wish to yearn and re-live that love because of your memories.

Part IV

Chapter 2

A MATTER OF PHILOSOPHY, LIFE AND GOD

Why the 'Message & Essence' are MORE important than the 'Messenger & Vehicle' used to deliver it

"There is nothing wrong in religion if one were to focus on the 'Message & Essence' which is meant to guide us, rather than use 'Messenger & Vehicle' as tools to divide and rule people."

–Author

"The 'Message & Essence' are MORE important than the 'Messenger & Vehicle' used to deliver it."

–Author

Introduction

I was in 7th Grade and studying at *D.A.V School* (Gopalpuram, Chennai Branch), one of the premier schools in Chennai, INDIA. In the 1980s, the School was considered one of the best in the city. It was considered one of the best, not because it had the best facilities or had showy buildings or furniture, but because it had some of the most dedicated teachers and a fine principal in Mr.Ram Kalia.

Facilities were spartan, but there was no mistaking the dedication of the staff. Standards were high and not lowered an inch. The discipline enforced was strict. Most of us students, in jest, called it a 'Military Camp'. The rumor was the Principal had retired from the military. I don't know if that was true, but one thing I know was that the discipline enforced was such, it did not leave us in any doubt.

By virtue of its reputation, it attracted the best students. Students who were ready to make any sacrifice to attain the mindset and discipline required to truly succeed. No one was going to complain. We were just going to deliver, period. Most in the current generation might deem this cruelty. For me, the discipline I gained at school laid a foundation that allowed me to face my toughest challenges later in life without flinching. When I look back, it provided a foundation that prepared me for the challenges that, I would face later on. That discipline made my subsequent life a breeze!

I joined the school in my 6th grade. I had taken an entrance exam to get in. It was incredibly challenging. Only 2 seats were available, yet it seemed like half of Chennai was attempting the entrance exam to secure a spot. I spent the entire summer preparing to bridge my knowledge gaps. My sister assisted me in refining my preparations. As things turned out, I got in.

The school days began with an assembly, which featured a speech and a world news briefing, both delivered by pre-selected students. This was followed by any comments or announcements from the staff or principal.

In my 7th grade, one of my teachers chose me to deliver a speech at the assembly on a specific date. The speaker had the freedom to select their topic and was usually given a week or two to prepare.

On the morning of the big day, I was up and ready. It was set to be my first speech ever on the podium and the microphone, with the entire school and all staff tuning in. Those 10-15 minutes were solely mine.

I was nervous, not because of facing an audience, but due to the content of my speech. The school was run by *Arya Samaj,* an organization founded by Maharishi Dayananda Saraswathi (1824-1883). One of his teachings emphasized his belief that idol worship in 'Sanatana Dharma' (Hinduism) held no value, and thus, followers of Arya Samaj distanced themselves from that aspect of Hinduism.

Here I was, heading to the assembly to deliver a speech challenging the belief that idol worship was nonsensical. I was about to give a speech that would question the very foundations and beliefs upon which the institution, that I attended, was built.

The Speech

As I took the podium, I began by discussing the *Gunas* (basic nature) of humans. I touched on *Sattvic*, *Rajasic*, and *Tamasic* Gunas, then directly delved into the essence of what idol worship was truly about. The crux of my speech highlighted the following:

All the Gods and Goddesses in '*Sanatana Dharma*' (Hinduism) are merely pictorial representations of profound life philosophies. Stories centered around these Gods, Goddesses, *Devas*, and *Asuras* are designed to communicate these intricate philosophies in a manner accessible and comprehensible to the general populace.

The Sages and Saints who penned the *Vedas*, *Puranas*, *Upanishads*, and many other texts understood that not everyone was equipped to read, internalize, and apply these vast philosophies. Furthermore, 'a picture was worth a thousand words'.

Mythological tales surrounding the Gods and Goddesses, along with other characters, not only made those stories more relatable, but also provided an effective medium to convey those insights to the community.

These representations, whether as sculptures, pictures, or stories, were meant to communicate, in a distilled fashion, the essence of the philosophies of life. The stories can be narrated as bedtime stories to children or delivered as discourses to adults. While these stories were enjoyable at one level, they conveyed teachings at multiple levels and depths. One's level of understanding of the depth of the philosophies depended on where one was in his/her spiritual journey. It had its many layers, and one could relate and apply these philosophies depending on where, and at what stage one was, in one's respective spiritual journeys and evolutions.

Children, with their limited experience of life, would enjoy them as fun stories with colorful characters and, in the process, also develop an imprint. They would then be able to recognize the value of these stories and apply the lessons as they went through their lives. Adults, on the other hand, would be able to relate to these philosophies at a deeper level. The ability to absorb and apply those stories to one's life depended on how open one was to learning and on how developed one's spiritual side was.

The diversity and multitude of the Gods and Goddesses allowed one to benefit from the teachings without surrendering one's identity and individuality. One could then easily relate to these philosophies through the stories attached to them. In the process, one would be able to learn and grow both philosophically and spiritually in one's life. Having chosen a path according to one's situation and applying the lessons one had learned, one could then lead a happy and fulfilling life.

The Gods and Goddesses were depictions meant to remind us of the deeper philosophies they and the stories associated with them represent. The problem was not with 'Sanatana Dharma' (Hinduism). The issue arose from what got lost in translation.

Over time, the 'Message & Essence' became obscured, as followers shifted their focus to the 'Messenger & Vehicle' used to convey it. What remained was not application, but blind belief, superstition, and "Idol Worship".

Why the 'Message & Essence' is More Important than the 'Messenger & Vehicle' used to deliver it

The problem of the 'Message and Essence' getting lost with the focus shifting to the 'Messenger and Vehicle' is not unique to Hinduism alone. The problem spans all religions. The message of every religion has been about peace, togetherness and the happiness of the human race.

But that translation was lost, and the argument of which 'Messenger or God' was or is superior and whose message is correct or superior has gotten rooted in the psychics of the population. The whole concept, message, and purpose of religions have gotten hijacked and misdirected, delivering 'hate' instead of 'love'. This completely misses 'the woods for the trees'. The point is, it is irrelevant which god, messenger, or vehicle was used to deliver the message. Neither is it relevant as to WHICH GOD is superior.

What really matters is the 'Message and Essence'. It is like passing the cane of a sugar cane through the mashing machine, throwing away the sugar cane juice ('Message & Essence'), and chewing on the left-over *Shakkai* or cane fibers ('Messenger & Vehicle').

The point is that the 'Messenger & Vehicle' (sugar-cane fibers) had done their job of delivering the 'Message & Essence' (sugar-cane juice). Now we have the beautiful sugarcane juice nectar in our possession, and we need to appreciate and relish it. The 'Messenger and Vehicle' are not as relevant anymore.

The debate over which sugar cane and where it came from is largely irrelevant. Smart people know that all that matters was that the sugar-cane juice tastes good and was for us to enjoy. It does not matter from where it came or who brought it.

To smart people, the 'Nector of Wisdom' is all that is relevant, and it is theirs to taste and enjoy!

To illustrate the argument that Gods and Goddesses were depictions of philosophy, I provided a few examples.

For instance, consider a depiction of Lord Shiva where he is in perfect poise and calm, meditating with the snow-covered Himalayas as his backdrop. He meditates with his eyes half open and half closed. His neck is blue (*neelkanta*), with a snake wound around it, and often there's a clear reflection of him in the melting water at his feet. The Lord is frequently shown with a *trishula* or trident beside him.

The white background symbolizes the absolute purity of the mind. His posture and poise represent the utter tranquility of the mind and his inner harmony. The eyes, half-closed and half-open, indicate HOW he attained that state of inner harmony and self-realization.

Closing the eyes suggests a detachment from the world. Fully opening them implies complete immersion in it. Having them half-closed means he is engrossed in his inner self (always rooted in God-consciousness) while also interacting with the outer world (managing his worldly duties and responsibilities).

The snake represents his 'ego serpent'. The 'ego serpent' harasses one with its venom of desires. Worldly people are victimized by the demands of their ego. A perceiver-feeler-thinker has a limited mind and is pressured by the demands of the body, mind, and intellect. The 'ego serpent' adorns Lord

Shiva's neck without harming him. This symbolizes Lord Shiva conquering his 'ego serpent' and being unaffected by it. (A common Indian custom is for men to wear a folded cloth around their neck, which is to remind them to keep that 'ego serpent' in check). A snake, by its nature, can sense any vibration or tensing of a person near it. Lord Shiva, in a tranquil state, is unaffected by the snake, and yet it adorns his neck. This is a representation of his attached-detachment to the world around him.

His tranquility is depicted by his clear reflection in the water in front of him, denoting a clear and tranquil mind. (One can't see one's reflection in murky or disturbed water). His tranquil mind allows him to reflect on his thoughts with clarity.

The trident denotes his conquest of the self, composed of the mind, body, and intellect. While mastering his inner self, he also engages with the outer world, denoted by his *Samabhavee-mudra* (half-closed and half-open eyes). Lord Shiva's neck is blue, and he is often referred to as *Neelakanta.* This has its own significance with a story and adjunct philosophy attached to it.

I went on to give a few more examples and concluded the speech. The whole point I was trying to make was that 'Sanatana Dharma', just like all other religions of the world, was sliding down a path of irrelevance. This is because, like all other religions, the focus was on the 'Messenger & Vehicle' rather than the 'Message & Essence'.

There was actually NO incongruence between Maharishi Dayananda Saraswathi's observation and mine. I agreed 'Sanatana Dharma' was blindly heading down a road to a dead end.

However, while Shri Dayananda Saraswathi, in my opinion, was right in questioning idol-worship and the rituals that were the surviving shakkai (cane fibers), dismissing idol worship was akin to 'throwing the baby out with the bathwater'. It just needed a re-look.

Having stated all this, as I finished my speech, I began to worry about its reception. As I stepped down and as the principal, Mr. Ram Kalia, took to the podium, I grew a bit jittery.

However, much to my surprise and delight, Mr. Kalia praised the speech and its delivery. Even though it completely upturned one of the core tenets of the Arya Samaj, he praised not only the diction but also how I had built the case and offered another perspective.

After that moment, my respect for my principal grew manifold. He did not shoot the messenger, and he appreciated the message delivered without prejudice.

The truth is, on the personal front, then or now, I don't have strong opinions on anything. I have learned that knowledge grows and opinions evolve. As a human race, if we have to climb up a ladder, we need to step up, while at the same time taking our foot off the past.

Why Maharishi Dayananda Sarawathi abhorred Idol worship

As an eight-year-old boy, Shri Dayananda Saraswathi was initiated into formal education with the *Yajnopavita Sanakara* ceremony. His father was an ardent devotee of Lord Shiva, and young Shri Dayananda Saraswathi was taught the rituals and fasts associated with the festive occasion of *Shivaratri.* In accordance with the custom of staying awake the whole night on the night of *Maha-Shivaratri,* young Shri Dayananda Saraswathi remained vigilant.

As young Shri Dayananda Saraswathi sat awake in front of the idol of Lord Shiva, he happened to see a mouse eating the offerings and running over the idol. After this incident, he began to question how Lord Shiva could be a world savior if he could not defend himself against a mouse.

That argument, however, misses the point. The essence of 'Sanatana Dharma' was to keep the focus on the 'Message & Essence' and NOT on the 'Messenger & Vehicle'. That is the reason even Gods and Goddesses in the stories are rarely depicted as 'perfect models'.

They are depicted with their vulnerabilities. If you take Lord Shiva himself, he is depicted in the story involving *Bhasmasura,* as falling for his own vanity.

Bhasmasura & Lord Shiva

One interesting story is that of *Bhasmasura.* Bhasmasura prays to Lord Shiva and undergoes severe penance to have Lord Shiva appear before him. Lord Shiva is extremely pleased and appears before Bhasmasura to grant him a boon.

Bhasmasura wanted a boon that allowed him to destroy and reduce ANYONE to ashes if he placed his hand on their head. Bhasmasura, through his prayers and penance, had stoked Lord Shiva's ego so much that Lord Shiva did not think twice before granting Bhasmasura his wish.

Having been granted his wish, Bhasmasura runs riot on earth. When Lord Shiva questions him, Bhasmasura chases Lord Shiva himself with the intention of placing his hand on Lord Shiva's head. Poor Lord Shiva is forced to run and hide from Bhasmasura, taking refuge with Lord *Vishnu.* He pleads with Lord Vishnu to do something about it.

Lord Vishnu now takes the form of the ravishing beauty *Mohini,* who is not only stunning and charming but also an attractive dancer. The moment the irresistible Mohini appears before Bhasmasura, he is taken. Suitably smitten by Mohini, Bhasmasura is led by Mohini to perform a dance with her. He follows her, step by step, in a dance called *Muktanrtya.* At some point, the dance requires one to place one's right hand on one's head.

Completely in love with Mohini, Bhasmasura is no longer thinking. He follows her steps. As Mohini strikes 'the pose', Bhasmasura follows her steps. He is led to place his right hand on his own head. The moment he does that, he turns instantly to ashes.

The story humanizes Lord Shiva and makes him more relatable. It goes on to show how even the best, even Gods themselves, can fall victim to their own vanity and ego.

The point that mattered was the 'Message & Essence' of various philosophies were so beautifully contained in the hand-crafted woven fabric of 'Sanatana Dharma'. All this was done in an inclusive and beautiful way to encapsulate the essence and philosophies necessary for leading a happy, prosperous, and balanced life.

However, what remained after thousands of years was 'blind following', devoid of learning, thinking, and application. This promoted mindless rituals and herd mentality, leaving very little room to apply those wonderful teachings.

Conclusion

'Sanatana Dharma' (Hinduism) as a religion or way of life was not unique in all this. All religions of the world suffered from this because they had ABANDONED reasoning, logic, and their very purpose behind.

They were now ABOVE any reasoning, logic, or questioning. Religion became a tool to control the herd. It became a tool to assemble groups of people against carefully selected targets. Targets selected to further the vested interests of a few craving for power and control. Religion became a tool to further 'self-serving' interests and agendas, all in the name of GOD.

People who claimed to have sanction from God or sacred texts could get away with anything. While some had ulterior motives, others simply deluded themselves into believing that they were ordained by God to carry out His work.

There is no problem with this, except that it created tremendous suffering that mankind is still grappling with. There is nothing wrong in religion if one were to focus on the 'Message & Essence', which is meant to guide us, rather than use the 'Messenger & Vehicle' as tools to divide, rule, and control people.

The fact is, what matters to the world is the universal message of all religions, the message of WHAT it was MEANT to be. Once the focus is brought back to the 'Message & Essence' in all religions, humans would be able to come together and reach their greatest potential. There would be peace, happiness, love, camaraderie, friendship, and prosperity for all.

Isn't LOVE and HAPPINESS the consistent message of all religions and faiths?

Time for some FUN

Time for the song **'Don't Worry, Be Happy'** sung by **American** world, reggae, and jazz singer and songwriter **Bobby McFerrin** from his fourth album, **'Simple Pleasures' (1988).** Enjoy!!

'Don't Worry be Happy'

Bobby McFerrin, [Album **'Simple Pleasures' (1988)]**

SCAN above to see **YOUTUBE** ***Video of the Song***

Lyrics

[Don't Worry be Happy]

Here's a little song I wrote
You might want to sing it note for note
Don't worry be happy
In every life we have some trouble
But when you worry you make it double
Don't worry be happy
Don't worry be happy now

Ooh-ooh-hoo-hoo-ooh hoo-hoo-ooh-ooh ooh
Don't worry
Woo ooh-woo-ooh-woo-ooh-ooh
Be happy
Woo ooh-ooh-ooh-ooh
Don't worry be happy
Ooh-ooh hoo-hoo-ooh hoo-hoo-ooh-ooh ooh-ooh
Don't worry
Woo ooh-woo-ooh-ooh-ooh-ooh
Be happy
Woo-ooh-woo-ooh-ooh
Don't worry be happy

Ain't got no place to lay your head somebody came and took your bed
Don't worry be happy
The landlord say your rent is late he may have to litigate
Don't worry
Ha-ha ha-ha ha-ha
Be happy
Look at me I'm happy

Ooh-ooh-hoo-hoo-ooh ooh-ooh-ooh-ooh ooh-ooh-ooh
Don't worry
Ooh-ooh-ooh-ooh-ooh-ooh-ooh...
Be happy
Ooh-ooh-ooh-ooh-ooh
Here I'll give you my phone number
When you're worried call me I'll make you happy

Ooh-ooh-hoo-hoo-ooh ooh-ooh-ooh-ooh ooh-ooh-ooh
Don't worry
Woo ooh-ooh-ooh-ooh-ooh-ooh
Be happy
Woo ooh-ooh-ooh-ooh

Ain't got no cash ain't got no style
Ain't got no gal to make you smile
But don't worry be happy
'Cause when you're worried your face will frown
And that will bring everybody down
So don't worry be happy
Don't worry be happy now

Ooh-ooh-hoo-ooh-ooh ooh-ooh-ooh-ooh ooh-ooh-ooh
Don't worry
Ooh-ooh-ooh-ooh-ooh-ooh-ooh
Be happy
Woo ooh-ooh-ooh-ooh
Don't worry be happy

Ooh-ooh-ooh-ooh-ooh ooh-ooh-ooh-ooh ooh-ooh-ooh
Don't worry
Woo ooh-ooh-ooh-hoo-ooh-ooh
Be happy
Woo ooh-ooh-ooh-ooh
Don't worry be happy

Now there is this song I wrote
I hope you learned it note for note like good little children
Don't worry be happy
Listen to what I say in your life expect some trouble
When you worry you make it double
Don't worry be happy be happy now

Ooh-ooh-hoo-hoo-ooh ooh-ooh-ooh-ooh ooh-ooh-ooh
Don't worry
Ooh-ooh-ooh-ooh-ooh-ooh-ooh
Be happy
Woo ooh-ooh-ooh-ooh
Don't worry be happy

Ooh-ooh-ooh-ooh-ooh ooh-ooh-ooh-ooh ooh-ooh-ooh
Don't worry
Woo ooh-ooh-ooh-hoo-ooh-ooh
Be happy
Woo ooh-ooh-ooh-ooh
Don't worry be happy

Ooh-ooh-hoo-ooh-ooh ooh-ooh-ooh-ooh ooh-ooh-ooh
Don't worry (Don't worry, don't do it)
Ooh-ooh-ooh-ooh-ooh-ooh-ooh
Be happy
Woo ooh-ooh-ooh-ooh
(Put a smile on your face, don't bring everybody down like this)

Ooh-ooh-ooh-ooh-ooh ooh-ooh-ooh-ooh ooh-ooh-ooh
Don't worry
Woo ooh-ooh-ooh-hoo-ooh-ooh
It will soon pass, whatever it is
Woo ooh-ooh-ooh-ooh
Don't worry be happy

Ooh-ooh-ooh-ooh-ooh ooh-ooh-ooh-ooh ooh-ooh-ooh
I'm not worried

Part IV

Chapter 3

LESSONS FROM GANESHA

Why having the right approach to a problem is important

"You will find only what you bring in."

– ***Yoda,*** *Star Wars Movie*

"Challenges are what make life, while Overcoming them is what makes life meaningful."

– ***Unknown***

There was a person I knew who was struggling in his business, and to correct things, he offered puja to Lord Ganesha (God with an elephant head who helps one overcome obstacles). He performed the puja (prayer and offering) diligently every day, yet his business did not improve. He was hoping that somehow Lord Ganesha, who was *'Nir Vignam'*, or the remover of obstacles, would clear the path for him.

In essence, it was the 'easy way out'. The expectation was that Lord Ganesha would do all the 'hard work', while this gentleman could simply perform a 10-minute prayer and appease Lord Ganesha with offerings of flowers, coconuts, and sacred water, and be done with it. If, after all this "great effort" from the devotee, things did not work out, then the devotee would approach Lord Ganesha and inquire why the Lord was seemingly displeased with him, and invariably, one of two things would happen.

One response would be to increase the "bribe" to the Lord. For instance, the devotee would say to Lord Ganesha, "If you do this for me, Lord, I would offer to break 108 coconuts in your name", and so on. (Now, don't ask me why

Lord Ganesha would be tempted. Considering that the Gods have created a universe with billions of galaxies and trillions of stars, I have no clue why Lord Ganesha would fold for 108 coconuts!).

On the other hand, another option would be to persistently implore the Gods. In the worst-case scenario, one could perform extensive rituals like *yagna* or consult an astrologer (my school friend would refer to astrologers as those who played the role of shrinks or psychologists in the 'Sanatana Dharma' ecosystem).

Even if, after all these efforts, things don't work out as expected, another option is to petition ANOTHER God.

There's nothing wrong with any of this; it's all part of growing up, learning, and evolving. I have personally been through these phases myself!!

Now, back to our devotee.

Ironically, though, Lord Ganesha, every day and in every moment, was conveying a consistent message to that person. It's just that the person was not listening. To cut to the chase, all idols in Hinduism are nothing but representations of a deeper philosophy.

Lord Ganesha was no different. He was the 'remover of obstacles' for a reason. In his 'elephant-headed form', Lord Ganesha conveyed deeper philosophies for success. The only problem was that the work had to be done by the person praying. Lord Ganesha is the guru. Essentially, his job is to lead the horse to the water. The horse must be ready to drink and drink well. Lord Ganesha has a long trunk, but asking him to drink for us is asking for too much. The devotee should also take some responsibility. In this case, the devotee is the one who has to drink, considering the thirst is his. He is the one who has to run the business. He is the one who needs the nectar of wisdom, NOT Lord Ganesha.

Coming back to the **consistent message** being delivered by Lord Ganesha

Lord Ganesha, for instance, has large ears symbolically screaming PLEASE LISTEN. He has small eyes for the size of his head, saying PLEASE FOCUS & CONCENTRATE. He has a big head, crying out loud PLEASE THINK, and he has a flexible trunk denoting FLEXIBILITY, with the ability to 'pick a needle' or even 'uproot a tree'.

While the gentleman doing pooja could not understand why Lord Ganesha was not helping him, the fact was that Lord Ganesha had always been sending the same consistent message. If you have obstacles in your path, then listen, focus, think, and be flexible. Such was the message of Lord Ganesha.

The rituals around Lord Ganesha were meant to help one look inward and reflect on the deeper philosophies that Lord Ganesha conveyed. The rituals also provided a way to contemplate our problems and then break a coconut, symbolizing a fresh start with the removal of past failures. Breaking the coconut was symbolic of opening up one's mind, devoid of all negative baggage, including past failures, ego, and doubts, and starting with fresh thinking.

Thus, 'invoking Lord Ganesha' actually involves 'invoking all those qualities' that are needed for success and imbibing them.

In the culture of 'Sanatana Dharma', any task is initiated with an invocation of Lord Ganesha. The concept of invoking Lord Ganesha was NOT merely an academic exercise or a superficial ritual. It was intended for ALL those involved in the puja or ritual to reinforce in their minds the teachings represented by Lord Ganesha and to seek happiness and success.

Lord Ganesha

A few more tidbits about Lord Ganesha (for interested readers): In its deeper layers, Ganesha's large head symbolizes his wisdom. A wisdom gained through *sravana* (listening to the eternal truths of Vedanta) and *manana* (independent reflection upon them).

At a deeper level, the trunk is representative of Lord Ganesha's intellect and faculty of discrimination. It signifies his ability to provide the correct treatment for a problem, akin to a trunk's powerful capacity to either pick a needle or uproot a tree.

Depiction of Ganesha's TRUNK

If you want to go even deeper. Man's intellect is of two types, namely the 'Gross' and the 'Subtle'.

'Gross intellect' is an aspect of discrimination which is applicable in the 'realm of the terrestrial world' while 'Subtle intellect' is an aspect of discrimination which is handy when one has to 'understand the transcendental'.

'Gross intellect' for instance helps to distinguish between pairs of opposites in the world. Example daylight and night, joy and sorrow, white and black.

'Subtle intellect' lets us phantom stuff like finite and infinite, real and unreal, transcendental and terrestrial.

The trunk at a much deeper level is supposed to denote *Lord Ganesha's* mastery over these two aspects of the intellect, which are namely the 'Gross intellect' (like ability to uproot a tree) and at a finer level the 'Subtle intellect' (like ability to pick a needle).

Lord Ganesha's intellect penetrates BOTH realms of the material and spiritual world.

Lord Ganesha is also depicted in a seated position with one leg on the ground and the other leg folded up. While the leg on the ground depicts his engagement with the world, the other folded leg off the ground depicts his engagement with the supreme reality.

A man of realization, like the depiction of Lord Ganesha, is rooted in supreme wisdom. He is NOT victimized by *raaga* (likes) or *dwesha* (dislikes). He is not swayed by agreeable or disagreeable circumstances, pleasant or unpleasant happenings, or good or bad environments. Neither does heat and cold, joy and sorrow, honor and dishonor, etc., have an effect on him. None of these, influences or troubles him. In other words, he is NOT a victim of the pairs of opposites, pulling in multiple directions. He stays his course and homes in on his tasks or targets.

Lord Ganesha is one who has transcended the limitations of the opposites and has gone beyond them. In Sanskrit, Lord Ganesha is therefore referred to as "*dwandwa-ateetha*", or beyond the opposites. This particular aspect is depicted by his possession of one broken tusk, where his two tusks represent the opposites, and the broken tusk symbolizes his overcoming of those opposites.

This concept is also illustrated in one of the mythological stories where Lord Ganesha breaks one of his tusks and uses it to write the *Mahabharata*. The Mahabharata is one of the great epics from the Indian subcontinent, dealing with the struggles and complexities of the challenges that life presents. It is a story of honor, war, and the triumph of dharma (justice).

Initially, Lord Ganesha used a stylus when he began writing the epic, but when the stylus broke, he didn't hesitate to break his own tusk and use it to continue writing. Symbolically, this act represents that sacrifice is sometimes necessary to gain knowledge and wisdom.

The large belly of Lord Ganesha symbolizes that a person of supreme wisdom can easily consume and digest whatever experiences life throws at them.

Lord Ganesha's large belly symbolizes his ability to digest the good and bad experiences that life presents. Whether it's heat or cold, birth or death, war or peace, or any trial or tribulation, Lord Ganesha maintains his grace and poise through all the fluctuations, ups and downs, successes, and challenges that the world throws at him. He effortlessly digests them and continues to move forward.

Story of 'Young Baby Ganesha's BELLY'

In Hindu mythology, *Kubera,* the God of wealth, once invited the young baby Ganesha to a feast at his palace. However, young Ganesha had a ravenous appetite. He not only consumed all the food that had been prepared for him but also polished off all the food intended for the other guests. Even after this, the young baby Ganesha remained hungry and began eating the festive decorations. At this point, Kubera was at his wit's end, unsure of what to do.

At that moment, Lord Ganesha's father, Lord Shiva, appears and offers the young baby Ganesha a handful of roasted rice, which he gratefully accepts. Upon eating it, his hunger is finally satiated.

As a child, this story was incredibly entertaining to me. However, the deeper philosophy behind it teaches us that a person can never be content with the joys offered by worldly possessions, symbolized by Kubera's feast. The more one acquires, the more one desires.

The "material world" can sometimes resemble a mirage in a desert. Pursuing it is akin to an endless chase, where the mirage always seems just a bit further ahead, and one never truly arrives. Material pursuits can never fully satisfy one's hunger for more; they are bottomless and insatiable.

Therefore, material pursuits, whether wealth, fame, or power, CAN NEVER provide peace, contentment, or lasting happiness to humanity. The happiness derived from them is transient in nature.

When Lord Krishna describes the material world as *'Maya'* (an illusion or mirage) or unreal, he is referring to what we perceive. This concept delves into the realms of the real and unreal, representing a deeper philosophy for another day.

The destruction of excessive desires, known as *vasanas,* is symbolized by the 'roasted rice' that Lord Shiva presents to the young baby Ganesha. Once roasted, the rice loses its capacity to germinate.

The handful of rice given by Lord Shiva represents 'need', whereas Kubera's feast represents 'greed', which is always insatiable. Even Kubera, the God of wealth, could not satisfy the hunger of the young baby Ganesha. Yet, it took nothing more than a handful of roasted rice given by Lord Shiva to his son to fully satiate that hunger.

To quote Mahatma Gandhi "The Earth provides enough to satisfy every man's need, but NOT every man's greed."

The endearing story of young baby Ganesha simply illustrates the profound philosophy of 'need' versus 'greed' and the wisdom it encompasses. It shows how young baby Ganesha grasps this wisdom early in life and successfully overcomes that challenge. This is why you will ONLY see a joyful Lord Ganesha. He has triumphed over the material world.

Frequently, at the feet of Lord Ganesha, there lies an array of plentiful food. Adjacent to this abundant spread of food is a tiny rat that refrains from partaking in the meal. The rat remains in place, seeking permission from the master to eat.

The lavish display of food symbolizes the abundance of material wealth, power, and prosperity. When individuals adhere to the elevated principles of living suggested, they indeed attain substantial material success. Lord Ganesha's indifference to the abundance of food at his feet serves to illustrate his detachment and mastery over his achievements and wealth.

The choice of using a rat as a depiction is to symbolize a thought or desire that initially begins small, but can then grow into excess. The rat is a creature characterized by its excessive cravings, representing the very essence of excessive desire. Regarded as one of the greediest creatures, it possesses an acquisitive nature and an insatiable greed that drives it to steal and hoard more than it can ever consume. Often, it hoards grains in burrows, nooks, and crannies, only to forget where it stored them in the first place.

The portrayal of the rat, patiently awaiting its master's approval in front of the bountiful feast at Lord Ganesha's feet, serves to illustrate that Lord Ganesha has his insatiable desire under control. He does not allow the rat, however small, to jeopardize his material or spiritual well-being.

The inclusion of the rat in this context serves to acknowledge that greed is an inherent aspect of human nature; it should not be denied. However, the rat's portrayal under observation and reasonable restraint signifies Lord Ganesha's mastery over his desires, without denying it's (desires) existence.

The practice of paying obeisance to Lord Ganesha at the outset of embarking on a journey or a task is rooted in the intention to invoke, internalize, and manifest his qualities. It involves listening attentively to the problem at hand, maintaining unwavering focus on the issue, engaging in profound and thorough contemplation, and exercising fluid intelligence during the execution of solutions. These are the profound lessons that Lord Ganesha imparts to the world.

When one achieves success, Lord Ganesha's message is to exercise control over any excesses and maintain a state of attached-detachment with regard to success, fame, wealth, or power. The desire, represented by the rat, may initially be modest but can grow unchecked, potentially consuming and undoing all the gains. Much like an uncontrolled rat devouring the abundant spread of food. Thus, the concept emphasizes the importance of maintaining equilibrium.

So, the next time you encounter an obstacle, invoking Lord Ganesha should not merely involve prayer; it should also entail invoking and internalizing the wisdom of Lord Ganesha. This practice enables you to confront obstacles and challenges with greater ease.

When you come across an image or idol of Lord Ganesha, take a moment to reflect on his philosophies and reinforce and internalize his wisdom. Allow his wisdom to permeate and radiate within you, aiding you on your journey. In doing so, you will not only find success but, more significantly, attain lasting balance and happiness in life.

Quoting Yoda from Star-wars, "May the FORCE be with You".

Time for some FUN

Time for **Jamaican** singer-songwriter and the king of reggae, **Bob Marley,** with a song he wrote and sang titled **'Three Little Birds'.**

The song **'Three Little Birds'** is from the album **'Exodus' (1977)** by the group **'Bob Marley & The Wailers'.** Enjoy!!

'Three Little Birds'

Bob Marley & The Wailers, [Album **'Exodus' (1977)]**

SCAN above to see **YOUTUBE** ***Video of the Song***

Lyrics

[Three Little Birds]

Don't worry, about a thing
'Cause every little thing, gonna be all right
Singin', don't worry, about a thing
'Cause every little thing, gonna be all right

Rise up this mornin'
Smile with the risin' sun
Three little birds
Pitched by my doorstep
Singin' sweet songs
Of melodies pure and true
Sayin', "This is my message to you, whoo-hoo"

Singin', don't worry, about a thing
'Cause every little thing, is gonna be all right
Singin', don't worry, don't worry 'bout a thing
'Cause every little thing, gonna be all right

Rise up this mornin'
Smile with the risin' sun
Three little birds
Pitched by my doorstep
Singin' sweet songs
Of melodies pure and true
Sayin', "This is my message to you, whoo-hoo"

Singin', don't worry, about a thing
Worry about a thing, no
Every little thing, gonna be all right
Don't worry
Singin', don't worry, about a thing
I won't worry!
'Cause every little thing, gonna be alright

Hmm, don't worry, about a thing
'Cause every little thing, gonna be all right
I won't worry
Baby don't worry, about a thing
'Cause every little thing, is gonna be all right
Say, don't worry about a thing, no girl

'Cause every little thing gonna be all right

Part IV

Chapter 4

LESSONS FROM HANUMAN

Why picking the RIGHT solution to the problem is important

"In matters of style, swim with the current; in matters of principle, stand like a rock."

– *Thomas Jefferson*

"The challenge of leadership is to be strong, but not rude; to be kind, but not weak; to be bold, but not a bully; to be thoughtful, but not lazy; to be humble, but not timid; to be proud, but not arrogant; to have humour, but without folly."

– *Jim Rohn*

Hanuman

Interestingly, the Honor'ble Former President of the United States, Mr. Barack Obama, also carries, among other things, a *Hanuman* figurine in his pocket. The Hindu deity Hanuman is not just about strength and bravery. He is about *'Chatur Buddhi'* or a mind like lightning. While he is about strength, he is also about compassion, as seen by the mounds of butter devotees place on his heart and chest in many temple settings.

While Lord Hanuman, the Monkey God, is an interesting character, the stories around him are even more interesting. In the epic Ramayana, Hanuman is assigned the task of finding Sita by Lord Rama. Sita was Lord Rama's wife who was kidnapped by Ravana and taken to Sri Lanka across the sea from South India.

In preparation to find Sita and needing to cross the ocean to get to Sri Lanka, Lord Hanuman used his powers to make himself large in stature and yet light in weight. This was an important symbolism, as Lord Hanuman had a near-impossible task. He had to maximize his wisdom while keeping his ego light to overcome all the obstacles that would come his way. His large stature and size were symbolic of his wisdom, 'huge'. While his light-weight was symbolic of his lack of ego. The ocean was symbolic of the large amounts of attachments and desires one has to cross to attain one's goals. Crossing such an ocean requires large amounts of wisdom and lack of ego. Hanuman's large size, yet lightweight, was nothing but a symbolism of just that.

While on his way and crossing the ocean to meet Sita, Lord Hanuman first encounters *Surasa*, the demon. Demon Surasa insists that no one could pass him WITHOUT first going into his mouth. Even though challenged and in a hurry, Lord Hanuman, devoid of any ego, used his intelligence and wisdom, rather than strength, to overcome the obstacle in his path.

Lord Hanuman calmly challenged the demon by growing larger and larger in size, attaining mammoth proportions. In response, the demon began to open his mouth bigger and bigger. At some point, BEFORE the demon could react, Lord Hanuman suddenly became very tiny as a fly and entered the mouth of the demon, then emerged. The demon's condition was satisfied, and he had to let Lord Hanuman go. Lord Hanuman had passed the test of wisdom and intelligence over strength.

As he flew onward in his journey, Lord Hanuman was offered to rest on the golden mountain *Mainaka*, which belonged to the Sea God. This was representative of desires and attachments. Hanuman refused the kind offer and stated that he would do so after his mission. He refused to fall into the trap of compassion or attachment, despite having a heart of butter. This illustrates the power of intelligence/wisdom over temptation, compassion, or attachments. In light of attempts to distract him from his mission, Hanuman refused to lose focus on his mission.

As Lord Hanuman flew, his shadow was caught by a Rakshasi (demoness) called *Simhika*. She used Lord Hanuman's shadow on the waters to pull him towards her. Lord Hanuman tried to break away, but the harder he tried, the more power Simhika derived, pulling him closer. Lord Hanuman this time used his intelligence and strength. He turned around and flew towards the force that was pulling him. This doubled his momentum, and he smashed into the mysterious source of the force with great power, destroying Simhika. This again shows how Lord Hanuman assessed the situation correctly and took corrective measures.

The reason why the story of Lord Hanuman crossing over to Lanka was highlighted was to point out that not all problems can be tackled using the same strategy. There is really NO 'one-size fits all'. There is no one template or fixed method or quick formula to tackle problems that come one's way.

Having a large number of great qualities simply increases the options one has in one's arsenal. The first step is to develop and practice those qualities. Like most things in life, it is a 'process' and not a 'destination'.

The second challenge is understanding the problem at hand and then administering the correct solution. Using a sledgehammer to stitch cloth might not be the best option. Similarly, using a fridge in Antarctica might not be of much use.

While sometimes one would have to use force, most of the time, one may have to use intelligence and wisdom.

Many problems can be best tackled by the application of wisdom. In order to do so, one must be big in stature as far as intelligence and wisdom are concerned, and light in ego. Problems tackled otherwise would only lead to disaster.

It is therefore important to use the right tools and strategy to give the problem the right treatment for success. Being weightier in wisdom and light on ego would allow one to cross the ocean of attachments and temptation, as highlighted in the story.

Hence, the story of Lord Hanuman crossing the ocean would always need to be kept in mind when one is faced with having to provide solutions to problems. The 'correct treatment' of the problems or obstacles would allow for 'quick and timely' resolutions and better outcomes.

'Dumb Examples' vs 'Smart Examples'

I just gave a few OBVIOUS examples like:

a. Using a sledge hammer to stitch cloth may not be the best option.
b. Using a fridge in Antarctica may not be of real help.

I know you are laughing at me for such dumb examples. Not really, I have just given you obviously stupid examples to bring out the stupidity. But, how about I give some real life examples.

Take a.) Using a sledge hammer to stitch cloth may NOT be the best option

Why would someone use a sledgehammer when what was needed was a needle? Well, have you ever seen road rage incidents where all it took was an apology, but somehow something that could start as something very minor escalates into an argument and then into a brawl and finally ends in murder?

Suppressing one's anger and ego and bringing out the apology (needle to stitch) would have mended the tear in the cloth, but what happens is that the persons involved, bring out their huge egos (sledgehammer) and bludgeon each other up.

Take b.) Using a fridge in Antarctica may not be of real help.

Why would someone need a fridge in Antarctica? hmm... Have you seen people who are already extremely wealthy, but give up relationships and health for more money? Why, why would they do that! Well they are like the person who buys a refrigerator in Antarctica.

Now, are you laughing at all the wealthy people who come to your mind, when you read that? Well, how about we also look in the mirror.

Ok a slight diversion. Do you know what the definition of the great salesman is?

A great salesman is one who can, "Sell a refrigerator to an Eskimo!"

Now, haven't we all been sold things we do not really need? Haven't we bought an endless number of clothes only to never wear them? Well, I will put my hand up before you do! So don't feel too embarrassed to look dumb. You have plenty of company!

Ok, the reason I brought up the 'Dumb Examples' Vs 'Smart Examples' is to make a point that the philosophies of 'Sanatana Dharma' are encapsulated in fun stories with depictions of God, Goddesses, *Asuras,* and *Devas* and their interactions and conflicts. The idea behind this design was to convey the philosophies and wisdom of the *Vedic* and *Puranic* texts in a fun and easy-to-relate manner.

The point was that not everyone would be able to completely read all the texts, digest them, and then apply them to better their lives. Hence, the mythological figures and the mythologies (whether they actually took place, is irrelevant) were vehicles used to deliver deeper wisdom for the benefit of mankind. The sages and munis who came up with these philosophies were men of greater wisdom and showed the way in a relatable and fun way, with the idea of leaving a deep impression without sounding like they were pontificating.

Unfortunately, the focus over thousands of years had shifted to the messenger and the vehicle used to deliver the message. This was NOT the original intent. These depictions and stories are layered in such a way that a child will find them fun to listen to as a bedtime story and yet make complete sense to an adult who has experienced life. This, in turn, will engage the children, creating deep impressions which they carry into their lives even as they grow up. Adults, on the other hand, would begin to relate to the philosophies and wisdom involved as they go through their respective life experiences.

The multitude of Gods and Goddesses and their diversity allows one to relate to them irrespective of our background or individuality. This can be done without giving up one's identity because the focus was always on the message.

'Sanatana Dharma' in design was meant to accommodate a multitude of opinions and depictions. There is never perfect or imperfect, white or black, perfectly right or completely wrong. The philosophies capture the entire spectrum of possibilities, and yet, it is able to balance opposite opinions, keeping Dharma (principles) in sight. There are no simplistic rules, only principles. It allows for questioning and accommodates the evolution of those principles. It allows for diverse paths to *Moksha* or salvation.

Questioning and debating was however, central.

The early texts even dabble with the question of whether God exists or not and are comfortable holding the ideas of the believer and non-believer in the same palm of the hand. Such verses were meant to open the mind of the person reading the text. It is designed like God himself questions his existence. As difficult to grasp as this may seem, what God himself was conveying was that he/she was/is unimportant and what one needed to focus on was the 'message and essence' of the philosophies and wisdom that was handed out, even as God humbly shifts focus away from himself/herself (God), and puts the spotlight on the message.

A 'Universal Wisdom' radiates from these depictions, and this can only be captured by the mind that is open to receiving it. It can then be seen in the way that it was intended to be seen.

While to cursory observers, the examples depicting an elephant-head, a rat, a snake, and a *trishul,* etc., may seem primitive or just mumbo jumbo, that is ONLY 'a reflection of their ignorance' encapsulated by the 'arrogance that follows that ignorance'.

A smart observer will focus on the message and essence of these stories and representations. This will allow him/her to gain from it and to be able to lead a happy, healthy, and prosperous life, which is what the inherent design in 'Sanatana Dharma' intended to do.

Time for some FUN

Time for **American** song-writer, singer, and actor **Lenny Kravitz** to rock you with his hit song, **'Are You Gonna Go My Way'**. It was his first single from his third studio album, **'Are You Gonna Go My Way' (1993)**. The song was cowritten by **Lenny Kravitz** and **Craig Ross**. Enjoy!!

'Are You Gonna Go My Way'

Lenny Kravitz, [Album **'Are You Gonna Go My Way' (1993)**]

SCAN above to see **YOUTUBE** ***Video of the Song***

Lyrics

[Are You Gonna Go My Way]

I was born long ago
I am the chosen, I'm the one
I have come to save the day
And I won't leave until I'm done

So that's why, you've got to try
You got to breathe and have some fun
Though I'm not paid, I play this game
And I won't stop until I'm done

But what I really want to know is
Are you gonna go my way?
And I got to, got to know, eh

I don't know why, we always cry
This we must leave and get undone
We must engage and rearrange
And turn this planet back to one

So tell me why, we got to die?
And kill each other one by one
We've got to hug, and rub-a-dub
We've got to dance, and be in love

(But what I really want to know is)
Are you gonna go my way?
And I got to, got to know

C'mon!
Are you gonna go my way?
'Cause baby, I got to know, yeah

Part IV

Chapter 5

SOME FUN: 'LOCKER ROOM TALK'

Why picking the right solution to the problem is important, like not thinking too much!

"Women marry men hoping they will change. Men marry women hoping they will not."

– Albert Einstein

"After the chills and fever of love, how nice is the 98.6 degrees of marriage."

– Mignon McLaughlin

WARNING SIGN

(**GIRLS** please **SKIP** this Chapter!)....

'LOCKER ROOM TALK' in progress,

STOP

'TRADE SECRETs' being exchanged

Tip for the guys

"Experience is the comb that life gives you, after you have gone bald"

– Navjot Singh Sidhu

"Whenever you're wrong, admit it; whenever you're right, shut up."

– Ogden Nash

If you find yourself in an argument with your wife or girlfriend, 'just apologize RIGHT AWAY', 'admit YOU are the idiot', and 'she IS right', and do so IMMEDIATELY without thinking.

Do not dilly-dally, as there is no thinking required. These are NOT matters of logic!

Hope you got what I am saying. If not, no problem, you will just have to suffer a little more before you get it. It is only a matter of time, so don't worry too much!

Also, swear that you will next time consult your wife/girlfriend on "everything" and drink from her "Wisdom". At least, you will be ALLOWED to sleep, rather than have to argue all night long.

Have you heard of the saying, "No one wins an argument!"? Sorry, it is a wrong statement. If you are in an argument with your wife/girlfriend, she has already crowned herself the winner BEFORE you are even allowed to open your mouth. You only have the right to open your mouth to confess that you are stupid, you made a mistake, and you will toe her line.

Your job now is to accept this situation and be happy, so that you are allowed to sleep. You need to sleep to survive or even live to fight another day! That is what *Lord Hanuman* or *Lord Ganesha* would have done in your place. This strategy in military terms is called a 'Tactical Retreat'.

Oh! I forgot that Lord Hanuman and Lord Ganesha are wise enough to be single. They have supreme wisdom. They know right away that even THEY cannot resolve this issue.

They just did the 'Strategic Retreat' and left this battlefield for fools like us!

Time for some FUN

(Pss... Girls, I know you read this for SURE, because girls too just want to have fun!).

(So here is a song for you girls!!).

Time for a song by **American** songwriter, singer and actress **Cyndi Lauper** with her lead hit single ,**'Girls Just Want to Have Fun'** from her album **"She's So Unusual" (1983).** The song was written by **Robert Hazard**. Enjoy!!

'Girls Just Want to Have Fun'

Cyndi Lauper, [Album **'She's So Unusual' (1983)**]

SCAN above to see **YOUTUBE** ***Video of the Song***

Lyrics

[Girls Just Wanna Have fun]

I come home, in the mornin' light
My mother says, "When you gonna live your life right?"
Oh momma dear, we're not the fortunate ones
And girls, they wanna have fun
Oh girls just wanna have fun

The phone rings, in the middle of the night
My father yells, "What you gonna do with your life?"
Oh daddy dear, you know you're still number one
But girls, they wanna have fun
Oh girls just wanna have

That's all they really want
Some fun
When the workin' day is done
Oh girls, they wanna have fun
Oh girls just wanna have fun (girls, they want)
(Wanna have fun, girls)
(Wanna have)

Some boys take a beautiful girl
And hide her away from the rest o' the world
I wanna be the one to walk in the sun
Oh girls, they wanna have fun
Oh girls just wanna have

That's all they really want
Is some fun
When the workin' day is done
Oh girls, they wanna have fun
Oh girls just wanna have fun (girls, they want)
(Wanna have fun, girls)
(Wanna have)

They just want, they just wanna (girls)
They just want, they just wanna (girls just wanna have fun)
Oh girls, girls just wanna have fun
(Just want, they just wanna)
They just wanna, they just wanna (girls)
They just want, they just wanna (girls just wanna have fun)
Oh girls, girls just wanna have fun

When the workin'
When the workin' day is done
Oh, when the workin' day is done
Oh, girls, girls just wanna have fun
Everybody
Huh, huh

They just want, they just wanna (girls)
They just want, they just wanna (girls just wanna have fun)
Oh, girls, girls just wanna have fun
(They just wanna, they just wanna) when the workin'
When the working day is done (they just want, they just wanna)
Oh, when the working day is done (girls, girls just wanna have fun)
Oh girls, girls just wanna have fun

(They just want, they just wanna)
(They just want, they just wanna)

Part IV

Chapter 6

CHARACTERS FROM INDIAN EPICS

Why Krishna's Wisdom is better than Ram and Ram Rajya?

"Wisdom is the knowledge of good and evil, not the strength to choose between the two."

–John Cheever

"The art of being wise is the art of knowing what to overlook."

– William James

Mr.Devdutt Pattanaik, India's leading mythologist, makes a fascinating observation about the characters in the Indian Epics of *'Mahabharata'* and *'Ramayana'*.

In the '*Ramayana*', Lord *Rama* upholds all rules and principles. In the process, he puts a lot of people — including himself, his wife, his father, brothers, and his people — through a lot of hardships. Lord *Rama* goes into exile to keep his father's word. He doesn't return even when his dying father, King *Dasharatha*, and pleading brother *Bharatha*, call him back. His wife *Sita* is put through *Agni Pariksha* (Fire Test) to prove her fidelity. In short, he and others around him were subjected to great suffering only to uphold the rigid rules and principles he had set for himself.

Again in the '*Ramayana*', Ravana, though a pious and god-fearing man and a great devotee of Lord *Shiva*, follows no rules or principles. He tricks Lord *Rama* into leaving *Sita* alone, guarded only by *Lakshmana*. He further tricks *Lakshmana* into leaving *Sita* unguarded, and finally tricks and abducts *Sita* against her wishes. *Sita's* abduction leads to a war, killing many and eventually annihilating Ravana, who was defending his wrong. The war to get the abducted *Sita* back led to destruction and suffering all around.

In the '*Mahabharata*', *Duryodhana* is a man of rules, even if it means he has to compromise on the principles of dharma (or justice). He debates about the technicalities of the law. He refuses to budge even though Shree *Krishna* asks him to return the kingdom to the exiled *Pandavas* based on principles. *Duryodhana* argued about rules as he dragged *Draupadi* to the court and attempted to disrobe and humiliate her.

Interestingly, in the same '*Mahabharata*', Shree *Krishna* is a person of principles yet is ready to bend the rules if necessary to uphold Dharma (Principles of Justice). Though Yudhistra had lost *Draupadi* in a game of dice, Shree *Krishna* protects *Draupadi* even as she prays to him. Similarly, in every situation in the '*Mahabharata*', Shree *Krishna* upholds Dharma and principles even though he bent the rules as and when necessary. The table below explains the different characters and their beliefs and consequent actions.

Krishna Upholder of Principles over just rules	**Rama** Upholder of Rules & Principles	↑ **Principles**
Ravana Rules and Principles don't matter	**Duryodhana** Upholder of Rules but ignores Principles	
Rules →		

Table 1. The Rule and Principle Grid

It is interesting to note that while both Ravana and Lord *Rama* were highly intelligent, they both caused immense suffering. Ravana used his intelligence to further his evil deeds, while Lord *Rama* created similar sufferings to uphold his rigid righteousness.

Duryodhana and Shree *Krishna* were intelligent. While *Duryodhana's* intelligence only caused him to be more foolish, Shree *Krishna's* knowledge had wisdom with the need and end goal of protecting Dharmic principles.

From the four different characters in '*Ramayana*' and '*Mahabharata*', one can see the lessons for our lives play out. Each character was wrong and right in their ways. However, it becomes evident that upholding Dharmic principles is more important than just blindly upholding rules.

Time for some FUN

Time for lead singer **Steven Tyler** of the **American** hard rock band **Aerosmith** to rock you with their hit pop rock song, **'I Don't Wanna Miss A Thing'** from the motion picture soundtrack of the movie **'Armageddon' (1998).** Enjoy!!

"I Don't Wanna Miss A Thing"

Aerosmith, [Motion Picture Soundtrack **'Armageddon' (1998)**]

SCAN above to see **YOUTUBE** *Video of the Song*

Lyrics

[I Don't Wanna Miss A Thing]

I could stay awake just to hear you breathing
Watch you smile while you are sleeping
While you're far away dreaming
I could spend my life in this sweet surrender
I could stay lost in this moment forever
Every moment spent with you is a moment I treasure

Don't want to close my eyes
I don't want to fall asleep
'Cause I'd miss you baby
And I don't want to miss a thing
'Cause even when I dream of you
The sweetest dream will never do
I'd still miss you baby
And I don't want to miss a thing

Lying close to you feeling your heart beating
And I'm wondering what you're dreaming
Wondering if it's me you're seeing
Then I kiss your eyes
And thank God we're together
I just want to stay with you in this moment forever
Forever and ever

Don't want to close my eyes
I don't want to fall asleep
'Cause I'd miss you baby
And I don't want to miss a thing
'Cause even when I dream of you
The sweetest dream will never do
I'd still miss you baby
And I don't want to miss a thing

I don't want to miss one smile
I don't want to miss one kiss
I just want to be with you
Right here with you, just like this
I just want to hold you close
Feel your heart so close to mine
And just stay here in this moment
For all the rest of time

Don't want to close my eyes
I don't want to fall asleep
'Cause I'd miss you baby
And I don't want to miss a thing
'Cause even when I dream of you
The sweetest dream will never do
I'd still miss you baby
And I don't want to miss a thing

Don't want to close my eyes
I don't want to fall asleep
'Cause I'd miss you baby
I don't want to miss a thing
'Cause even when I dream of you
The sweetest dream will never do
I'd still miss you baby
And I don't want to miss a thing

Part V

YOUR INNER 'GPS' [GURU POSITIONING SYSTEM]

<u>Part V</u>

Chapter 1

GUIDING PRINCIPLES

Guiding Principles to help us CENTRE ourselves leading us to Holistic Happiness and Prosperity

"Hatred is so much easier to win than love – and so much harder to get rid of."

– ***Enid Blyton,*** *Six Cousins again*

"The web of our life is of a mingled yarn, good and ill together."

– ***Shakespeare*** *(All's Well That Ends Well, Act 4, Scene 3)*

Mahatma Gandhi, with his infinite love for humanity, had internalized humanity's most pressing and difficult moral conflicts. He had suffered for the whole of humanity, as he churned internally and wrung his 'heart & mind' out to give us these beautiful guiding principles, that could help to alleviate human suffering.

When understood and imbibed, these principles will free the hearts of humans from the shackles of their bondage, while liberating society from its limitations. Thus, they will enable humanity to rise to its happiest, healthiest, and most prosperous state.

Mahatma Gandhi helps us to center and brings us back to the core values that would help humanity survive and not self-destruct. He brings us to our base line, reminding us of the need to strike a balance, lest we crash and burn.

The more things change, the more they remain the same. In this constant flux, it would help to recall the words of the great Mahatma Gandhi.

Quoted as the '7 Deadly Sins'

The

7 Deadly Sins

Wealth *without* work,
Pleasure *without* conscience,
Science *without* humanity,
Knowledge *without* character,
Politics *without* principle,
Commerce *without* morality,
Worship *without* sacrifice

While these concepts may seem abstract, it is necessary for us to take a step back and ponder philosophically about human civilization and WHERE we are taking it.

In the face of disparities in society, unresolved conflicts, festering wounds from the past, lack of consensus, a shortage of wisdom guiding decisions, a barrage of technological advances challenging the way we live, exacerbating differences in ways we are unable to comprehend and grasp, and a lack of direction in which global leadership is grappling with multi-dimensional dilemmas, we NEED TO CENTER ourselves with the teachings left by that great soul who lived a century ago.

I would like to quote a few *Sanskrit Slokhas* that emphasise the similar thoughts.

A

'Sanskrit Slokha'

Describing how to navigate in an imperfect world

चरेद्धानकटुकोमुञ्चेत्स्नेहंननास्तिकः।
अनृशंसश्चरेदर्थंचरेत् काममनुद्धतः॥ - Mahasubhashitsangrah

carēddhānakaṭukō muñcēt snēhaṃ na nāstikaḥ ।
anṛśaṃsaścarēdarthaṃ carēt kāmamanuddhataḥ ॥

Meaning:

One should do righteous acts without being bitter,
Give up attachment without being an atheist,
Earn material prosperity without being cruel,
and
Enjoy carnal pleasure without being reckless.

We need to do this so that humanity survives these tough challenges and is not swept so far away from its moorings that it begins to drift without direction or purpose into oblivion and impending doom.

A

'Sanskrit Slokha'

Describing how to navigate in an imperfect world

शान्तितुल्यंतपोनास्तिनसन्तोषात्परंसुखम्।
नतृष्णायाःपरोव्याधिःनचधर्मोदयापरः॥ - चाणक्यनीतिः

śāntitulyaṃ tapō nāsti na santōṣāt paraṃ sukham ।
na tṛṣṇāyāḥ parō vyādhiḥ na ca dharmō dayāparaḥ ॥

Meaning:

There is no Penance like peace, no Happiness like contentment,
no Disease like lust and there is no Dharma like kindness.

Conclusion

It is to be noted that NONE of what Mahatma Gandhi said or what the Sanskrit verse tells us EVER condemns or demonizes the material world. It only states that whether it be wealth, pleasure, science, knowledge, politics, commerce or worship, one should engage in them, while balancing the responsibilities that go with it.

For us to survive and thrive, our society should NOT abandon its core principles as outlined by the Mahatma. I leave you with these thoughts as I end this chapter.

Time for some FUN

Time for a song by **American** singer and actress **Vanessa Williams,** with the third single, **'Save the Best for Last' (1992),** from her second studio album **'Comfort Zone' (1991).** The song was written by **Phil Galdston, Wendy Waldman,** and **Jon Lind.** Enjoy!!

'Save the Best for Last'

Vanessa Williams, [Album **'Comfort Zone' (1991)**]

SCAN above to see **YOUTUBE** *Video of the Song*

Lyrics

[Save the Best for Last]

Sometimes the snow comes down in June
Sometimes the sun goes 'round the moon
I see the passion in your eyes
Sometimes it's all a big surprise

'Cause there was a time when all I did was wish
You'd tell me this was love
It's not the way I hoped or how I planned
But somehow it's enough

And now we're standing face to face
Isn't this world a crazy place?
Just when I thought our chance had passed
You go and save the best for last

All of the nights you came to me
When some silly girl had set you free
You wondered how you'd make it through
I wondered what was wrong with you

'Cause how could you give your love to someone else
And share your dreams with me
Sometimes the very thing you're lookin' for
Is the one thing you can't see

But now we're standing face to face
Isn't this world a crazy place?
Just when I thought our chance had passed
You go and save the best for last

Sometimes the very thing you're looking for
Is the one thing you can't see

Sometimes the snow comes down in June
Sometimes the sun goes 'round the moon
Just when I thought our chance had passed
You go and save the best for last
You went and saved the best for last

A

'Sanskrit Slokha'

On Conquering desire and staying on top of it

आशायाःयेदासाःतेदासास्सर्वलोकस्य।
आशायेषांदासीतेषांदासायतेलोकः।। - कवितामृतकूपः

āśāyāḥ yē dāsāḥ tē dāsāssarvalōkasya ।
āśā yēṣāṃ dāsī tēṣāṃ dāsāyatē lōkaḥ ॥

Meaning:

Those who are enslaved to desires are enslaved to the whole world.

But for those to whom desire is enslaved, to them, the entire world is enslaved.

Detachment

While excessive attachment to desires is unhelpful and leads to misery, for most of us, complete decoupling from the material world isn't an option either. While asking for complete disengagement is obviously not practical, one can still navigate the world with a heightened state of spiritual evolution and yet be engaged in the material world.

Once one recognizes and understands the limitations of the material world, one would then be able to navigate life much better. The material world has its limitations, and keeping one's head above the water will allow one to reclaim one's life and lead one to health and true happiness.

Shri Krishna in the *Bhagavad-Gita* uses the symbolism of the horses, the chariot, the reins, and the charioteer to describe how one needs to navigate the world.

A

'Sanskrit Slokha'

<u>Describing how one should navigate one's life</u>

रथःशरीरंपुरुषस्यराजत्रात्मानियन्तेन्द्रियाण्यस्यचाश्वाः।
तैरप्रमत्तःकुशलीसदश्वैर्दान्तैःसुखंयातिरथीवधीरः॥

rathaḥ śarīraṃ puruṣasya rājatrātmā niyantēndriyāṇyasya cāścāḥ ।
tairapramattaḥ kuśalī sadaśvairdāntaiḥ sukhaṃ yāti rathīva dhīraḥ ॥

Meaning:

The Soul is the master of the chariot – Final decision maker.
The Body is the chariot.

Buddhi (Intellect) is the charioteer who helps the soul to decide the direction to take.

Mana (Mind) is the reins with which the soul, controls the horses with the help of Intellect.

The Horses are our sense organs (eyes, ears, nose, tongue & skin) through which we experience the world.

The path on which we tread in life of attractions and distractions.

The person who holds them carefully, cleverly and wisely travels happily in the world like a superior *Rathwan* (Skilled Charioteer).

Attached-Detachment

Most of the symbolism in Sanatana Dharma, whether related to Lord Ganesha (seated with one leg on the floor and the other folded on his lap, and disengaged) or Lord Shiva (in tranquillity and peace even with the ego serpent around his neck), symbolizes the same philosophy.

It is the philosophy of 'Attached-Detachment'.

Attached-detachment is the ability to be immersed in the material world and yet be untouched by it. To navigate one's life with one's intellect and mind in control of the reins (as described by Shri Krishna in the Bhagavad Gita) would lead one to that elusive happiness and peace.

A

'Sanskrit Slokha'

On the 'Ultimate Truths'

नास्तिविद्यासमंचक्षु: नास्तिसत्यसमंतप:।
नास्तिरागसमंदु:खंनास्तित्यागसमंसुखम्।।

nāsti vidyāsamaṃ cakṣu: nāsti satyasamaṃ tapa: ।
nāsti rāgasamaṃ duḥkhaṃ nāsti tyāgasamaṃ sukham ॥

Meaning:

There is no eye like knowledge, no penance like truth,
no sorrow like attachment and there is no happiness like a sacrifice.

Maintaining that 'Gap'

Sadhguru talks in his book 'Inner Engineering' about how one can maintain one's composure and inner peace by maintaining a 'Gap' between one's 'inner self' and one's 'emotions or outer self'.

Sadhguru correctly points out that most suffering is in one's head. Interestingly, it is actually a choice. One can actually choose to manage, diminish, and minimize it rather than suffer unnecessarily in one's head.

I would say that happiness and peace are possible only when one does not take one's self too seriously. Having that attached-detachment, and sense of humor would go a long way in mitigating the suffering of oneself and, consequently, the suffering of people around us.

We are just in a better and enhanced 'mental space' to think through and focus on solutions rather than unnecessarily replay the negativity in our own minds.

Emphasis on Action and NOT Results

Shri Krishna gives invaluable guidance in the Bhagavad Gita when he asks one to detach from the potential outcomes of one's actions and instead shift focus to our actions. When one leaves the 'burden' of the 'potential outcomes' of one's actions to the Almighty, one is unencumbered and lightened.

A

'Sanskrit Slokha'

कर्मण्येवाधिकारस्तेमाफलेषुकदाचन।
माकर्मफलहेतुर्भूर्मातिसङ्गोऽस्त्वकर्मणि॥ २-४७

Karmanye vadhikaraste Ma Phaleshu Kadachana,
Ma Karmaphalaheturbhurma Te Sangostvakarmani

Meaning:

You have the right to work only but never to its fruits.

Let not the fruits of action be your motive, nor let your attachment be to inaction.

It is a powerful message and is the first step in becoming a *Karma-Yogi.* A Karma Yogi is one WHO practices Lord Krishna's advice. Such a person is a person of action WHO engages in the world to do good WITHOUT motive from outside. Such a person maintains 'tranquillity of the mind' and 'nobility in action'.

Such a person's actions are unencumbered by the potential fruits of his actions, and such a person's joy is not weighed down by the expectations of results. Shri Krishna's advice unshackles one from the burden of the expectations (of results) and liberates one to rise and attain one's greatest potential and happiness in one's lives.

Time for some FUN

I would like to end this chapter with a song from the **1978** blockbuster **Hindi** movie **'Muqaddar Ka Sikandar'**, starring one of **Bollywood's** greatest movie stars of all time, **Amitabh Bachchan,** a.k.a. **Big B**. The Movie was directed by **Prakash Mehra.** The Music is by the duo **Kalyanji-Anandji** and the voice is that of the legendary **Kishore Kumar.** Enjoy!

<table>
<tr><td colspan="2">SONG
'Rote hue aate hain sab'
MOVIE
Muqaddar Ka Sikandar (1978)
(The conqueror of his destiny)

SCAN above to see **YOUTUBE** ***Video of the Song***</td></tr>
<tr><td>*Lyrics*
['Rote hue aate hain sab']</td><td>*Translation*
[Everyone comes crying into this world]</td></tr>
<tr><td>Rote hue
aate hain sab
Rote hue
aate hain sab
Hasta hua joh jayega
Woh muqaddar ka sikandar
Woh muqaddar ka sikandar
Jaan-e-man kehlayega</td><td>Everyone comes here crying (into this world)
Everyone comes here crying (into this world)
The one who leaves laughing from here
He'll be the conqueror of his destiny
He'll be the conqueror of his destiny
He will be known as such, my dear</td></tr>
</table>

Rote hue aate hain sab Rote hue aate hain sab Hasta hua joh jayega	Everyone comes here crying (into this world) Everyone comes here crying (into this world) The one who leaves laughing from here
Woh sikandar kya tha jisne zulm se jeeta jahaan Woh sikandar kya tha jisne zulm se jeeta jahaan Pyar se jeete dilon ko woh jhuka de aasmaan Joh sitaron par kahani pyar ki likh jayega Woh muqaddar ka sikandar Woh muqaddar ka sikandar Jaan-e-man kehlayega	A conqueror who is cruel to the world is nothing A conqueror who is cruel to the world is nothing He who wins the hearts with love can bow the sky down He who will write the story of love on the stars He'll be the conqueror of his destiny He'll be the conqueror of his destiny And so will his name be, my dear
Rote hue aate hain sab Hasta hua joh jayega	Everyone comes here crying (into this world) The one who leaves laughing from here
Zindagi toh bewafa hai ek din thukrayegi Zindagi toh bewafa hai ek din thukrayegi Maut mehbooba hai apne saath lekar jayegi Marke jeene ki adaa joh duniya ko sikhlayega Woh muqaddar ka sikandar Woh muqaddar ka sikandar Jaan-e-man kehlayega	Life is like an unfaithful lover, one day it'll let you down Life is like an unfaithful lover, one day it'll let you down Death is our faithful lover, one day it'll take us with it The one who even in death will yet teach the world the style of living He'll be the conqueror of his destiny He'll be the conqueror of his destiny And so will his name be, my dear

Rote hue aate hain sab Hasta hua joh jayega Woh muqaddar ka sikandar Woh muqaddar ka sikandar Jaan-e-man kehlayega	Everyone comes here crying (Into this world) The one who leaves laughing from here He'll be the conqueror of his destiny He'll be the conqueror of his destiny And so will his name be, my dear
Humne maana yeh zamana dard ki jageer hai Humne maana yeh zamana dard ki jageer hai Har kadam pe aasuon ki ik nayi zanjeer hai Haal-e-gham par joh khushi ke geet gata jayega Woh muqaddar ka sikandar Woh muqaddar ka sikandar Jaan-e-man kehlayega	I agree that this world is full of pain I agree that this world is full of pain On every step there are new shackles of tears The one who sings songs of joy when he's sad He'll be the conqueror of his destiny He'll be the conqueror of his destiny And so will his name be, my dear
"Rote hue aate hain sab Rote hue aate hain sab Hasta hua joh jayega Woh muqaddar ka sikandar Woh muqaddar ka sikandar Jaan-e-man kehlayega".	Everyone comes here crying (into this world) Everyone comes here crying (into this world) The one who leaves laughing from here He'll be the conqueror of his destiny He'll be the conqueror of his destiny He will be known as such, my dear".

Part V

Chapter 3

POSITIVE VIBRATION

Be the Change..... Be the Light ..... Be the Celebration

"Everything in life is vibration."

– Albert Einstein

"I am a believer of butterfly effect. A small positive vibration can change the entire cosmos."

– Amit Ray

Positive Vibration

Here is a small poem 'POSITIVE VIBRATION' to end this section on a positive note. Hope you like it. Enjoy!!

Poem
'POSTIVE VIBRATION'
Book
'FACETS'
(Poetry for All Seasons)

SCAN above to see **YOUTUBE** ***Lyrical Video of the Poem***

Lyrics

[POSITIVE VIBRATION]

When the dark days of winter are past
When the blue skies are here to last
When the flowers open up and bloom
When the sun shines away all the gloom

When the butterfly owns every flower
When over the hive the bees hover
When the grasslands sway to the breeze
When the trees shake off the winter freeze

When you wear that smile to start the day
When you remember me even when far away
When you smell the aroma of morning coffee
Looking forward to a day full of discovery

With lot of wonderful surprises u did not expect
Big or small your life's cup is full without regret
When you start the day with energy n passion
The day stays bright in an uplifting fashion

When you open your heart and embrace the world
When you raise the flag of love and let it unfurl
With every hug you multiply the joy manifold
Love is the lingua franca whether young or old

When efforts of yours are soulful n with meaning
Your vibrations are universal and deeply healing
Change the world with a little positive vibration
Be the change, Be the light, Be the celebration!!

Time for some FUN

Time for a song by **American** singer, song-writer and musician **Marc Cohn,** with the song **'Walk Through this World'**, from his second album **'The Rainy Season' (1993)**. Enjoy!!

'Walk Through this World'

Marc Cohn, [Album **'The Rainy Season' (1993)**]

SCAN above to see **YOUTUBE** ***Video of the Song***

Lyrics

[Walk Through this World]

I'm writing you this letter from some old hotel
I can feel the distance between us
From the Spanish Steps to the Liberty Bell
I know the angels have seen us, seen us, baby

They see you down on Seventh Avenue
While you're just hanging by a thread
And I'm sitting in a lonely room without a view
Wishing I was there with you instead

Won't you walk through this world with me
Walk through this world
Over the miles of mystery
Walk through this world with me

I'm staring out across the rooftops, baby
I've seen the writing on the wall
Heard a little bit of thunder at the seventh wonder
But everything is bound to rise and fall, that's all

Walk through this world with me
Walk through the world
Over the mountains and the shining sea
Walk through this world with me
Walk on, walk on, walk on

Let me get this ringing out of my ears
Let me get these stars out of my eyes
'Cause I just want to look back over all the years
With you right there standing by my side
Could you just

Walk through the world with me
Walk through the world
Over the miles of mystery
Walk through this world with me

Walk through the world with me
Walk through the world
Over the mountains and the shining sea, yeah
Walk through this world with me
Come on, now

Walk through the world
Walk through the world
Walk through the world

Walk through the world
Oh, yeah, yeah
Walk through this world with me
Come on baby
Walk through the world

Part VI

The WORLD is ONE-FAMILY

Part VI

Chapter 1

VASUDHAIVA KUTUMBAKAM

'The World is One Family'

"The true civilization is where every man gives to every other, every right that he claims for himself."

– Robert Green Ingersoll

"There is nothing noble in being superior to your fellow man; true nobility is being superior to your former self."

– Ernest Hemingway

The oldest of the texts in the Vedic tradition mentions *'Vasudhaiva Kutumbakam'*, which translates into the meaning that 'ALL living beings on the earth are a part of ONE family'. ('Vasudhaiva Kutumbakam' is a Sanskrit phrase derived from the *Maha-Upanishad*, which reiterates that 'The World is One Family').

In the eyes of God, all humans, whether the leper asking for alms on a busy street or the richest and most powerful people dining in their beautiful mansions, are ALL EQUAL and deserve equal respect. Ultimately, give or take, we are all children of God.

Basic respect for a fellow human being should be at the core and guiding principle of all our actions. This respect should come from a space untainted by differences stemming from Gender, Ethnicity, Creed, Nationality, Religion, Sexual Orientation, Race, Color, Status, Linguistic preferences, Location (urban, suburban, or rural), Lifestyle (liberal or moderate), and Political Leanings (left, right, or center).

Inculcating basic respect for others and treating others with empathy will be equal to respecting ourselves. When respect is fundamental, it will promote a more conducive atmosphere to exchange perspectives and concerns. Empathy will allow us to understand other's perspectives while being truly sensitive to other's circumstances, concerns, and feelings.

As humans, we all have the capacity for empathy and respect. This is a capacity all of us possess innately. We just need to tap into these, activate, sensitize, and nurture these capacities.

It would then be easier to understand differences and apply the infinite ingenuity innate to us as humans to find solutions to those specific concerns and problems. The amazing gift that God has given us is this ingenuity and unlimited imagination in an unlimited universe. When every human on this planet is empowered, and when this human potential is unlocked, no situation ever needs to be a zero-sum game. Every problem is an opportunity, and every concern can be approached in a win-win manner.

In this way, a powerful and enabling atmosphere will be created, which will bring out the best qualities in each one of us. It will help each one of us realize our greatest potentials in terms of health, wealth, and happiness. We will then blossom as individuals and as a comity of nations. In this way, we can together build a happy and healthy world for all of us, our families, and our children.

These perspectives are NOT born out of idealism. These are pragmatic approaches that we need to imbibe because we can see further ONLY when we rise higher. Hence, we need to rise higher and go above our superficial differences that are clouding our judgment.

The truth is every civilization of the world is great in its own way. No civilization or grouping is superior to the other. Every civilization has just adapted to its geographic location, climate, circumstances, and place in the history of time. Every nationality is great in its own way. Ultimately, scratch the surface and we are all just the same humans.

Just as having pride in one's culture, nation, or economy is a wonderful thing, having a non-judgmental approach and an inquisitive mind will allow us to see the best in other cultures, nations, and economies. When we approach these experiences with an open mind, opportunities to learn will open up to us. We can then learn and grow from those teachings and experiences. This, when accompanied by humility, will allow us to grow our collective wisdom. Together, the human race can then grow and blossom, bringing prosperity to all.

Accepted, that the world was limited in its approach for thousands of years in the past. Wars have been fought and blood has been spilled, even as it was justified with every conceivable reason possible. We have viewed resources as scarce and always had a winner-takes-all approach. It has always been an 'us against them' approach. It however, does NOT have to be that way anymore.

With cooperation, trust, patience, and a better understanding, guided by wisdom, humility, empathy, and faith in the 'human capacity and ingenuity', we can together 'invest and focus' our efforts towards a better and brighter future for all. When we are no longer held hostage by past grievances or current superficial differences, we are free to soar together and reach our potential as a human race and for humanity.

The limited world and closed mindset approach of the past is a very old approach born in a scarce era seen by limited minds. The truth is God has a large heart, and he has created an unlimited world and gifted us with infinite imagination and ingenuity. This has been and is ONLY limited by our limited views and perspectives.

The trick really is not just about opening our minds but starts with opening our hearts and doing it with love, sincerity, empathy, and humility. Our differences and concerns at that moment will become insignificant. Opening our hearts would open our minds to see the unlimited world filled with abundance and love. It was SUCH a world that God had truly envisioned for us.

Some call it the 'Dawn of the Golden Era' or *'Amrit Kal'*. We are at the cusp of it. So, let each of us do our part and reach out for it!

I will end this chapter by leaving you with this beautiful and soulful poem, cradled in crisp prose, conveying in simple but powerful words the concept of 'Vasudhaiva Kutumbakam' (World is One Family).

"We are made of air, water and each other,

What we do to the air, we do to ourselves

What we do to the water, we do to ourselves,

What we do to each other, we do to ourselves".

– ***Lekha Washington***

Time for some FUN

Time for a song by **American** singer and songwriter **Norah Jones,** with second single **'What am I to You?'**, from her album **'Feels Like Home' (2004)**. Enjoy!!

'What am I to You?'

Norah Jones, [Album **'Feels Like Home' (2004)]**

SCAN above to see **YOUTUBE** ***Video of the Song***

Lyrics

[What am I to You?]

What am I to you?
Tell me, darlin', true
To me, you are the sea
Vast as you can be
The deepest shade of blue

When you're feeling low
Oh, to whom else do you go?
See, I'd cry if you hurt
I'd give you my last shirt
Because I love you so

Now if my sky should fall
Would you even call?
I've opened up my heart
I never wanna part
I'm givin' you the ball

When I look in your eyes
I can feel the butterflies
I will love you when you're blue
But tell me, darlin', true
What am I to you?

Now if my sky should fall
Would you even call?
I've opened up my heart
I never wanna part
I'm giving you the ball

When I look in your eyes
I can feel the butterflies
Could you find a love in me?
Would you carve me in a tree?
Don't fill my heart with lies

I will love you when you're blue
Tell me, darlin', true
What am I to you?

Part VI

Chapter 2

PRAYER FOR THE WORLD

A Prayer for Universal Peace and Well-Being

TWO *Sanskrit Slokhas* (Verses)

for

Universal Peace & Prosperity

ॐ सर्वेभवन्तुसुखिनः। सर्वेसन्तुनिरामयाः। सर्वेभद्राणिपश्यन्तु। माकश्चित्दुःखभाग्भवेत्॥ ॐशान्तिःशान्तिःशान्तिः॥
Om, Sarve bhavantu sukhinaḥ *Sarve santu nirāmayāḥ* *Sarve bhadrāṇi paśyantu* *Mā kashchit duḥkha bhāgbhavet*

May all be Prosperous and Happy
May all be Free from Illness
May all see what is Spiritually Uplifting
May No one Suffer
Om Peace, Peace, Peace

Shanti **(Peace) Mantra**

ॐ द्यौः शान्तिरन्तरिक्षं शान्तिः
पृथिवी शान्तिरापः शान्तिरोषधयः शान्तिः ।
वनस्पतयः शान्तिर्विश्वेदेवाः शान्तिर्ब्रह्म शान्तिः
सर्वं शान्तिः शान्तिरेव शान्तिः सा मा शान्तिरेधि ॥
ॐ शान्तिः शान्तिः शान्तिः ॥

Om Dyauh Shaantir-Antarikssam Shaantih
Prthivii Shaantir-Aapah Shaantir-Ossadhayah Shaantih |
Vanaspatayah Shaantir-Vishve-Devaah Shaantir-Brahma Shaantih
Sarvam Shaantih Shaantireva Shaantih Saa Maa Shaantir-Edhi |
Om Shaantih Shaantih Shaantih ||

May peace radiate there in the whole sky as well as in
the vast ethereal space everywhere.
May peace reign all over this earth, in water and
in all herbs, trees and creepers.
May peace flow over the whole universe.
May peace be in the Supreme Being Brahman.
And may there always exist in all peace and peace alone.
Aum peace, peace and peace to us and all beings!

Time for some FUN

We end this book with a song performed by **American** Jazz Legend and Vocalist, **Louis Armstrong** called **'What a Wonderful World' (1967).** The words and music were by **George David Weiss** and **Bob Thiele**. This song was inducted into **'Grammy Hall of Fame'** in **1999.** Enjoy!!

'What A Wonderful World'

Louis Armstrong [ABC records **(1967)**]

SCAN above to see **YOUTUBE** ***Video of the Song***

Lyrics

[What A Wonderful World]

I see trees of green
Red roses too
I see them bloom
For me and you
And I think to myself
What a wonderful world
I see skies of blue
And clouds of white
The bright blessed day
The dark sacred night

And I think to myself
What a wonderful world
The colors of the rainbow
So pretty in the sky
Are also on the faces
Of people going by
I see friends shaking hands
Saying, "How do you do?"
They're really saying
I love you
I hear babies cry
I watch them grow
They'll learn much more
Than I'll ever know
And I think to myself
What a wonderful world
Yes, I think to myself
What a wonderful world
Ooh, yes

Part VII

Vibrations and the Universe

Part VII

END NOTE

VIBRATIONS AND THE UNIVERSE

Why Every 'Small Vibration' Matters

"If you want to find the secrets of the universe, think in terms of energy, frequency and vibration."

– Nikola Tesla

"Every moment there are a million miracles happening around you: a flower blossoming, a bird tweeting, a bee humming, a raindrop falling, a snowflake wafting along the clear evening air. There is magic everywhere. If you learn how to live it, life is nothing short of a daily miracle."

– Sadhguru

It is interesting that in *Sanatana Dharma*, Lord *Shiva* is shown with a ***Damaru*** in his hand. The *Damaru* is a two-sided small drum that fits into his hand. Lord *Shiva* in this depiction is seen to be playing the *Damaru*, as he sends out the spiritual vibrations. According to the Sanatana Dharma philosophies these Spiritual Vibrations were used to create the Universe and are used to regulate it.

While these may seem as a Spiritual depiction or even Mumbo Jumbo (to the uninformed), it will be prudent to note that this does have some deeper meaning and truth to it. The Universe that seems complex on the face of it, actually rests on some simple but fundamental basic building blocks.

To quote Albert Einstein,

"The most incomprehensible thing about the universe is that it is comprehensible."

The Universe right from the dawn of creation, which we refer to as the BIG BANG, started from a single point and expanded to form the visible universe and beyond. As the Universe grew in diversity and complexity, it built upon basic building blocks while sticking to certain fundamental principles.

Somewhere along the way, these 'small vibrations' manifested into mass and energy vibrating at diverse and varying frequencies. These manifestations grew, while expanding and becoming the Universe we see today.

ATOMS and WHAT THEY CONTAIN

"The best armour of old age is a well-spent life preceding it."

– Charlie Munger

"Love is your quality. Love is not what you do. Love is what you are."

– Sadhguru

In the scientific world when atoms ('*Anu*' as described in early Sanskrit Verses) were observed at a very small granular level it was found to contain Electrons, Protons and Neutrons.

However, what is interesting is that when observed even more deeply 99% of an atom is just actually empty space and what we have are just vibrations happening at a very minute granular level.

In fact, we and the things around us are nothing but made up of zillions of these small vibrations.

Where PHYSICS meets PHILOSOPHY

"Act only according to that maxim whereby you can, at the same time, will that it should become a universal law."

– Kant

"Happiness is not based on achievements. It's an attitude cultivated by appreciating the simple things in life and valuing relationships over possessions."

– Gaur Gopal Das

At one level the entire universe can be fundamentally looked on as mass, energy and ether. At the minutest level (beyond atoms, neutrons, protons, electrons and even quarks, leptons, gluons), the universe is made up of zillions of small vibrations. It is the aggregate of those small vibrations that determine the characteristics of that manifestation.

Mass is like 'knots' in the field of these energies. Mass can also be seen as the concentration of energy at points in space.

While all mass in the world is ultimately an aggregate of these small vibrations, the difference between inanimate and animate objects is 'consciousness' or *Chit,* as in ancient Sanskrit texts.

The consciousness or *Chit* (as described in Sanskrit texts) allows us to modify or regulate our integrity framework of the aggregate small vibrations that constitute ourselves. These aggregate vibrations tend to draw similar vibrations and help us grow our collective destiny.

Physicist Albert Einstein did propose the 'Theory of Relativity.' While this worked when applied to the larger Universe, it failed to explain what happened at the 'Atomic Level.' At an 'Atomic level,' this theory failed to explain and capture what was happening, leading Albert Einstein to work on a theory that could explain the Universe at the 'Atomic' and 'Larger levels.' Albert Einstein spent his last days trying to complete this work, but sadly, he passed away before he could close the loop.

On the other hand, the laws of 'Quantum Mechanics' proved to be more apt to reliably explain what happened at the 'Atomic Level.' However, it could NOT explain what was happening when applied to the larger Universe.

Since then, physicists have been looking for a theory that would bring the 'Theory of Relativity' and the 'Theory of Quantum Mechanics' to a common platform. A platform that is often called the 'The UNIFIED THEORY of EVERYTHING.'

Science has found that LIGHT PHOTONs, for instance, can behave BOTH like a PARTICLE and a WAVE. Further theories, such as ENTANGLEMENT and STRING THEORY, have left physicists baffled and more confused.

Also, a UNIFIED theory that connects the 'Relativity' and 'Quantum Mechanics' has still been elusive to Scientists.

However, if we begin to see the UNIVERSE as made up of zillion vibrations with 'Mass and Energy' being just different manifestations of these vibrations, we may just begin to see the connections leading to a 'UNIFIED THEORY of EVERYTHING.'

Ultimately, Both MASS And ENERGY are made up of zillions of these small vibrations. When a bunching of these vibrations occurs within an integrity framework, particular manifestations of energy and mass are created. Mass are just concentrated knots in the Energy fields.

BOTH Energy and Mass are just made up of small vibrations vibrating at different and diverse frequencies. At the minutest level, each manifestation maintains an integrity framework unique to its grouping. Hence these small vibrations while vibrating at a diverse set of frequencies, go on to exhibit their own unique characteristics.

Interestingly, Mass and Energy are ultimately interchangeable as and when we are able to move them from one integrity framework to the other. When the 'dense and tight knot' we call Mass is unravelled, huge amounts of energy is unleashed.

UNIVERSAL VIBRATIONS

"The most beautiful moments in life are moments when you are expressing your joy, not when you are seeking it."

– Sadhguru

"What you do makes a difference, and you have to decide what kind of difference you want to make."

– Jane Goodall

Interestingly, each and every Universe (among the ones in the infinite 'Alternative Universes') has a 'Certain Vibration' as central to its Integrity framework. Within the Universe, there are many stars and galaxies that have their own vibrations. The 'sum of parts,' however, makes up the whole.

On similar lines, EACH and EVERY human being has a SMALL VIBRATION in him. In various forms of Religion or Philosophy, these are referred to as the SOUL. It is NOT just individuals that have a SOUL, but so do all particles that make up the UNIVERSE in our reality. However, humans have consciousness, which allows them to shape these vibrations.

Ultimately, these vibrations do and can change. We are made up of zillions of atoms having their own small vibrations which can respond to change originating within.

At an individual level, all of us have an 'integrity framework.' When we move in directions that are NOT in sync with it, our inner vibrations will feel torn in different directions.

The point I am making is that if our actions are driven by LOVE and a CONCERN for each other we will create such a VIBRATION framework for us on EARTH. This is something that we send out into the UNIVERSE. This would for instance attract other POSITIVE nurturing frameworks in our immediate environment and in our UNIVERSE.

For example, at the extreme level, either LOVE or HATE can be the predominant vibration we send out (as a planet) into the Universe. Consequently, we are more likely to attract other aliens who have the SAME TYPE of Vibration. This may lead to COLLABORATION or DESTRUCTION, depending on WHO we end up attracting. This in turn is a function of our aggregate vibrations as a humanity.

For instance, if our actions are driven by HATE and DESTRUCTION, we may end up with collective vibrations that may ultimately lead us on a path to the end of us as a human race. For instance, if we are driven by hate, we are more likely to attract aliens who are ALSO driven by hate. We may end up self-destructing or in mutual destruction.

Ironically the Universe would actually help and facilitate us to do the same. The Universe is only in the business of giving us what we ask for and consequently deserve as a species.

If we choose LOVE, we will survive and thrive. While if we choose HATE we will get exactly that and end up destroying each other. Progress and technological development only serve to AMPLIFY our innate inner vibrations.

A society, civilisation or species gets what it deserves. The only rules that matter are those of the 'KARMIC balance of the UNIVERSE.' That balance gets restored at the appropriate time, no matter what.

The point is that, "The Universe does NOT care for HUMANs in particular". Now, that is a humbling thought.

There is really no privileged position assigned to humans. The status of superiority that humans assign themselves is just our delusion. This may stem from our temporary dominance and consequent arrogance that is born out of that position of dominance. While we need the Universe to exist, the Universe does not need us to survive.

Hence, we can nurture ourselves and care for each other or go ahead hate and destroy each other. The fact is the Universe does not care. The Universe has its laws and cares about only maintaining the Karmic Balances. We can choose our collective fate. In someways, we are actually in control of that.

For instance, there are nuclear weapons and AI (Artificial Intelligence). If humanity cannot develop an INTEGRITY framework of TRUST built on CONCERN for fellow human beings, it is NOT difficult to see WHERE this would end. Both nuclear weapons and AI (Artificial Intelligence) are examples of Technology that would only AMPLIFY our CORE VIBRATIONS.

Whether those 'CORE VIBRATIONS' are of HATE or LOVE is really up to us as countries, as communities and at an individual level.

The choice is ours as humanity. The universe is just a facilitator. The Onus is on us as an intelligent species to make sure that in our rush, our SUPREME INTELLIGENCE does NOT get ahead of our COLLECTIVE WISDOM.

DIMENSIONS of the PROBLEM

"Life can only be understood backwards, but it must be lived forwards."

– Kierkegaard

"Too many people are hungry, not because there is a dearth of food. It is because there is a dearth of love and care in human hearts."

– Sadhguru

The sobering thought is that the power we wield today is nothing compared to what is going to be in our hands as we go forward. It would be imperative for us humans to anchor and base our work from a place of LOVE and NURTURING. We need to develop an INTEGRITY FRAMEWORK that is nurturing and caring, rather than based on mistrust and hatred.

The tools of science and technology we have, even today alone, are enough to destroy the human race many times. As we go forward, we are going to see the potential for 'Amplified Outcomes' at levels we can't even fathom today.

Now the question is are we going to SEED the future with LOVE or base it on HATE? WHAT are we going to teach and pass on to our children? The SEED we lay today, whether LOVE or HATE will determine our future and the future of our children. The choice is before us, and we have the power to shape our COLLECTIVE DESTINY.

The most frightening part is that if we do not get our foundations right, and do it right now, we may end up moving forward with HATE in our hearts. 'HATE and GREED' in our hearts is guaranteed to make us all perish and die, as we hurtle towards SUCH a collective destiny.

A society or civilisation GETS what it DESERVES. If we choose hate, the way the Universe works is that it will give us exactly what we ask for. It is just that this will be at ANOTHER LEVEL. If you consider how technology can amplify HATE or LOVE, it becomes clear why.

For instance, take atomic weapons (which was described as 'harnessing the power' of the 'Creation of the Universe' by former US President *Franklin Roosevelt*). Humans discovered that a small amount of mass can be converted to huge amounts of energy. The same tech can be used for destruction or to generate energy; we had and have a choice.

The atomic weapon was really a 1st generation weapon. We then went on to develop the 2nd generation weapon and called it a 'Thermo-nuclear' weapon. Now, we all know how destructive that can be.

The 2nd generation 'Thermo-nuclear weapon' is on an exponential curve when compared to the 1st Generation 'Atomic weapon.' Now, if I told you that we had barely begun to get started, and it is possible to have a 9th generation weapon. What would your reaction be?

You read right, 9th generation weapon.

For one moment here, let us step back and take a deep breath as we begin to grasp the magnitude of that kind of weapon. Each Generation of Weapon can pack a punch that is exponentially greater than the punch of the previous one.

A 9th generation weapon, when set off, will be so powerful that it would end OUR UNIVERSE (This UNIVERSE being our reality in the multitude of ALTERNATIVE UNIVERSEs). Such a weapon, when set off, would simply cause a REVERSE BIG BANG. It would bring our Universe back to a SINGLE POINT. Well, that is what 'HATE WHEN AMPLIFIED' looks like.

As we use our intelligence to build bigger and more powerful technologies, we are going to have tremendous power in our hands. The question then is, "Given such power, what are the choices we are going to choose to make?" Those decisions would ultimately determine, whether we are going to NURTURE or DESTROY each other.

All this starts with that SMALL VIBRATION in EACH ONE of us. Are we going to choose nurturing qualities of LOVE, UNDERSTANDING and EMPATHY, or are we going to let HATE be our predominant emotion? Because those 'Small Vibrations' in us determine how we choose to approach our lives.

Even as we interact in this world, those small vibrations in us together are being collectively transmitted outwards and into the UNIVERSE. While 'Positive Vibrations' attract positive forces, 'Negative Vibrations' attract negative forces.

Every day, and with every decision we make, we make choices that strengthen the LOVE or HATE in us. These vibrations of LOVE or HATE then get transmitted outside and projects itself outward and into our immediate world and into the Universe. Even as they project outward they become more amplified as they seek similar vibrations, that then comes back to us many times over.

PROGRESS in TECHNOLOGY just facilitates the amplification of our 'inner' little vibrations. A simple example is SOCIAL MEDIA. It helps us to sit and type on a keyboard and amplify our hate or love as it appears on the screen of millions of others, who in turn respond. Technology can amplify our qualities as human beings, whether good or bad; the choice is ours.

Honestly, the UNIVERSE DOES NOT CARE. It is ONLY programmed to give us what we desire as a human race. Whether we send out LOVE or HATE from our individual hearts, we get back the same, just at higher concentrations.

As the saying goes, "What GOES around, DOES come around."

So, WHAT is that SMALL VIBRATION in your hearts going to be?

LOVE or HATE.

The choice is Yours!

Time for some FUN

We end the chapter with a melody-love song to set the mood. This is from the movie soundtrack of the *Tamil* movie *'Anbe Sivam'* **(2003)**. The movie actors are the legendary **Kamal Haasan** and **Kiran Rathod**. The Movie is directed by **C. Sundar**.

The song *'Poo Vaasam Purappadum'* or **'Fragrance of a flower'** is penned by **Vairamuthu** and sung by **Sadhana Sargam and Vijay Prakash.** The Music composer is **Vidya Sagar.**

SONG

'Poo Vaasam Purappadum'

(Fragrance of a flower)

MOVIE

'Anbe Sivam' (2003)

(Love is God)

SCAN above to see **YOUTUBE** ***Video of the Song***

Lyrics ['Poo Vaasam Purappaddum']	*Translation* **['Fragrance of a flower']**
Male: Poo vaasam porapadum pennae Naan poo varainthaal Thee vanthu viral sudum kannae Naan thee varainthaal	**Male:** A flower would come to life and spread its fragrance as I paint it A fire comes to life and (be careful) it could burn your fingers as I paint it

Female: Uyirallathellaam uyir kollum endraal Uyirulla naano ennaaguven..	**Female:** If (as you paint them) non-living things come to life then what would happen to the likes of me? (Do we stand a chance?)
Male: Uyir vaangidum oviyam neeyadi...ee	**Male:** (Why are you worried) when you are the one that gives life to these paintings of mine
Male: Poo vaasam porapadum pennae Naan poo varainthaal	**Male:** A flower would come to life and spread its fragrance as I paint it
Thee vanthu viral sudum kannae Naan thee varainthaal	A fire comes to life and (be careful) it could burn your fingers as I paint it
Male: Mmm.. pulli sernthu.. pulli sernthu oviyam Ullam sernthu.. ullam sernthu kaaviyam	**Male:** Just as when a line is formed as dots are connected An epic poem is formed when hearts connect
Female: Kodu kooda oviyathin Bhagamae	**Female:** As much as lines are drawn to connect and complete a picture
Oodal koda kaadhal endru aagumae	Quarrels also are just a part of the journey in matters of love and life

Male: Oru vaanam varaiya neela vanna	**Male:** When we think of painting the sky, we think of azure blue
Nam kaadhal varaiya enna vannam	What colours should we use to describe our love?
Female: En vetkathin niram thottu.. Viral ennum kol kondu Nam kaadhal varaivomae vaa aaaa	**Female:** Just use the brush as you would use your fingers touch the colour of my shyness Let us forge ahead and make this painting of our love ......
Male: Poo vaasam porapadum pennae Naan poo varainthaal	**Male:** A flower would come to life and spread its fragrance as I paint it
Thee vanthu viral sudum kannae Naan thee varainthaal	A fire comes to life and (be careful) it could burn your fingers as I paint it
Female: Oviyathin jeevan engu ulladhu..	**Female:** Where is the soul of the painting?
Male: Uttru paarkum aalin kannil ulladhu..	**Male:** It is in the eyes of the person looking at it
Female: Penn udambil kaadhal enghu ulladhu	**Female:** Where is love in a Woman's Body?

Male: Aan thodaadha bhaagham thannil ulladhu	**Male:** It resides in a part that no man can touch or grab (implying love can only be earned by man)
Female: Nee varaiya therindha oru navina kavignan Penn vasiyam therindha..oru nalindha kalaignan	**Female:** You are a modern poet who can also paint You are a legend who fascinates women
Male: Megathai yemaatri mann serum mazhai Polae Madiyodu vizhundhaayae... vaa aaaaa	**Male:** Just like raindrops that touch the ground by deceiving the cloud, you fell and dropped into my lap
Male: Poo vaasam porapadum pennae Naan poo varainthaal...	**Male:** A flower would come to life and spread its fragrance as I paint it
Mm hmm hmm Thee vanthu viral sudum kannae Naan thee varainthaal	A fire comes to life and (be careful) it could burn your fingers as I paint it
Female: Uyirallathellaam uyir kollum endraal Uyirulla naano ennaaguven..	**Female:** If (as you paint them) non-living things come to life then what would happen to the likes of me? (Do we stand a chance at all?)
Male: Uyir vaangidum oviyam neeyadi...ee	**Male:** (Why worry) Aren't you the painting that takes life

PUBLICATIONS

100% of 'AUTHOR EARNINGS' Go to CHARITY

SOCIAL MEDIA Links

ABOUT THE AUTHOR

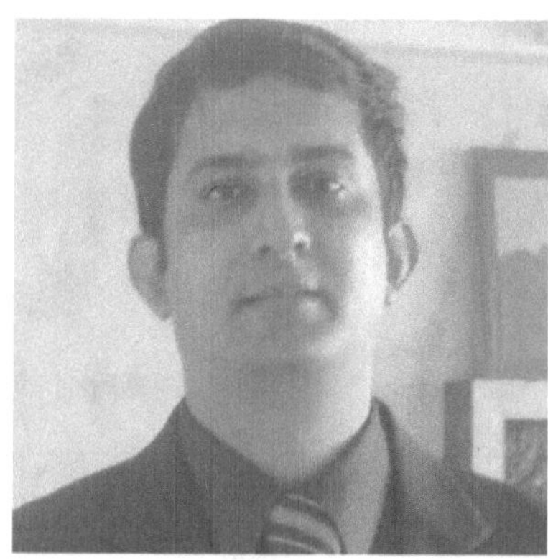

Mr. A.Venkatasubramanian a.k.a. 'A.V.' has **authored 13 books,** including **'9 Non-Fiction Books'** and **'2 on Poetry and Songs'**. He has also **penned several articles** that were **published online** and **featured in newspaper columns.**

Mr. A.Venkatasubramanian is an **engineer** and **management graduate,** having done his **B.E.** from **India,** his **M.S. in Engineering** and **M.B.A. in General Management** and **Finance** from the **US**. He has also completed **CFA (Chartered Financial Analyst, USA)** until **Level II.**

While he made a start to his career in the **technology industry,** his experience spans a number of industries, including **automobiles, airlines, information technology, retail, banking, market research, real estate** and **finance.**

Mr. A.Venkatasubramanian is currently an **entrepreneur** in the **technology space** and loves **travel, photography, music** and the **arts.** He is an **avid reader** and **enjoys sports.**

PUBLICATIONS

100% of 'AUTHOR EARNINGS' Go to CHARITY

Real Estate	Investing & Real Estate	Finance & Philosophy
	 	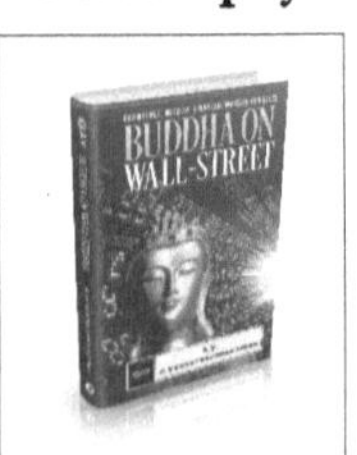

Technology & Society	Entrepreneurship
	 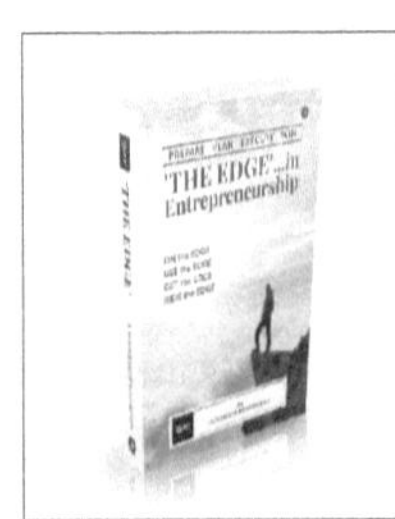

PUBLICATIONS

100% of 'AUTHOR EARNINGS' Go to CHARITY

Poetry & Songs

Poetry & Songs

Love & Humanity

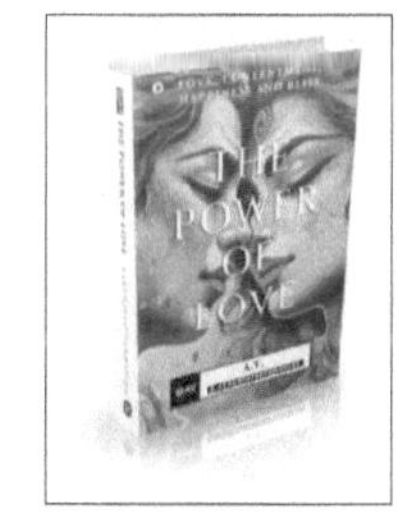

PUBLICATIONS

100% of 'AUTHOR EARNINGS' Go to CHARITY

Administrator's Hand Book

Self-Improvement

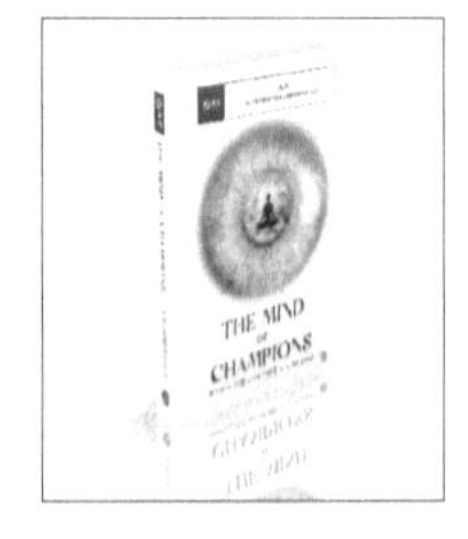

PUBLICATIONS

100% of 'AUTHOR EARNINGS' Go to CHARITY

Biography [Part - I]	Biography [Part - II]

@

YouTube

Find us on **YouTube**

@

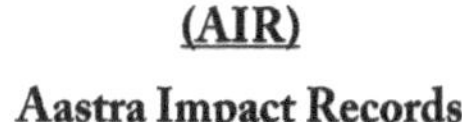 **(AIR)** **Aastra Impact Records**	**(AIM)** **Aastra Impact Media**	**(AID)** **Aastra Impact Dreams**
 YouTube @ 	 YouTube @ 	 YouTube @ 
100% of Author's Earnings Go to Charity	**100% of Author's Earnings Go to Charity**	**100% of Author's Earnings Go to Charity**

LinkedIn

Find us on **Linkedin**

@

(AIR) Aastra Impact Records	(AIM) Aastra Impact Media	(AID) Aastra Impact Dreams
		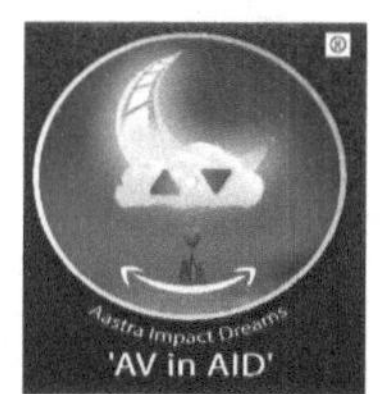
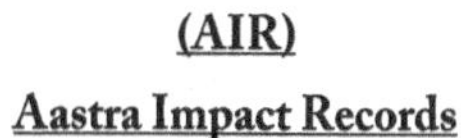 @	Linkedin @	Linkedin @

100% of Author's Earnings Go to Charity	**100% of Author's Earnings Go to Charity**	**100% of Author's Earnings Go to Charity**

PUBLICATIONS

100% of 'AUTHOR EARNINGS' Go to CHARITY

a	COVER	TITLE	Books
		1. **The Real Deal** ***(All You Need to Know about Investing in Real Estate)*** Genre: Real Estate investing	
		2. **Nuggets of Wisdom** ***(Invest in Real Estate with Wisdom)*** Genre: Investments	
		3. **Buddha On Wall-Street** ***(Knowledge Wisdom Moksha Bliss)*** Genre: Finance and Philosophy	
		4. **You Better Watch Out!** **(*Technology Change Society Culture*)** Genre: Technology & Culture	

PUBLICATIONS

100% of 'AUTHOR EARNINGS' Go to CHARITY

a	COVER	TITLE	Books
		5. **The Art of Public Good** ***(Power Wisdom Prosperity Balance)*** Genre: Public Policy	
		6. **FACETS** ***(Poetry for all Seasons)*** Genre: Poetry & Songs	
		7. **The Power of Love** ***(Love Happiness Contentment Bliss)*** Genre: Love & Humanity	
		8. **The G-Forces** ***(Gita Governance Goodness Godliness)*** Genre: Self-Improvement	

PUBLICATIONS

100% of 'AUTHOR EARNINGS' Go to CHARITY

a	COVER	TITLE	Books
		9. **The Mind of Champions** ***(Where Fire & Ice are Forged)*** Genre: Self Improvement	
		10. **The Edge** ***(Prepare Plan Execute Win)*** Genre: Entrepreneurship	
		11. **Hopscotch** ***(Poetry for all Reasons)*** Genre: Poetry & Songs	
		12. **Pepper Bright - I** ***(Snippet of an Adventure)*** Genre: Biography	

www.ingramcontent.com/pod-product-compliance
Lightning Source LLC
LaVergne TN
LVHW041137150826
845673LV00001B/22

9798890667687